THE PURSUIT

OF HAPPINESS

Evolving A Soul

THE PURSUIT

OF HAPPINESS

Evolving A Soul

William J. O'Malley

ThomasMore®
– *An RCL Company* –

Allen, Texas

Send all inquiries to:
Thomas More®
An RCL Company
200 East Bethany Drive
Allen, Texas 75002-3804

Toll Free 800–888–3065
Fax 800–688–8356

Printed in the United States of America

ISBN 0–88347–333–X

1 2 3 4 5   02 01 00 99 98

Let me find
the serenity
to accept the things that can't be changed,
the courage
to change the things that can
and the wisdom
to know the difference.

—Reinhold Niebuhr

This book is for

JACKIE AND JOE DE MARIA
and long overdue.

Contents

Introduction

<hr/>

SO MANY DEAD-ENDED EYES

<hr/>

"Ah! Look at all the lonely people!"
The Beatles— *"Eleanor Rigby"*[1]

Walk 42nd Street west, from fabled Broadway to 8th Avenue. Not in the fantasies of Cole Porter or Sondheim or anyone else who passes through in a cab or a limo, but really. Then amble up to, say, 55th Street and across to Broadway and back down again. Eye the slack-eyed flesh peddlers: "Ennybody wan' it?"

Check the ads for the skinflicks; walk, if you dare, into a porn shop, and study the faces of people exercising First Amendment rights. Look at the wary steel eyes of the cops. Cruise strip-miles from Vancouver to Miami, from Bangor to Baja, and try to figure what city you're in: same brand names, same menus, same movies.

Pick a mall, any mall, and watch the slack-jawed kids casting lazy eyes at the other slack-jawed kids. Wander the chi-chi shops on Rodeo Drive. Hover around the blackjack tables in Vegas and scan the empty faces. Killing time before time kills them. So many inanimate souls. So many dead-ended eyes.

Abraham Maslow writes of an old psychology textbook he used as an undergraduate, "awful book, but it had a wonderful frontispiece. The lower half was a picture of a line of babies, pink, sweet, delightful, innocent, lovable. Above that was a picture of a lot of passengers in a subway train, glum, gray, sullen, sour. The caption underneath was simply, 'What happened?'"[2]

What, indeed?

Humanity adds an invitation to our animality, but it is only an invitation, a potential which need not be activated, like one's potential to play football or have children or murder. That potential is the human soul. As infants, we pulsed with wonder, with the urge to reach and touch and explore. But by second grade, that's gone, a victim of efficient, soulless, job-oriented education. (Rare to see a student read an unassigned book. Or an assigned one, for that matter.)

Before long we settle for a "realistic" acceptance of what seems incontrovertibly "the way things are"; we "adjust" to the humdrum and practical, which then becomes the norm, the stunting we share with everybody else, and therefore we don't even notice how impoverished we are (though, somewhere in the depths of what might have been, we feel it).

Psychologist Robert Johnson says: "Each person's psyche has an inborn evolutionary urge to grow, to integrate the contents of the unconscious, to bring together all the missing parts of the total individual into a complete, whole, and conscious self."[3] I know few schools, ever or now, that attempt to help young people integrate a self instead of adjusting to fragmented pieces of a self. And we were all in school, all pregnant with that potential, once. Families try, without knowing really what they're about, to make a child become a person, and most often with little more than gut instinct to go on. "I want them to have the best life they can have"—without ever sitting down and pondering what "the best life" really means, except for what "everybody says" is "the best life."

Our evolution into fully human beings is prevented not only from the outside—jungle-cities, infantile propaganda, uninvolving education, anesthetic entertainment-chemicals-sex, but also from the inside. For thirty-five years I've tried to convince bright young people there's more to life than the nonpassing lane on the way to a ranch house in the suburbs. They roll their eyes as if I'm wearing a sign that says, "Repent! Your doom is nigh!" Which is pretty much on target. I have a hunch also that their parents would pull them out of my classes if they knew the heresy I preach. For that very reason, the administration might pull me out of my classes, given the real priorities. If they knew what I taught!

Part of the reason for settling for terminal mediocrity is also fear of "pride"—a universally accepted mistranslation of the Greek hubris, which doesn't mean pride at all but rather arrogance. Not that we don't want to "be somebody"; that's built right into our very human potential. It's just that we want to be like everybody else at the same time.

Perhaps that's why folktales always made heroes out of the third brother with a porcupine head and Cinderella weeping at dishpan hands: to show that anybody can be somebody. Surely Albert Schweitzer and Eleanor Roosevelt got up a few mornings mumbling, "I'm tired of being somebody." Yet they slogged on. Those of us more fearful of the human invitation also fail to realize that, to be confident, one has to act *as if* one is in order to find out it is true.

But part of the cause is also fear of the cost, effort, sacrifice. "I have no time for all that ruminating and brooding and reading books. A journal? I hardly write my mother! I don't like being alone; the quiet gets on my nerves. And they'll think I'm loony." Thus, as John W. Gardner writes: "By middle life most of us are accomplished fugitives from ourselves."[4]

The root of the problem is not creeping socialism or science or technology. "The fault," as Cassius tells Brutus, "is not in our stars, but in ourselves that we are underlings." It is an attitude of mind which hasn't changed since the time pharaohs forced slaves to build their pyramids: a willingness to sacrifice humanity to other objectives—but now a willingness not only in the manipulators but in the manipulated.

Just as Hitler did, Madison Avenue, Hugh Hefner, and Madonna simply discern which way the parade is heading and get in front of it. If integrity, honesty, truthfulness, chastity, and charity sold cars and tickets and commercial time, they'd give us those. If audiences indicated by their choices at the box office, the remote control buttons, and the cash registers that external validations of self-worth (like cars, clothes, paychecks, sex, grades, awards) were *not* what we really cared about, the hucksters would be out of business.

But they've researched the crowd. They've known without ever reading "The Grand Inquisitor" that "man has no more agonizing anxiety than to find someone to whom he can hand over, with all speed, the gift of freedom with which the unhappy creature was born."[5] They know we are all too willing to give up our birthright to a sovereign soul for a mess of pottage.

In urging the effort to go in quest of a soul and mining its richness, I am not speaking of religion, much less proselytizing for any denomination. I am speaking of finding and evolving the only self one will ever have. Erik Erikson says that the very

purpose of adolescence, as a natural crisis of human development, is to discover an identity: a personally validated self,
at once just like every other human being, yet in an unduplic-
able way.

Our public schools at first set up shop not just to produce
managers and workers for industries but to form good citizens,
ethical people of conscience and character: trustworthy and
trusting, honorable, fair, committed—what politicians so cava-
lierly advert to as "family values," rarely having the slightest idea
what those values really are. Just some vague yearning to get
back to what the Waltons were.

But in the popular—and even sophisticated—mind, teaching ways to evolve the self and its ethics somehow intrudes
religion into what is essentially a secular institution, thereby
infringing on the rights of parents who disbelieve in any kind
of Higher Power. Nothing could be further from the truth.

Whether there is a God or not, the two basic questions any
human being must face are (1) Who and what am I? and (2)
How do I fit into all this? What will fulfill the one life I have
to live, and how do I deal with all the other human beings with
whom I share it? These are *the* most basic human questions, yet
they are the two questions no public school can openly deal
with, despite their claim to teach "the humanities."

Confronting one's unique human psyche (soul) and
evolving a personal ethic does not make one a good Jew or a
good Christian or a good Muslim. We have to undertake that
quest just to discover how to be good *human* beings. God or no,
we live in a horizontal web of relationships with every other
human being with whom we share this fragile planet.

What I do ripples out into that web and affects every part
of it, however slightly. If I throw one hamburger box out the car
window (and if everyone else does), we all suffer: a trash-filled
world. If I lie whenever I have need and opportunity (and if

everyone else does), we all suffer: a world in which no one can trust anyone else. To be good adult human beings, we have to be responsible—to our own consciences and to all the others who share this web of the moral ecology, even if all the scriptures of all the religions that ever existed are just so much self-delusive rubbish.

It is too reductionist by far to say human beings are merely more complex mechanisms than rocks and carrots and monkeys, a belief reflected in the anonymous statement made in pre-Nazi Germany that

> the human body contains a sufficient amount of fat to make seven cakes of soap, enough iron to make a medium-sized nail, a sufficient amount of phosphorus to make two thousand match-heads, enough sulfur to rid oneself of one's fleas.

Is that all Shakespeare and Bach and Helen Keller were worth? With tragic irony, that reductionism led to precisely what happened in the Nazi camps: turning human beings into soap.

Since Aristotle, the definition of humans has been "rational animals," and it is an unquestioned shibboleth of education that school will produce a *mens sana in corpore sano,* ("a sound mind in a sound body"). We can, of course, arrive at some insight into ourselves by comparing ourselves to other animals. Biologically, anatomically, physiologically, there are countless resemblances. Yet the contrasts are even more remarkable. The question is not about our animality, but what we do *in spite* of our animality. As Abraham Heschel asks, "Would it be valid to define an ape as a human being without the faculty of reason and the skill of making tools?"[6]

We are not just "rational animals," beasts with implanted computers. We have at least the potential for uniquely human activities which cannot be rooted in either the body or the mind. Selfless love, for instance, is neither physical nor rational. So, too, honor, decency, altruism. A sociologist or executive is free to treat humans as merely "factors" or "workers and consumers." Military leaders are free to treat their underlings as merely "personnel," rather than as sons and daughters. Physicians are free to treat patients as merely interesting biological specimens. But they are not. If it were true, the only difference between a physician and a veterinarian would be the clientele.

Moreover, when we refer to humans as "brutal," we are usually describing an action of which no brute is capable.

Human wisdom begins with calling things by their right names, without self-deceit or vested interests. Human evil begins by calling a thing by a wrong name—and accepting the lie we tell ourselves. We all know a skunk is not a cute black kitty with a white stripe, like Flower in *Bambi*. But we can convince ourselves (or be convinced) that self-indulgence, greed, and lust are not just universally acceptable but also praiseworthy.

God or no, we cannot absolve ourselves from legitimate guilt for calling people and things by the wrong names and then using them in illegitimate ways. Without guilt, we get Auschwitz.

This book is not about religion but about humanity. The word *religion* comes from the Latin *religare:* to bind fast, a connection not only to other human beings but also to a Higher Power—no matter what that Power's sectarian mask. It adds to the horizontal web of relations we have with all other humans a vertical dimension which transcends time and space. Until the final chapters, this book is not about that vertical dimension.

Similarly, there is a significant difference between moral evil and sin. Any human—believer or unbeliever, child or adult—is capable of moral evil, upsetting the balance of the web of moral, human relationships which is society. Strictly speaking, however, no unbeliever can sin, since sin would rupture not

man relationship but also a relationship an unbe-
never does not have: to a Divine Being. This book is not about
sin, but it is about moral evil, acting less than human.

Any human being has the legitimate right to be irreligious.
But no human being has the legitimate right to be inhuman,
that is, to be immoral.

Until about forty years ago, every society in history—in its
own unique ways—had accepted that, and in America, the
Protestant work ethic of thrift, honesty, hard work, and sacrifice
established an ordered interlocked system and spread it across
the country with miraculous rapidity.

But now a Norman Rockwell family transported to the
end of the twentieth century would be aghast, not only at the
gadgets but at the inhumanities we pay little more attention to
than changes in the weather: drive-by shootings, battered and
murdered infants, drugs, suicides, commonplace divorce, nonstop
litigation, serial killers, terrorist bombings—not in some remote
and "uncivilized" backwater, but in "The Greatest Land of All."

How did that radical turnabout occur in little more than a
generation? Because our society lost its bearings, its soul.

A world which, since the beginning, had been accustomed
to scarcity changed almost overnight into a world of overabun-
dance, to the point where we now pay farmers *not* to produce
and glut the market, lowering prices. And profits. A world in
which anyone who doesn't sport Nikes, drives a five-year-old
car, or hasn't bade farewell to virginity by age eighteen is a loser.

The question now becomes: What comes *after* satisfaction?

From Joe DiMaggio
to Daryl Strawberry

People who can remember when our country was an altruistic
community are all over fifty years old. Before World War I,

America, like most countries, was fragmented into small communities: farm towns, neighborhoods, blocks. Everybody knew everybody else; everybody pitched in at a death or a fire or the birth of a new baby. No law; we just did it because it was "the right thing to do." The two wars and the Depression pulled the segments together, not always willingly, but we all had a continuing series of problems no small group could solve alone.

Factions didn't disappear, but for a long while they became less important. On the battlefield, as in (idealized) old black-and-white war movies, the baseless antagonisms between the redneck, the tough from Brooklyn, the Boston Brahmin, and the towhead from Iowa yielded to the more pressing problem of staying alive.

At home, women were mobilized and worked in factories, making money and achieving a self-esteem beyond the realm of homemaking. Kids went round the neighborhood collecting newspapers, cans, melted-down fat. It was an honor to be a Scout. We were enlivened by an altruistic spirit of national unity we never felt before and quite likely will never feel again.

In the years after the World War II, we never realized we were living in the Golden Age. Then the avuncular Eisenhower gave way to the Golden Boy, a president who embodied all we thought good about ourselves: youth, energy, bravery, good looks, intelligence, humor, determination. But at 12:32 p.m. on November 22, 1963, that ideal shattered, and with him, our altruism. For three days the whole world stood still, and we all sat staring at the television. We found he'd been shot by a pasty-faced nobody, who in turn was gunned down by a strip-joint operator. It was obscene.

Then the betrayals began to come in battalions: Martin Luther King Jr., Bobby Kennedy, Anwar Sadat, Indira Gandhi;

Vietnam, Agnew, Watergate; riots and demonstrations by all kinds of alienated segments of the population; My Lai, Three-Mile Island, the Iran hostages, the Beirut hostages, Nicaragua, AIDS.

Meanwhile, without our realizing, the media succeeded in making the trivial important and the important trivial. Can a nation with a *National Reporter* fascination ever have heroes? It all became too much, too depressing, to digest. So gradually, we withdrew like Candide to cultivate our own gardens and let the rest of the world go to hell, not realizing it was dragging the whole web—and each of us—with it.

In *The Invasion of the Bodysnatchers,* alien pods took over humans' bodies and lives, and it was impossible to tell which people were, what they seemed or aliens. Not a bad metaphor for today's relationships. How much of what people say is true, and how much is façade? How much of what I send to Save the Children will get to children?

We've come routinely to *expect* everyone with a vested interest to lie. We expect politicians to be insincere, to be scripted by pollsters. If we trip, we know no one will catch us. The America of the '50s still rings in the rhetoric of the '90s, but the voices invoke an ideal as a reality which no longer exists, or at least no longer appeals.

The real ideal seems Crito in Plato's *Dialogues*—decent, upright, unintrusive—who tells Socrates he owes it to his family and friends not to be too eager to suffer for an ideal. In effect, his basic philosophy is "Look, I don't meddle in anybody else's business, except maybe the scandal pages, and they deserve all the muck they get. I don't bother you, so don't you bother me. To each his own. Live and let live, that's my motto."

As the chorus in Eliot's *Murder in the Cathedral* laments: "living . . . and partly living."

In Search of a Soul

Just as we use the words *love* and *value* and *faith*, we use the word *soul* as if we knew what it meant. There are many words that cluster around the idea of the human soul: *psyche, spirit, self, who-I-am, conscience, essence, character, life-force.* And I would like to use *soul* to encompass all those realities within each one of us. So it would be unwise to expect these pages to "nail down" that elusive reality within each of us into a clean-cut, left-brain dictionary definition. Rather, it is a series of clues to a better right-brain *understanding* of the soul and how one might go about enlivening it and enriching it.

What do we find when we seek within? A junk shop of sensations, half-formed ideas, unfocused fears, unexamined convictions? A viper's tangle of synapses and reflexes? Knots of resentments, wounds, anxieties? Probably. But far more. What is the soul who wraps them all into a unique spiritual organism?

Many claim they can access their "real self" only on a chemical high or at a rock concert. But who are they the rest of the week? That "real self" which emerges only on the occasional high is most often little more than the raw, unfettered animal Id.

My soul—my real self—is what in me remains the same despite all the changes and transformations to which I'm subject. The soul-self is the sum of all the divergent forces within each of us which makes us who-we-are, a scheme of values that gives a sense of rootedness to life, one's center of gravity, a capacity not only for self-acceptance but also for self-transcendence.

This book purports to do little more than invite you to wander around in the humanity we share and which you possess in a way no one else has ever experienced. It invites you to accept your unique story and the unique people who have been significant players in it, as they *are*, free of the wish that it could have been different, free of victimhood, and to sense that your self-story is integrated into a wider history. Who and what am I? And how do I fit into all this? What will fulfill the one life I have to live, and how do I deal with all the other human beings with whom I share it?

Perhaps as good a way as any of describing human growth toward wholeness is this: it is the process of clearing title to one's self. An adult, then, is one who exercises exclusive ownership rights and responsibilities for oneself. The self may be freely shared, but there is no question of either ownership or responsibility: adults own and take responsibility for themselves. In a word, an adult is self-possessed. For most of us the process of clearing the title takes a lifetime.[7]

As a workaholic of certifiable intensity, I spend every summer writing all day and evening, sandwiching in my vacation in two-hour segments every afternoon, reading in the sun, tanning my Don Knotts body, and cultivating uncountable wrinkles. One summer, every afternoon, this big-bottomed black Labrador retriever would amble up to my chaise with a stick in her mouth and shoulder me out of repose to throw it into the lake for her.

Well, I threw it, and she went gallumphing into the water after it. She'd return, hide behind a tree (so I couldn't see she'd dropped the stick to shake off the water). Then she'd sidle back, and we'd start it all over again until she was hacking and panting, and my arm was as limp as linguine.

But she was still wagging that old tail like a hairy black metronome gone amok. Whatever joy a black Lab can entertain, she entertained to the max. Even when she was exhausted. Why? Because she was doing what she was *born* to do: retrieve.

That's the question this book sets out to pursue: What will make us wag our tails with wild abandon, even when we're exhausted?

Chapter One

⸺ ❧ ⸱⸱ ❧ ⸺

THE DECLINE AND FALL

OF THE SOUL

As Gregor Samsa awoke one morning from a troubled dream, he found himself changed in his bed to some monstrous kind of vermin.

He lay on his back, which was as hard as armor-plate, and, raising his head a little, he could see the arch of his great brown belly, divided by bowed corrugations. The bed cover was slipping helplessly off the summit of the curve, and Gregor's legs, pitiably thin compared with their former size, fluttered helplessly before his eyes.

Franz Kafka—*The Metamorphosis*[1]

Even though he has just awakened to find he is now an enormous cockroach, Gregor, a traveling salesman, lies helplessly on his back, trying occasionally to turn over, ruminating:

> And apart from the business itself, this plague of
> traveling, the anxieties of trains, the irregular,
> inferior meals, the ever-changing faces, never to be
> seen again, people with whom there was no chance
> to be friendly. To *hell* with it!

Something monstrous—but nonetheless real—has happened to
him. He's become an insect, an automaton, a slave of instincts
and of other people. His attitude toward dirt changes; he begins
to take pleasure in crawling, degraded and infantile. Which is what
he has been all along: a modern man, alienated and estranged.

What has happened now that the purely rationalist Myth of
Economic Progress has demythologized and disenchanted us
(in both senses of the word) from the sacred elements of all
those ancient myths? We are left with . . . nothing.

If nothing I do is sacred or sinful, then nothing I do has
any importance at all. In the anthill of an apartment, in the
beehive of work, in the stampedes of our cities, in the silent
emptiness of endless space, I am, despite my hope, as negligible
as Gregor Samsa.

> Is that all there is?
> Is that all there is?
> If that's all there is, my friends,
> 　　then keep on dancing.
> Let's break out the booze and have a ball,
> 　　if that's all . . . there is.[2]

Although—even in modern secularized society—few
would admit to atheism, an alarming number of people, young
and old, at least seem to *act* as if "that's all there is": five days of
meaningless work, meaningless study, meaningless competition,
and two days to "break out the booze and have a ball."

Macbeth, no mean pragmatist, spoke the same soulless truth:

> Tomorrow, and tomorrow, and tomorrow,
> Creeps in this petty pace from day to day,
> To the last syllable of recorded time;
> And all our yesterdays have lighted fools
> The way to dusty death. Out, out, brief candle!
> Life's but a walking shadow, a poor player
> That struts and frets his hour upon the stage
> And then is heard no more; it is a tale
> Told by an idiot, full of sound and fury,
> Signifying nothing.[3]

Here we stand, hapless, hopeless, hairless apes stranded in a remote corner of a mindless reality. We live now pretty much in a postmetaphysical reality, seemingly without normative foundations or even any idea of a grounding theory.

The events sketched in this chapter might seem one more dry history lesson suitable only for the airy towers and minds of scholars, but actually they chronicle ideas that have filtered down into every woman and man on the street today, a gradual uprooting of society from traditions—religious, societal, ethnic—shedding what we long thought unquestionable absolutes, exchanging guilt for formless anxieties, unshackling ourselves not only from the tyranny of the gods but also from the enlivening of the gods. In eschewing the gods, we have become godforsaken.

From Druids to Darth Vader

For the wise men of old, the cardinal problem had been how to conform the soul to reality, and the solution had been knowledge, self-discipline, and virtue. For magic and applied science alike the problem is instead how to subdue reality to the wishes of men.[4]

The progress of civilization—from the bloody snarlings of near-beasts to the bloodlessly articulated theories of rarefied rationalism—has been, in an ironic but real sense, a process of dehumanization. Some believe experience of full humanity, for everyone from prince to peasant, peaked in the thirteenth century; since then, humanity gradually petered away, as naive beliefs eroded, while rational science and technology accelerated geometrically into the vacuum thus created. In so thoroughly vanquishing nature and the beast in us, we have vanquished our selves.

Throughout history, human value and meaning had for the most part been inextricably connected with the nature of "the gods," subject to their capricious benevolence or wrath. But since the end of the Renaissance, we have gradually distanced ourselves from the gods. As the power of the gods waned, it seemed the power of humans emerged from under "divine" influence into manifest independence. However, as Emerson suggested, perhaps we have paid for our refinement with a loss of divine energy.

History is a story of disenchantments, not only of correcting naiveté, but of taking the magic out of everything. In primitive cultures, gods, magic, ritual, enchantment permeated people's lives. They found meaning and purpose, as tribes and as individuals, by interacting with the powerful forces of nature.

The yearly *rhythm* of natural change gave a rhythm to their own lives—a sense of rightness, wholeness, meaning, like an artfully composed piece of music into which they blended. It gave them a center, connectedness, a shared vision, *coherence*. For them, that relationship with nature and life was I-Thou, and not I-It. No matter what unexpected setbacks, the people were rooted in a myth in which they were "at home."

But after fifty thousand years in which human life was at every turn entwined with nature and its anthropomorphic gods peering companionably down from the sky, the holy mountain, the sacred pyramid, a quite new and different idea of the gods— and thus of human beings—began to form independently in two widely distant places: under a bo tree in India and in the Athens marketplace.

India

After trying all the ways to find happiness in the midst of inescapable suffering—from bodily mortification, to philosophy, to hedonism, Siddhartha (d. 480 b.c.) achieved the fulfillment of Nirvana and became Guatama Buddha ("the Awakened One"). He arrived at the conclusion that the world we *believe* real and filled with gods is a delusion. Whatever is divine in reality is the Oversoul, nonpersonal, inexpressibly other and pure. Whatever divine presence we sense in nature and in ourselves are errant sparks of that "faraway" divine reality, imprisoned in defiling and corruptible matter. Therefore the path to happiness, true human fulfillment, is to deny matter through physical penance and abstractive meditation, to purify the soul of desire and liberate it—purged of individuality—into the absorptive Oversoul.

Greece

A century later, far away in Greece, with the emergence of leisured classes and thus the growth of sophisticated thought, the gods of Olympus began to seem almost embarrassing, a crude family of jealous manipulators—and the nature gods before them downright barbaric. As human dealings with the environment became less visceral and more cerebral, thinkers like Socrates (d. 399 B.C.), his student, Plato (d. 347 B.C.), and Plato's student, Aristotle (d. 322), came to a conclusion similar to Buddha's: earlier understandings of the divine in nature were far too *immanent,* that is, too "locked within" this world.

Instead, they pictured a single god as a distant creative intelligence in whom all the forces of the mind and the universe had their ideal and most real forms. The realities we see, as Plato showed in his parable of the cave, are only shadows, of imitations, of reality. As with the Buddha, they found such a perfect god too pure to become involved in the material world, since this world is everywhere corruptible—except for the human soul. It was this god of rarefied ideals who showed human beings, through reason, what was truly real, good, and beautiful: the meaning and fulfillment of human life. Happiness.

Thus you have two sets of polarities in human understanding of the nature of the gods and thus the nature of humanity: (1) the polarity between the immanent (this-worldly) gods of the primitives and the transcendent (other-worldly) god of the philosophers, and (2) the polarity between what seemed to be two radically different means to apprehend the purpose of human life: the visceral conviction of the primitive and the clear-eyed cerebral rationalism of the philosophers.

So many problems could be eliminated if we could only factor the gods out of the equation entirely and say, with Pythagoras, "Man is the measure of all things." Ultimately, we succeeded.

Israel

Meanwhile, along the eastern shore of the Mediterranean, there lived a people of quite different mind-set from their more sophisticated neighbors to the west and east: the Hebrews. They were far less heady than the Greeks in their ruminations about divinity and their divinely instituted purpose in life, and more down-to-earth than the Orientals. Overwhelmed by slavery in Egypt, they turned to a charismatic leader named Moses, who believed he had encountered the one and only God, Yahweh the Liberator, who dwelt with them, moved with them, protected them.

Their relationship with this God was far "warmer," more mutually personal than that of the Greeks to their unreachable First Cause or the Easterners to their nonpersonal Oversoul. For the Greeks, the truths of life came through rigid logic and reasoning; for the Orientals, through total escape from that same calculating intelligence.

For the Hebrews, truth dwelled not so much in the head as in the heart, not in logical exactitude nor in wordless contemplation, but in experience of trustworthiness. The divine was incontestably holy and "other," yet they "knew" Yahweh also dwelt in the center of their city, in the Temple: transcendent, yet immanent.

Christendom

Then near the middle of what became the first century of a new era, news began to spread through the Mediterranean basin of a quite new and different understanding of God—and therefore of the meaning and purpose of human life. A new sect emerged from Judaism which claimed that the infinite God had not only created the world and given purpose to each of its parts, had not only sent messages through privileged prophets, but that this time Divinity itself had *entered* human history as a human being. Divinity had somehow "emptied" itself of divine power and become an individual human, the transcendent totally immersed in the toil and sweat and frustration of immanent human life. *Emmanuel,* God-with-us.

For centuries after, philosophers argued about how that could happen—a tripartite single God? Fully transcendent but completely immanent? Yet no matter how they argued, battled, connived against one another, all agreed that—somehow—the transcendent had fused with the immanent. Not just the divine power they sensed in the storm or the divine serenity they felt by a quiet lake, but God walking among us and living the kind of life God expected men and women to live. The sacred had become secular in order to make the secular sacred.

Then for over a millennium, from the conversion of Constantine in 312 until the rise of Protestantism in the sixteenth century, the Catholic Church, with its theology and ritual, saints and feast days, shrines and crusades, supplied the background in which most of the European world found meaning and purpose. The rhythm of the liturgical year—from Christmas to Easter to Pentecost, with all kinds of saints' days between—gave a matrix within which communities or individuals could judge whether they were "synchronized" with "the order of things."

The rhythm of the "peak moments" of family life—birth, puberty, marriage, moments of moral failure, death of loved ones—also found meaning in the sacraments, especially in the meal that celebrated their community and their inevitable triumph over suffering and death. Even ravaged by plague, war, drought, invasion, schism, heresies, they found life was ultimately "holy," ratified by the salvific blood of the Son of God, who had immersed himself in that same life. All the segmented joys and sufferings of their lives somehow "fit" into a coherent, meaningful pattern. For centuries, to all intents and purposes, as with the pagan primitive, the sacred and the secular were one life: Christendom.

Then in the thirteenth century, through abrasion with the minds of the Muslim who had preserved him, Aristotle once again invaded Europe—intriguingly pagan and rationalistic in a Christendom dominated by clerics seemingly hungrier for power than for holiness or wholeness. But through the painstaking work of geniuses like Thomas Aquinas (d. 1274), the pagan rationalism of Aristotle was put in service of the Christian view of God and humanity, and for two more centuries, Christendom was "home" once again,

a myth that made everything—even the insupportable—
make sense.

There is no arguing Christendom was benighted, in uncountable significant areas of human being. It is true, since the
Renaissance we have achieved an enormous understanding and
control of nature, human suffering, and technology which
makes their lives seem punitive by contrast. But we seem to
understand and control our own selves far less well than a
feudal serf or a scullery maid. Surely less well than John Bunyan
or the Wife of Bath.

The Modern Era

An individual in a phone booth takes up nearly all the space,
fills it, dominates it. Put the same person in a crowded room
and his or her significance diminishes. All the more so in a huge
coliseum. Now with the rise of the new learning, especially in
astronomy, and the age of exploration which made a single
European village, or even a city, or the entire continent shrivel
in contrast, the human context became almost infinitely larger
than anyone had suspected, a background against which any
individual was proportionately depreciated. It is difficult to feel
"at home" in a limitless place.

Copernicus (d. 1543) had postulated that the earth—and its
passengers—was not the focus even of our cozy solar system,
much less the center of reality. His conviction found validation
through the telescope of Galileo (d. 1642) and a rudimentary
understanding of its movements through the mechanics of
Newton (d. 1727).

As Galileo said, God gave us two books, the Bible and
nature, to help us understand God's mind and will, and many
began to realize God had given us nature before God found
need to give us Scripture, much less an authoritative Church to
read it for us. Understandably, the guardians of Christendom

became more than apprehensive, not only about the sanctity of revelation (the basis of their power) but also about the diminution of human value which would result from admitting what became inescapable.

Meanwhile, missionaries were sending letters from all over the world, telling stories of non-Christian peoples who nonetheless lived exemplary moral lives without benefit of either Scriptures or the Catholic Church and its hierarchy and theologians. It began to appear that beneath the world's religious diversities there was a common body of beliefs about human fulfillment of a divine will, certain truths so manifest that all societies subscribed to them—independently of Christianity. It was not essential to be Catholic in order to be a good human.

About the same time, Descartes (d. 1650) began applying the critical rationalism of science and mathematics to philosophy, which liberated intelligent people to *doubt*, to call into question the hitherto unquestioned authority of Aristotle and ultimately of the Church (which had been threatened for a century already since Luther [d. 1546]). That skepticism focused finally on Scripture itself. After centuries of reassurance to ordinary folk, the myth of Christendom was cracking up.

The Enlightenment in the eighteenth century was a philosophical movement that spread over all of Europe. Its basic conviction was that, through reason, humankind could find happiness by understanding truths about nature—especially human nature—which had since the beginning been shrouded in the mysterious and impregnable will of the gods or God. It rejected the ancient world's cyclical view of history for a belief that history is a record of human *progress,* toward perfection through reason.

The tools of science, unbiased by questionable immaterial realities, could be brought to bear on all human questions and problems and eventually obviate them. Voltaire (d. 1778), in the name of Enlightenment, declared war on the Church, its dogmas, ethics, traditions, and especially its clergy. His views and those of his fellow *philosophes* triumphed in the French Revolution (1789–99) in which clergy were unfrocked and purged, and a harlot dubbed the Goddess of Reason danced naked on the altar of Notre Dame. It was a decade of the triumph—far more visceral than cerebral—of the ordinary man and woman in the streets.

The nineteenth century saw the fulfillment of unbiased rationalism in the rise of utilitarianism, empiricism, and the Industrial Revolution. Thomas Hobbes (d. 1679) had articulated a philosophy and economics dependent on a completely individualistic picture of human nature. Every moral decision is ultimately selfish and utilitarian; even what appears altruistic is merely disguised self-seeking. Giving alms to a beggar not only relieves his distress but, more importantly, my own distress at his plight.

Jeremy Bentham (d. 1832) and John Stuart Mill (d. 1873) saw all self-interest as ultimately in the public interest. My personal greed will drive me to strive harder, generate more desirable products, contribute through taxes to the general welfare. Therefore, just as with science, business must not be burdened with matters totally outside economics, surely not by any metaphysical or spiritual considerations.

The thinkers of the Enlightenment, however, still believed the order of the universe argued to a Designer; such a vast and intricate piece of clockwork demanded a Watchmaker, and many of the symbols of Freemasonry reflect their conception of the Divinity as a Cosmic Architect.

But like Plato they also saw such a sublime Entity as completely "other" from mutable, defiling, corruptible material life. God was instead a supremely powerful toy maker who set the universe spinning, then turned to disport himself with some other project. Therefore, no possibility existed of any kind of personal relationship with such a Deity, as there had been for primitive peoples, the Hebrews, and the citizens of Christendom. Thus "religion" for many lost its transcendent dimension and became only the Brotherhood of Man.

Human delusions of value came under further judgment from Charles Darwin (d. 1882), who argued that human beings had descended from apes and shared not only their physical attributes but their attitudes as well. Karl Marx (d. 1883) declared an individual life of paltry significance in the inevitable unfolding of the historical drive toward the Workers' Paradise.

Friederich Nietzche (d. 1900) finally wrote the death certificate for God, asserting there had never been an entity outside the mind to validate the *idea* of God to which humans had clung since the beginning. Along with God died the whole idea of an inherent rightness and wrongness. As Ivan Karamazov shouted, "If there is no God, *anything* is permitted!"

Who, then, can save society from anarchy? The Superman, the individual liberated from enslavement to a nonexistent deity or to bourgeois mannerisms which pass for morality. Might makes right, and as long as I am the strongest, I *legislate* right and wrong. That doctrine came to full flower in Adolf Hitler and Josef Stalin.

But such one-sided rationalist reductions of society, economics, and human purpose had and still has palpable results, captured in the novels of Charles Dickens (d. 1870), which George Bernard Shaw called at least as subversive as *Das Kapital*. Moreover, Dickens's pictures of the London slums in the mid–nineteenth century, with a few changes in detail, could serve as mirror images of Bedford-Stuyvesant or south-central L.A. at the close of the twentieth century. And his depiction of schools—which along with the family are the breeding grounds of a sense of ethics, humanity, and self-worth—bears an unsettling (if less genteel) resemblance to our own schools.

The following is a homily delivered by Mr. Thomas Gradgrind to the (quavering) pupils of Mr. McChoakumchild in Gradgrind's company school, a sorting-house to determine which children would become managers in his mills and which would be "hands":

> Now what I want is Facts. Teach these boys and
> girls nothing but Facts. Facts alone are wanted in
> life. Plant nothing else, and root out everything else.
> You can only form the minds of reasoning animals
> upon Facts: nothing else will ever be of service to
> them. This is the principle on which I bring up my
> own children, and this is the principle on which I
> bring up these children. Stick to Facts, sir![5]

No room in Mr. Gradgrind's school for fancy, imagination, intuition, the unquantifiable, the "sense" of something larger than "Fact." In his school, a horse was not a noble beast, a snorting steed with flaring eyes; it was "an equine quadruped." His students were not human spirits yearning for greatness, dreaming dreams, envisioning the unheard-of, exulting in the circus. They were not even known by name but as "Girl Number 23." They were "reasoning animals," nothing more nor less. No sin in Gradgrind's school or world but sloth and lack of productivity. Nothing sacred except financial profit.

Despite the self-gratulatory rhetoric of our modern school catalogues, the reality of education today is little different. There was a time in each student's life, long ago, when going to school was exciting: finger painting, building with blocks, learning to write your own name, reading all by yourself. Then without our realizing, it became serious business, because life is a serious business. Mr. Gradgrind took over.

Education has yielded to mere schooling, endured as the price of working credentials, with no interest in pursuing higher learning for its own humanly enriching sake. Everybody passes. On the other hand, administrators want extra class days. Why? To force-feed data students will never remember or have use for.

The purpose of learning these skills isn't—as it was in ancient Greece—to make youngsters virtuous and wise but to make them more efficient cogs in the Economy machine. Students are taught to label a sonnet Petrarchan or Shakespearean by men and women whose souls have never been moved by a sonnet. On the contrary, as Viktor Frankl insists, education must be education toward the ability to *decide*. And he might have added "responsibly."

As Morton Kelsey writes: "Superficial compulsory education has provided just enough consciousness to drive a great percentage of the people in the Western world out of Eden and leave them in the wastelands."[6]

Robert Fitch[7] summarizes this odyssey of the conquest of humanity by studying the five realities we can make central to our lives: God, Nature, Humanity, Society, and the Self. At least in the West, for thousands of years, the Hebrew-Christian God was at the core of the meaning of individuals and societies. But by the eighteenth century, that God was enfeebled by the increasing independence from the divine afforded by the sciences, and by the nineteenth century, God was definitively pronounced dead by Nietzsche.

The new idol became Nature, which had been competing with God at least since the fifth century B.C. Copernicus and Newton, Descartes and Voltaire slowly—and in some cases unwittingly—cut the thousands of strings that anchored us to a divine being and sent God drifting off into the cold space of Deism.

The Enlightenment deposed Nature for Humanity, whom Auguste Comte proclaimed the Supreme Being. Mill, Darwin, and Marx found in this Humanity the roots of an inevitable Progress. But its own inner contradictions toppled the doctrine of divine Humanity, since purely scientific studies proved being human was not that special after all. A human was little more than a complex machine, victim of heredity and environment, creature of unconscious drives and impulses: at best a more complex beast of prey.

Then the divinity of Humanity gave way to the divinity of Society in Nazism and Communism, which in turn ultimately shattered into many nations, each now shattered in turn by factionalism. Finally, we are fragmented into single, final, and irreducible individualists. Margaret Mitchell captured such a man in the hero of *Gone with the Wind:* "I believe in only one cause. I believe in Rhett Butler." And Frank Sinatra grounded that cult more recently and concretely: "I Did It My Way." The ultimate divinity: the Self. A culture of narcissists.

The Myth of Secular Progress

In America, hard-nosed, no-frills "religion" was first embodied in the Puritan, Cotton Mather: the way to righteousness and fulfillment—happiness—is upright character and hard work, the Protestant work ethic. That yielded to the practicality of Ben Franklin. To show how interchangeable Yankee shrewdness and "Christianity" have become, many believe Franklin's dictum "God helps those who help themselves" comes from the Christian Scriptures! That in turn devolved into the cynical advertising ploys of Phineas T. Barnum: "There's a sucker born every minute, and you'll never go broke underestimating their taste."

Barnum and Gradgrind still ride high in the boardrooms of Madison Avenue, the Tube, the billboards, the slide-out postcards in every magazine. You can't have too much. Image outweighs substance; nothing succeeds like the appearance of success; it is not the gods that bestow fulfillment but consumption.

The Economy is its own justification. *Anything* good for the Economy, is "of God." (I capitalize it to give it its due.)

The Law of the American Dream is more subtle in its statements and more sophisticated in its methods than the Law of the Jungle, but no less savage. It is less meticulous in its strictures than the Law of Moses, but no less demanding. It is less forgiving than Christendom, but no less pervasive.

The following analogy of the Economy to idolatry might seem at first forced, but it will show how absolutely thoroughly the secular has replaced the sacred in every corner of our lives.

Just as the gods gave meaning and a sense of coherence and purposefulness to more primitive societies, and Yahweh made sense out of life for Hebrews, and Christ's message validated even suffering and death for the medieval and renaissance Church, now the Economy serves that purpose.

Our lives are validated only insofar as we become grist for the Gradgrind mill: workers, consumers, managers, investors— who serve the "priests": scientists, inventors, financiers, advertisers who answer our prayers for more "new things," which our ancestors could not have dreamed of, much less coveted.

And yet we are, most of us, willing devotees of the Idol: Economy. Many of us uncritically accept the values of the modern world: blind faith in technology, gadgets, progress, slavery to the stupefying media. We are willing to accept that the "soul" of our society is not a shared spirit but a mass of electric circuits. Still, given the limits of the Monopoly game, we all benefit: the harder we work, the more we have to spend; the more we have to spend, the more the Economy thrives; the more the Economy thrives, the more we have to spend. Our self-interest serves the public interest. And on it goes.

Ironically, this fanatic religious campaign has even been able, in a kind of *1984* "Newspeak," to completely turn around the very meaning of the word *Economy.* Before, it had always meant thrift, conserving, buying carefully, frugality. Now it means precisely the opposite: expansion, spending, the bullish market, the golden calf. As with all religions, the Economy through its advertisers is a work of *conversion,* a complete turnaround of values—even a complete inversion of what "value" now means.

Besides priests, there are highly valued "scriptures." For the hierarchy, there are *The Wall Street Journal* and *Forbes;* for the lower levels of the faithful, there are *People* and *Newsweek.* They tell us what's important and who's important, who are the "saints" who have "made it." And there are audiovisual "scriptures" as well, proclaiming the good news everywhere we turn: "THE MORE THINGS YOU HAVE, THE HAPPIER YOU'LL BE!"

Like any religion, the Economy offers fulfillment: newer, improved, bigger, livelier lives. It has successfully evangelized and secularized not only institutions but the very *consciousness* of the "congregation." We genuinely *want* what the "priests" and "scriptures" want us to want: more tangible proofs of our success. Thus, the supernatural and sacred are as nonsensical as astrology and fortune cookies.

No drill sergeant, no voodoo hypnotist, no Siberian brain-washer—not even Hitler or Big Brother—ever had such coverage, such compliant subjects, or such sophisticated and successful methods as the huckster-priests of the unquestioned Economy. And we don't mind, really. After all, it's good for all of us. It's very thorough evangelization.

The moral code of the idolatry is strict: work and compete, that is how you will find fulfillment, your real *value*—SATs, report cards, salaries, promotions, new cars, designer jeans (which used to be poor people's pants). Efficiency and speed become demigods in their own right, to the point one would rather have a tried-and-true fast burger than enjoy a meal. On the assembly line, one plugs this part to a piece someone else has assembled, hands it on to a faceless someone who paints it, someone else to ship, someone else to sell, someone else to drive. Soulless, but efficient. And we all "profit."

There are also secular rituals that celebrate competition and the Economy: Super Bowls, Olympics, and World Series in which sport is no longer sportive; Academy Awards, Emmys, Tonys, Grammys, and Country Music Awards in which the point at issue is hardly art; political conventions in which the point is rarely character but more often image; rock concerts which are liturgies of the Id; shopping malls which are cathedrals of consumption. Even taking a walk is no longer a chance to "stop and smell the flowers" or sense the sacred in nature; that is short-circuited by the Walkman keeping us plugged in to "the divine."

One rarely mentioned flaw in this secular religion (which amounts to heresy) is to observe that so many "saints" who have really devoted themselves wholeheartedly to the pursuit of its goals and promises, who have really "made it" in the idolatry of the Economy, so often find need to anesthetize themselves from life with drugs and very frequently end up killing themselves: Elvis Presley, Marilyn Monroe, Janis Joplin, Jim Morrison, John Belushi, Howard Hughes, Jimi Hendrix, Kurt Cobain, River Phoenix . . . and the beat goes on.

Despite the promises of the secular gospel, there was something missing from their lives which made them unable to accommodate "having it all," something integral and important. Perhaps what was lacking was a soul, a self. Perhaps they had "sold their souls"—their honest selves—to a false god. Not that there necessarily is a real transcendent God to validate our ideas of God, but that this god—the Economy—has not validated its claims to our allegiance.

With nothing but a calculatedly "soulless" background against which to measure themselves—unlike the sacred myth systems of the primitive, the ancient, the Hebrew, Christendom—the modern man or woman finds life segmented, one-damn-thing-after-the-other, with no sense of meaningful coherence, no story line.

The surgeon often treats us merely as biological specimens in need of repair, the politician as so many votes to open a door and then be forgotten, a general as so many dogfaces to accomplish a task rather than sons and daughters of somebody. The battle-weary teacher can deal with (admittedly peevish) human beings as so many educands to get through the system, and the Economy's Gradgrinds can treat them as merely "economic factors."

For all our speed and efficiency, for all our goods and services, for all our defenses against even inconvenience, for all our better nutrition and medical care and life-expectancy, are we demonstrably any *happier* than the primitive squatting among so many enchantments, the Hebrew clutching his prayer shawl and muttering to Yahweh, the medieval peasant leaning her hoe on the furrow to say the Angelus? Do we have a more genuine sense of self, a more heartfelt sense of belonging to a community and a cause greater than the limits of our own skins, a true sense of living purposeful lives—than those simpler folk, benighted in simplicity, superstition, and magic? Are we missing something?

The world to which unbalanced rationalism has led us, the demystified world given us by the Enlightenment and Scientism, the utilitarian world of Gradgrind and Barnum and the Economy seems a cold place indeed. It is empirical, this worldly, secular, pragmatic, contractual, hedonistic, disenchanted. "Is that all there is?" Something seems to be missing, something integral and important.

We are the hollow men
We are the stuffed men
Leaning together
Headpiece filled with straw. Alas![8]

The curse of liberated modern society seems to be a sense of short-term goals and long-term aimlessness. Yet the quest for Eden, for "home," is the root of human history—the pioneers, our grandparents who set sail for the New World, our parents who fought world wars to build security for their children. They had an intuitive "sense" things could be better: a dream to validate their lives, and, in the going, they were "already there."

But, since the '60s, we have been derailed from questing into a kind of dull resignation, from striving to mere survival. Our hearts are not restless, just frustrated, by our inescapable but unfed hunger. Yet it is precisely our stubborn refusal to adapt, our snotty conviction we could prevail, which *made* us human and keeps us human. When we let it go, our humanity—and the humanity of our cities—slips away with it. No need for more evidence of that dull resignation to a life without hope than the surly attendant who shoves change at you in the subway.

Now, only one goal: more. Once our hero was a farm boy named Lincoln, for whom the human appetite had a goal: human dignity. Now our hero is a farm boy named Presley, who "had it all," but killed himself. Yet years after his suicide, two thousand people visit his shrine every day. "The King!"

If the agents of the Economy have the answers, why are millions in third-generation Welfare? Why do so many wander streets with dead-ended eyes, bumming change and sleeping on grates? Why so many divorces, so many suicides, especially among teenagers who "have it all"? Why do the young, who used to embody our hope, drop out, turn to drugs and crime?

Why do the privileged cling to cool, indifference, disconnect-
edness? Why do we all settle for bland food, education, TV?
Why do half our citizens find voting not worth the effort?

Something is missing. Something integral and important.

The absolute *reductio ad absurdum* of unbalanced rationalism
is George Lucas's Darth Vader, whom Joseph Campbell describes:

> Darth Vader has not developed his own humanity.
> He's a robot. He's a bureaucrat, living not in terms
> of himself but in terms of an imposed system. This
> is the threat to our lives that we all face today. Is
> the system going to flatten you out and deny you
> your humanity, or are you going to be able to
> make use of the system to the attainment of
> human purposes? How do you relate to the system
> so that you are not compulsively serving it? It
> doesn't help to try to change it to accord with
> your system of thought. The momentum of
> history behind it is too great for anything really
> significant to evolve from that kind of action. The
> thing to do is learn to live in your period of
> history as a human being. That's something else,
> and it can be done. . . . By holding to your own
> ideals for yourself and, like Luke Skywalker,
> rejecting the system's impersonal claims on you.[9]

Is that all there is?
Is that all there is?
If that's all there is, my friends,
   then keep on dancing.
Let's break out the booze and have a ball,
   if that's all . . . there is.

Chapter Two

A Society without a Soul

Things fall apart; the centre cannot hold;
Mere anarchy is loosed upon the world,
The blood-dimmed tide is loosed, and everywhere
The ceremony of innocence is drowned;
The best lack all conviction, while the worst
Are full of passionate intensity . . .
And what rough beast, its hour come round at last
Slouches towards Bethlehem to be born?

William Butler Yeats—*"The Second Coming"*[1]

To those untroubled by much reading or thought, cultural customs, taboos, and moral strictures seem something like dancing. At one time, groups danced in patterned, geometrical

45

figures: schottische, minuet, waltz. There was a time within some memories when the man led, the woman followed, and that was that. (Few realized Ginger did everything Fred did—but backwards and in high heels!) Today, moral strictures, like today's dancing, at least seem as if every participant is improvising as he or she goes along, because there is no pattern anymore.

As Herbert Marcuse persistently pointed out, scientific thought—not only so-called "hard" sciences like physics and chemistry but "softer" sciences like psychology and sociology—had to free clearheaded analysis from value judgments. Philosophical values contributed nothing to the subjugation of nature, and in fact too often hindered it. When you face the problems of constructing an atomic bomb, for instance, including human victims into the equation can be distracting.

Therefore, unadulterated science (scientism) freed nature from any inherent purposes, stripped reality down to only quantifiable values. It chose to ignore in humans what had been considered the "natural" values of self-esteem and interpersonal relationships and redefined us in terms of quantifiable values: units of labor during units of time. "The historical achievement of science and technology has rendered possible the translation of values into technical tasks—the materialization of values."[2]

This utilitarian option negates the difference between quite mutable cultural taboos and the immutable nature of human beings, denying some actions are of their very nature destructive to human beings, no matter what "society allows," because of their inherent nature. Fire burns; rape ravages; murder is unfair—no matter who's temporarily in charge.

Humanity doesn't change at societal whim. Males and females still go through the same life cycles as Cro-Magnons and have to deal with one another just as they did. Like them, we need to develop a meaning-system, a myth, which gives a felt value in work, which binds men and women to one another and to their children, which settles problems when individual desires and priorities conflict with the community's, whether in a family or tribe or, now, in the Global Village.

But the meaning-system that governed us until the '50s has eroded away until it is thin as the smoke blown at us by politicians in search of "a return to family values"—none of which they are ready to define lest the definition conflict with the feelings of the ACLU, NRA, NAACP, GM, IBM, or the dependable contributors to some PAC.

Moreover, the Connecticut clubwoman today is different from even a modern Navajo woman. A woman's *ideas*—especially about what is morally acceptable—are actually culturally conditioned. In a patriarchal society, for instance, it is easier for a girl to *feel* inferior, even if she really is not, while a woman living in a *non*repressive society will feel free to make moral, human decisions different from those of the heroine of a Jane Austen novel.

The crucial question is what is *objectively* unfitting, no matter what the time or culture. Is there something objectively abnormal about a boy with an earring, a female crane operator? If our society sanctions flag burning or public pornography, does that make these acts human? Was slavery ethical in the antebellum South but taboo today? Is acceptability of abortion, divorce, casual sex merely a matter of societal whim?

In 1953, there were about 400,000 divorces in the United States; in 1993, nearly 2 million. In 1953, there were 7,880 homicides; 1993, 26,570. Then, 18,000 rapes; now, 109,000. Then, 63,000 robberies; now, 672,480. In 1953, there were no abortion statistics since it was a crime, but in 1993 there were 1,528,930.[3] Our society has changed. Has what the word *human* means changed as well?

As Nietzsche pointed out clearly, in a world without willful gods or a purposive God, such questions are inoperative. If two knowledgeable people stand on opposite sides of, say, the capital

...1e, and there is no Higher Power to arbitrate ...then they are *both* right. The only way to settle ...their differences is to duke it out. Might makes right.

Not many even of the unchurched would be bold enough to assert "There is no God"—however practically impertinent such an Entity is to their everyday lives. And when it comes to practical decisions, their professed "belief" has little or no influence on any choice. "Church is church; business is business."

When asked if in business one must routinely compromise personal moral principles, the majority of (religiously trained) students respond "Yes" without hesitation. When asked if their religious "convictions" will have anything whatever to do with their choice of careers, the majority respond "No" with equal lack of hesitation. The way you choose shouts so loudly I can't hear what you claim. To all intents and purposes—though they would resolutely deny it—they are functional atheists.

No problem at all with that. The only difficulty is one of hypocrisy: claiming character, virtue, and religiosity (even to oneself) and at the same time basing all choices on egocentric motives. "I am an honest person who cheats and lies only when I have need and opportunity." From a society or individual without firm principles, such statements are lies told to the self and—worse—accepted by the self as true. No problem with being an egotist, only with claiming at the same time to be an altruist.

In order to live with ourselves, we have to feel "comfortable" within ourselves, "okay," "at home," with no outstanding "debts," guiltless. But without principles grounded outside the self—whether in the will of the gods or the objective natures of things (natural law), free choice becomes self-justifying, no matter what the choice or its consequences.

In the days of Elmer Gantry hellfire sermons, guilt brought the wayward back to the beaten path—at the cost of corroding souls with self-laceration: stunted, anxious, angry, unfulfilled.

Within little more than a generation, the pendulum came full swing to the point where guilt itself is the only "sin"—and with identical results: stunted, anxious, angry, unfulfilled souls.

When we get rid of the gods—effectively if not admittedly—we get rid of guilt. Without the gods, "anything is permitted." But when we get rid of guilt, what we get is Auschwitz.

Soulless Societies

The Camps

During World War II, the Nazis gassed and worked to death not only 6 million Jews but at least 10 million Slavs as well. They eliminated at least 150,000 homosexuals and about as many Gypsies as *Untermenschen,* less than human according to the philosophy and policies of that society. There were at least 2,700 priests in the Dachau camp, half of whom died. Gas accounted for "relatively few" deaths compared to the monstrous total; by far the majority were overworked as slaves and starved to death.

These men and women could not be allowed to sit idle; they were valuable commodities in a rational economy. Thus they were rented out as slaves to German war industries in the area: BMW, Messerschmidt, Krupp, I. G. Farben—many of them still profitable businesses today and contributing their fair share to the German economy and to the nation in taxes. The Oskar Schindlers were few, and even Schindler initially employed Jewish slaves out of self-interest. It was simply shrewd business practice, profitable for the war effort, the SS, and the industrialists.

Manpower meant money. A prisoner in the Dachau Camp found and kept a record of how valuable each worthless man and woman was to the Third Reich. (RM = Reichsmarks.)

Daily rental of prisoner =	+ RM	6.00
Deduction for food =	– RM	.60
Deduction for use of clothes =	– RM	.10
Value of prisoner per day =	+ RM	5.30
x Usual life span (270 days) =	+ RM	1,431.00
Average proceeds from rational disposal of corpse (fillings, clothes, bones, valuables held by bursar) =	+ RM	200.00
	+ RM	1,631.00
Cost of cremation =	– RM	2.00
Total value of prisoner =	+ RM	1,629.00[4]

The usual life span was nine months. But some lived four or five years, worth nearly 10,000 Reichsmarks each. This economy was most economical, extracting fillings, using hair for mattress stuffing, bones for fertilizer. That, to the rational economics of the Third Reich, was the "value" of a human being, each of whom was a son or daughter of someone, with dreams, hopes, a need for respect, each of whom had a soul, a self. But not in the Third Reich. *Untermenschen*. Gregor Samsas. Rational animals.

The question rankles. The men and women who carried out those atrocities were not Vandals come hot-eyed from the steppes in search of rapine and blood. They were for the most part out-of-work haberdashers and bakers, peach-faced boys and girls in swastika armbands, who would never even kick their neighbor's dog, who went home from work and played Mozart on the piano. They too were, supposedly, rational animals. The relative few who were tried after the war had as their sole justifying defense: "I was only following orders."

Perhaps being a rational animal is not enough.

In *Eichmann in Jerusalem,* Hannah Arendt came to the conclusion that the root of all Nazism meant and did was "the banality of evil." As George tells Lenny in *Of Mice and Men,* it's not wicked people who cause all the trouble; it's dumb people.

In what seems exaggeration, yet with enough echo of truth to make one ponder, Eugene Ionesco wrote:

> The world of the concentration camps . . . was not an exceptionally monstrous society. What we saw there was the image, and in a sense the quintessence, of the infernal society into which we are plunged every day.[5]

Hiroshima

On August 6, 1945, the first atomic bomb exploded over Hiroshima, a city in southwest Honshu, Japan. Within seconds, the combined heat and blast pulverized everything in the immediate vicinity, generated spontaneous fires some distance away, produced winds so powerful the flames burned out nearly four and a half square miles and killed between 70,000 and 80,000 and injured 70,000 more. Ninety percent of the city was leveled. Several days later, a second bomb, dropped on Nagasaki, killed between 35,000 and 40,000. The bombs were dropped on people, when they could have been dropped on deserted acreage.

President Truman argued that what seemed an atrocity to some, even to some of the bomb's inventors, brought the Japanese to their knees and that the bombs saved at least a half-million lives on each side. The mathematics are unarguable. The cost-effectiveness is beyond dispute.

My Lai

On March 16, 1968, U.S. soldiers led by Lt. William L. Calley invaded the South Vietnamese hamlet of My Lai, an alleged Vietcong stronghold. But the peasants must have been warned, since when the unit arrived no one was left but those who could not run: old people and infants. Nonetheless, since orders were to "Shoot anything that moves," the soldiers dutifully shot to death 347 unarmed civilians, then the cattle.

The incident did not become public until a full year later. Five soldiers were court-martialed, and Calley was sentenced to life at hard labor. But in September 1974, a federal court overturned the conviction and set Calley free, since he was only following orders. Whoever devised the mission and gave the orders was lost somewhere in the anonymity of military bureaucracy.

The event was horrific, and the question was how young men of a supposedly civilized society could so lose their humanity, their souls. However, had they killed far more people over a larger area, impersonally, with bombs, shells, rockets, white phosphorous, and napalm, they would have been following what is common military practice today, and the society which issued their orders could remain complacent of its rightness.

The Milgram Experiments

In the early '60s, Stanley Milgram, a professor of psychology at Yale, carried out a series of experiments on a cross section of volunteer males, from blue-collar workers to professionals. These paid volunteers were to act as assistants in experiments about the effect of punishment on learning. A subject was strapped to an "electric chair," and each time the subject missed a memory question, the volunteer in the next room pressed a button to deliver an electric shock, intensifying at each new wrong answer until the final calibration: "Danger: Brain Damage." Cries of the subject increased from murmurs, to gasps, to pleas, to shrieks of pain.

Actually, the experiment was not about learning but obedience. The "subject" suffered no pain; the cries were tape-recorded. The real subject was the volunteer at the console: how far would he go before compassion refused obedience?

Before the experiment, Milgram circularized 40 psychiatrists asking how many of 1,000 *teachers* would go all the way to "Danger: Brain Damage." Their estimate was one-tenth of one percent. Actually, 62 percent obeyed the commands when assured the experimenter took full responsibility. Teachers.

Milgram concluded:

> With numbing regularity good people were seen to knuckle under to the demands of authority and perform actions that were callous and severe. Men who in everyday life are responsible and decent were seduced by the trappings of authority, by the control of their perceptions, and by the uncritical acceptance of the experimenter's definition of the situation into performing harsh acts. The results, as seen and felt in the laboratory, are to this author disturbing. They raise the possibility that human nature, or more specifically, the kind of character produced in American democratic society, cannot be counted on to insulate its citizens from brutality and inhumane treatment when at the direction of a malevolent authority.[6]

American education does not train future citizens to think for themselves. We train in the Gradgrind method: ingest, disgorge, forget. Not, as Viktor Frankl argued, to make decisions. Rather we train citizens to conform.

Soulless Selves

A nation's soul is reflected in its art, which distills the anxieties, joys, warped ideas, and convictions of the majority of its citizens into the concrete-universal of single individuals.

Arthur Miller

The claustrophobic effect of the American Dream on the modern soul is captured as well as anywhere in Arthur Miller's *Death of a Salesman:* in the parents, Willy and Linda, and in the sons, Biff and Happy. Willy Loman bases his philosophy of life squarely on the guarantee that "personal attractiveness" will insure success and fulfillment. He sneers at the characters in the play who have substance, who plod onward step by step. What counts is making "the big deal." What counts is image. But Willy, who has worked all his life, is stifled in the city which has crept around his house like a predatory beast.

> WILLY: The way they boxed us in here. Bricks and windows, windows and bricks.
>
> LINDA: We should've bought the land next door.
>
> WILLY: The street is lined with cars. There's not a breath of fresh air in the neighborhood. The grass don't grow any more, you can't raise a carrot in the back yard. They should've had a law against apartment houses. Remember those two beautiful elm trees out there? When I and Biff hung the swing between them?
>
> LINDA: Yeah, like being a million miles from the city.
>
> WILLY: They should've arrested the builder for cutting those down. They massacred the neighbohood. *Lost!* More and more I think of those days, Linda. . . .

LINDA: Well, after all, people had to move somewhere.

WILLY: No, there's more people now.

LINDA: I don't think there's more people. I think—

WILLY: There's more people! That's what's ruining this country! Population is getting out of control. The competition is maddening! Smell the stink from that apartment house! And another one on the other side.[7]

In the end, plagued by hallucinations, out of a job, Willy finally kills himself so his wife can pay off the mortgage on a house no one will live in.

Willy's sons, Biff and Happy, have bought the American Dream too. But Biff can't cope with it, dropping out after high school, going from job to job and petty theft to petty theft. Now he works on a ranch and loves it, but he can't be happy because there's no money in it. Happy has a well-paying job, but he beds his friends' fiancées a week before their weddings.

BIFF: Are you content, Hap? You're a success, aren't you? Are you content?

HAPPY: Hell, no!

BIFF: Why? You're making money, aren't you?

HAPPY: All I can do now is wait for the merchandise manager to die. And suppose I get to be merchandise manager? He's a good friend of mine, and he just built a terrific estate on Long Island. And he lived there about two months and sold it, now he's building another one. He can't enjoy it once it's finished. And I know that's just what I would do. I don't know what the hell I'm workin' for. Some-times I sit in my apartment—all alone. And I

> think of the rent I'm paying. And it's crazy.
> But then, it's what I always wanted. My own
> apartment, a car, and plenty of women. And
> still, goddammit, I'm lonely.
>
> BIFF: Listen, why don't you come out West with
> me?
>
> HAPPY: You and I, heh? . . .
>
> BIFF: I'm tellin' you, kid, if you were with me I'd
> be happy out there.
>
> HAPPY: See, Biff, everybody around me is so false that
> I'm constantly lowering my ideals . . .
>
> BIFF: Then let's go!
>
> HAPPY: The only thing is—what can you make out
> there?[8]

That enslavement to false values was brought home to me by a well-to-do businessman who came for advice. He was wretched, hated his job, and his suppressed rage was threatening his marriage. I asked if he'd ever had a fulfilling job, and he said, "Of course. The job I had before I got promoted to this one. I couldn't wait to get to work Monday morning." I asked if he couldn't go to his boss, thank him for the confidence in promoting him, but ask if he could have his old job back.

He looked at me blankly. I asked how much he was making; $90,000. And how much at the previous job? $75,000. He began to see what I was driving at. "Wait a minute. You're asking me to give up fifteen grand!" I asked if it was making him happy. His face sagged. He kept bringing up objections: mortgage, kids' tuition. Move into an apartment; tell the kids to get jobs. Was his marriage worth a lousy fifteen grand? Seventy-five grand was not small potatoes.

Next day we talked for an hour again, round and round the same arguments. He left, and I never saw him again. Had he set himself free of the $15,000 and become happy again, I'm fairly sure he would have written to thank me.

Tennessee Williams

When *Cat on a Hot Tin Roof* appeared, Williams called it "the most highly, intensely moral work that I have produced."

The play takes place in a single evening, Big Daddy's birthday, on "twenty-eight thousand acres of the richest land this side of the valley Nile." Present are the Reverend; the doctor; the elder son, Gooper; his wife, Mae; and their five no-neck children. More importantly, there are Brick, the favored son who has broken his leg in a drunken attempt to run hurdles the previous night, and his wife, Maggie the Cat.

Brick and Maggie's sexual relationship is nonexistent, owing partly to Brick's anomalous feelings toward his lifelong, now dead friend Skipper, partly to Maggie's having once tried to sleep with Skipper, and partly to Maggie's earth-mother dominance of Brick, whom Williams describes as having "that cool air of detachment that people have who have given up the struggle." Brick encourages Maggie to take a lover, in fact he's "insultingly eager" that she do it.

Also, there is Big Mama, a perfumed and petulant rhino, and Big Daddy, the central engine of the play ("All of my life I been like a doubled up fist."), who has been told (wrongly) that he does not have terminal cancer. Big Daddy does not have a Norman Vincent Peale approach to life and humanity:

> When you are gone from here, boy, you are long gone and no where! The human machine is not no different from the animal machine or the fish machine or the bird machine or the reptile

machine or the insect machine! It's just a whole
God damn lot more complicated and conse-
quently more trouble to keep together.[9]

Big Daddy is a man who has made peace with "mendacity,"
pretending to love Big Mama when he can't "stand the sight,
sound, or smell of that woman for forty years now!" Pretending
to love "that son of a bitch Gooper and his wife Mae and those
five same screechers out there like parrots in a jungle."

BIG DADDY: *I've* lived with mendacity! Why can't
you live with it? Hell, you *got* to live
with it, there's nothing *else* to *live* with
except mendacity, is there?

BRICK: Yes, sir. Yes, sir, there is something else
that you can live with.

BIG DADDY: What?

BRICK: [lifting his glass] This! Liquor.

BIG DADDY: That's not living, that's dodging away
from life.

BRICK: I want to dodge away from it.[10]

For three acts, they loathe and lie to one another right to the
end, all victims of "moral paralysis." Unless Williams means to
create a group of characters—as Fellini did in *La Dolce Vita*—
so repellent in their excessive hedonism and self-absorption
that no sane person would want to emulate them, it is difficult
to justify "Cat" as a moral treatise, as Williams claims.
Theologian Robert Fitch examines his claim:

Since Tennessee Williams frankly declares himself
to be an evangelist, we may inquire what is the
gospel, the good news, which he has to offer. Man
is a beast. The only difference between man and

other beasts is that man is a beast that knows he
will die. The only honest man is the unabashed
egotist. This honest man pours contempt on the
mendacity, the lies, the hypocrisy of others who
will not acknowledge their egotism. The one irreducible value is life, which you must cling to as
you can and use for the pursuit of pleasure and of
power. The specific ends of life are sex and money.
The great passions are lust and rapacity. So the
human comedy is an outrageous medley of
lechery, alcoholism, blasphemy, greed, brutality,
hatred and obscenity. It is not a tragedy because it
has not the dignity of a tragedy. The man who
plays his role in it has on himself the marks of a
total depravity. And as for the ultimate and irreducible value, life, that in the end is also a lie.[11]

In our time, morality has become what Dr. Alfred Kinsey called
merely "social formalities" or "social restrictions." According to
such a view, one doesn't have sex on the front lawn as dogs do
merely from fear of what the neighbors might think. Therefore,
all customs, laws, and rules are relative, alien, arbitrary, and external to the individual. Sex is a purely biological action which
renders all guilt feelings superfluous. And, according to Dr. Kinsey,
the more frequently you flaunt the customs, the less the guilt.

There is no doubt that the work of Williams and others has
great power. The question is whether they offer any truth about
humanity other than humanity's refusal to evolve beyond
higher-level animals. The same might be said of the novels of
Genet, Jay McInerney, Kerouac, Burroughs, Ayn Rand, and so
many others who we are told *ad nauseam* in the reviews are
"brave, honest, audacious, sweeping, visionary, sensitive." As
Fitch asks:

Sensitive to what? Like a vulture to carrion?
Desire unsatisfied yields pain; desire satisfied yields
satiety *and* pain: this is the meaning of life.[12]

Paddy Chayevsky

Network (MGM, 1976) is Chayevsky's biting satire on the
people who provide us with television commercials to sway our
choices and also decide for us what we want to see—as well as
a satire on the people who eagerly gobble up what they provide.

Even the news no longer has anything to do with Ed
Murrow find-the-truth reportage. Max, the network news
chief, played by William Holden, says early on:

> Less than three percent read books. Less than 15
> percent read newspapers. An entire generation that
> doesn't know *anything* that didn't come out of this
> tube! We're in the boredom-killing business!

Howard Beall, played by Peter Finch, who won a posthumous
Oscar for his role, is the anchorman on Max's fourth-rated
network, and finally—on the air—he cracks: "I don't have any
bullshit left. I'm out of it, you see?" And he tells his shocked
audience that he's going to blow his brains out on the air the
following Tuesday.

At first the network executives are appalled and fire Beall
on the spot. But when they see what his bizarre claim has done
to their ratings, they have second thoughts. Because of the
arguments proposed by the icy, soulless Diana Christiansen (a
name fraught with ironies), played by Faye Dunaway, they not
only keep Beall but give him a show of his own, complete with
an orchestra and stained-glass windows. "They want someone
to articulate their rage," Diana says. And she's right.

And Beall performs to specifications:

> You've got to get mad! You've got to say, "I'm a
> human being, goddammit! My life has *value!*" So, I
> want you to get up now. I want you—all of you—
> to get up out of your chairs. I want you to get up
> right now and go to the window, and open it, and
> stick your head out and yell, "I'm mad as *hell,* and
> I'm not going to *take* this anymore!"

All over the country, windows fly up and heads emerge shouting, "I'm mad as *hell,* and I'm not going to *take* this anymore!"

But once you've shouted that, once you've vented your rage at being treated like a cockroach, what then?

Then Beall makes a deadly mistake. He begins to point his mad finger at precisely the proper villains: the corporate executives ultimately responsible for the chains of command which infantilize the American soul. The head of the corporation which has bought the network to turn a profit by any means (Ned Beatty) summons Beall into his presence and finally suborns him:

> You have meddled with the primal forces of
> nature, Mr. Beall! And I won't *have* it! Is that *clear?*
> . . . There *are* no nations; there is only one,
> holistic system of systems, vast and immense, inter-
> woven, interacting, a multinational dominion of
> *dollars!* It is the international system of currency
> which determines the quality of life on this planet.
> . . . There is no democracy. There is no America.
> There is IBM and ITT and ATT and Dupont,
> Dow, and Exxon. Those are the nations today. . . .
> The world is a *business,* Mr. Beall!

And who can gainsay him? The Economy has taken over our choices as the Law to the Hebrew, the Koran to the Muslim, the Church to the medieval peasant. Moneytheism creeps into every corner of our lives, sways our practical and ethical decisions. We merely substitute one slavery for another. As Dostoevsky's Grand Inquisitor shrewdly points out, there is no gift a human being will more gladly surrender than the curse of freedom.

When Beall finally becomes too much of an embarrass-ment, the network executives have a meeting to discuss their options. Diana offers a simple one, "Kill him." So they do. On the air.

The media have become the Superego of our society, permeating our attitudes about money, fame, sex, and, in general, what is important, desirable, moral, human. Nor do many mind. According to the Nielsen survey, children 2–18 watch 19 hours of television each week, children 12–17 watch 23 hours, males watch 18 hours, females 22 hours.[13] Of the 168 hours in the week, most of us sleep 56 and work 40, which leaves 72 hours free. Thus, most Americans spend 28 percent of their free time with the Tube.

Try to imagine what would happen if all the television and radio technicians went on strike for a month. Children watch it interminably, often without supervision. Equivalently, otherwise good parents allow their children to invite strangers into their homes and say and do anything they choose.

Something in *Network* spoke to the American people—and even to those who make their livelihood in the media and vote for the Academy Awards. The film won best actress, best actor, best supporting actress, best screenplay.

And it changed nothing. The foxes rule the henhouse.

Entitlement / Victimization

It is a good and just thing our society has finally recognized the objective victimization of women, blacks, raped women, abused children, the handicapped. But now that legitimate sense of victimization has broadened to become almost universal. When something bad happens to me, someone (else) must be blamed. Somebody's thwarted my God-given right to happiness. Although the framers of the Declaration of Independence restricted that right to the *pursuit* of happiness, we nonetheless have a kind of pseudo-psychology of entitlement. John Taylor writes:

> The central tenet of the postwar generation, reinforced by Dr. Spock, by television, and by advertising, was that every American was entitled not just to pursue happiness but to *be* happy, to enjoy steadily increasing prosperity, invigorating personal relationships, glowing health, a rich sex life, the respect of peers—in a word, fulfillment.[14]

Taylor also reports the following stories:

—Rose Cipollone developed lung cancer after smoking a pack and a half a day for forty years and sued three tobacco companies for it. The case got all the way to the Supreme Court.

—Mayor Marion Barry was caught smoking crack with a woman in a DC hotel and, like Adam, replied to arresting officers, "Bitch set me up." Then his friends claimed his arrest was racist.

—In March 1991, police made a frat-house drug bust at the University of Virginia, and Fred Carter, father of one of the arrested boys, shouted, "Why didn't investigators go to the University of Richmond or Norfolk State?" A clear case of discrimination.

—Doctors spend $117 billion a year for malpractice insurance.

—Books like *Obsessive Love: When Passion Holds You Prisoner* imply we have nothing to do with what we do.

—Dan White, who killed San Francisco mayor George Moscone, pleaded he was a victim of temporary insanity brought about by eating junk food.

—Members of ACT UP declared AIDS victims are killed not only by the disease but are "murdered" by the government's failure to find a cure.

—Both the ACLU and the NRA declared drug use a "victimless crime" and argued that the war on drugs "is no less than a war on the Constitution."

—A New York man was mutilated after he deliberately jumped in front of a subway but received $650,000 because the train hadn't stopped in time to avoid hitting him.

Amitai Etzioni, sociologist at American University, told Taylor: "The economy may work best if everyone is motivated by greed, but society doesn't." Today, it is difficult to separate "the economy" from "society." When negotiating with other world leaders, the American president at least doesn't appear to be arguing for the ordinary American woman or man. Of course, if big business prospers, we all prosper. That's a given. Depending on what "prosperity" means. And costs.

It is easy enough to say, as I have, we are victims of television. The more fundamental question is: How many of us are free to turn it off?

One is tempted, as so many intelligent students are, to the winsome pessimism of Kurt Vonnegut in *Cat's Cradle:*

> *The Fourteenth Book of Bokonon* is entitled, "What Can a Thoughtful Man Hope for Mankind on Earth, Given the Experience of the Past Million Years." It doesn't take long to read *The Fourteenth Book*. It consists of one word and a period. This is it: "Nothing."[15]

"Are Ya Havin' Any Fun?"

Aldous Huxley describes L. A., the City of Dreadful Joy:

> And what joy! The joy of rushing about, of always
> being busy, of having no time to think, of being too
> rich to doubt. The joy of shouting and bantering,
> of dancing and forever dancing to the noise of
> savage music. . . . The joy, in a word, of having
> what is technically known as a Good Time.[16]

One judges the validity of a philosophy not by its inner consistency or marketability to narcissists but by its results. What are the results of at least acting on (if not articulating) the principles guiding a society which eschews the human soul, a society resolutely empirical, this-worldly, secular, competitive, consumerist, pragmatic, utilitarian, contractual, and hedonistic?

To list only a few qualities in the general population at the end of the twentieth century, which at least did not seem as pervasive in the middle of it: we seem more insecure, neurotic, purposeless and uncommitted, fatalistic or fanatical, insensitive to genuine evil. In two words: spiritually anemic.

The competition essential to insure "the good life" engenders hostility, angry tensions, fear of inadequacy, and it pervades not only the workplace but social relations, families, athletics, education.

> The general feeling of insecurity is increased by
> the fact that for the most part neither tradition nor
> religion is strong enough today to give the indi-
> vidual a feeling of being an integral part of a more
> powerful unity, providing shelter and directing
> his strivings.[17]

Carl Jung insists neurosis occurs when one is unable or unwilling to cope with *legitimate* suffering, the natural crises that arise simply by our having bodies that change and by living in a world where "shit happens." Conversely, we achieve an adult self—a soul, character—by rising above those challenges. But we live in a society in which we are told, since we sat up in our Pampers to watch the Electronic Baby-sitter, we must not tolerate even *inconvenience*. We have come from fifty centuries in which scarcity was a given into an age when super-abundance is a given. Yet in 1993 alone, 5,000 Americans under 24 committed suicide. Perhaps they had been led to believe that life can deliver more than life *can* deliver.

Far too many work only at short-range goals and suffer from long-range purposelessness, afraid of commitment, preferring to "keep my options open" lest I miss out on something. It is what author Marya Mannes calls "the leukemia of non-commitment":

> Certain words are too troublesome for us now: sacrifice, nobility, courage. Only suckers give up something they want for something others need. Only suckers act purely from moral conviction. Only suckers stick their necks out for what they believe, when what they believe makes others uncomfortable. This is the cynicism of Play It Safe.[18]

We suffer also from fatalism. Nobody can do anything about anything. It's all just too big and out of whack. I'm nobody—which becomes a self-fulfilling prophecy. We forget that Martin Luther King Jr., Nelson Mandela, Lech Walesa, Mother Teresa, and anyone else who ever made a difference was once a nobody too.

Too often those who do refuse to knuckle under become fanatical, monomaniacally focusing on one side of one cause, intolerant of ambiguities. Every question is either/or and not more/less: Pro-Choice or Pro-Life, profits or welfare,

heterosexual or homosexual, white supremacy or black devi-
ousness. Most often such Teflon convictions are not personally
researched opinions but the "mind" of a group. "Less than three
percent read books. . . . An entire generation that doesn't
know *anything* that didn't come out of this tube!" They have the
delusion that thoughts acquired from hearsay and media are
their own ideas. They have no opinions; their opinions have
them. Thus, they abandon autonomous selves as free and
responsible beings.

Because of the glut of news every day about events that
would have been appalling a generation ago—drive-by
shootings, infanticide, terrorism, and the rest—we become
insensitive to evil. We notice it now only as we notice litter or
graffiti or noise, when they are especially blatant: Jeffrey
Dahmer, Jonestown, Waco, Oklahoma City. And if we are insensitive to an infant murdered every few days in New York City,
how indifferent can we become to our own peccadilloes?

> Western people are children of inner poverty,
> though outwardly we have everything. Probably
> no other people in history have been so lonely, so
> alienated, so confused over values, so neurotic. We
> have dominated our environment with sledge-
> hammer force and electronic precision. We amass
> riches on an unprecedented scale. But few of us,
> very few indeed, are at peace with ourselves,
> secure in our relationships, content with our loves,
> or at home in the world.[19]

We are free from superstitions, but we have lost our souls. We
have not turned to devils but to anesthesia. We no longer think,
as more primitive peoples did, of the earth as our Mother;
merely dirt under which there may be oil or uranium. The stars
lost their divinity as astronomy developed, and there is no need

for the blood of Adonis in a world of chemical fertilizers. And we know that the Rebel Without a Cause today is not going to hell. He is going nowhere.

Chapter Three

THE PURSUIT
OF HAPPINESS

If happy little bluebirds fly
beyond the rainbow
Why, oh, why can't I?

Arlen—*"Over the Rainbow"*[1]

Because you're not a bird, dummy.

The surest way to stall evolution of a human soul is to get caught in the game of If Only: "If only my parents had been different; if only I were white; if only I were taller (or shorter); if only I hadn't done that . . . "That game is so self-destructive because anything after those two words is, by definition, one of "the things that can't be changed." Wanting different parents or physique or past is as futile as flapping your arms to carry you over the rainbow. The inescapable result: frustration.

Yet we play If Only. Over and over. But unless you can live with things-as-they-are, you live an illusion. It may be consoling for a while, but sooner or later, reality bursts your self-induced cocoon. The house always wins. The only way to evolve a healthy soul is to accept yourself and the web around you for what they are—wounds, past mistakes, contrary agendas, unexpected setbacks: the lot—and get on with it.

Another warping game is Reductionism: fastening on a monochromatic "solution" to all the human problems and questions and negating all evidence to the contrary, even essential evidence. As we have seen, "rational animal" doesn't do the trick of capturing *all* being human means. No matter how that simplistic definition clears away the inconvenient philo-sophical and metaphysical mists that becloud the task of the sociologists, the physicians, the generals, the economists, and the politicians, human beings are far more complex and worthy of far more dignified treatment than the highest level apes or dolphins or dogs.

There are many with higher IQs and better degrees than mine who would dispute that. Therefore, we have to take time at this point to consider epistemology: What validates opinions? The only answer is: the-way-things-really-*are*.

Epistemology

If man has learned to see and know what really *is,*
he will act in accordance with truth. Epistemology
is in itself ethics, and ethics is epistemology.[2]

Whenever I begin a new course, my first task is to validate everything I'll claim for the rest of the year. So I begin: "I'm now going to say the most important sentence I'll say all year.

I won't say it until everyone has a pencil and paper." They all pull out pencils and paper (first day, you see; they have them). "Here it is: *The tree comes to me.*" They stop, squint up at me, jaws sag: Another loony, and we've got him for the whole year.

But that one sentence tells it all: I don't put the tree out there; I don't tell it what it is and how I can legitimately use it. It comes to me; it tells me. And if it falls in the forest when nobody's around to hear it (even me), it still makes a noise. Humbling to admit, but things are actually occurring at this very moment of which I'm totally unaware, but nonetheless they exist.

If I am to understand anything I do experience, I have to (1) perceive what's actually out there; (2) categorize it correctly with all others of its kind; (3) evaluate it fairly, without preconceptions, prejudice, vested interests; (4) call it by its proper name; and (5), if I'm wise, ask someone more knowledgeable to critique my opinion.

If I'm drunk and *perceive* the tree as "a big green ostrich, with no feet," my opinion is clearly foolish. If I see a man mincing along with his knees together and immediately *categorize* him "gay," I've left out the possibility he may have just suffered a cathartic accident and is scurrying to the nearest men's room.

If I see a black skin and immediately *evaluate* the person within it as "deadbeat," I've superimposed a prior bias on the facts.

If you offer me a thousand dollars and I write back that I "except" your gift, I shouldn't expect to get the grand; I've *said* precisely the opposite of what I meant.

And if I tell you, "There's a unicorn in the garden, and he just ate a lily," you can *critique* what I said by looking for yourself and will more than likely encounter a horse with an arrow in its forehead.

"My opinion's as good as anyone else's!" No, your opinion is only as good as the *evidence* and reasoning process that backs it up, and that evidence is "out there" *before* it's "in here."

There is a crucial difference between "objective truth" and "subjective truth." Objective truth—primary truth—is outside the mind; it remains true whether you agree with it or like it or are even aware it is the truth: Acid burns, dropped objects fall, too much tension gives you a headache. If there are intelligent beings on other planets, they're there even if we've never experienced them.

Subjective truth—secondary truth—is inside the mind; it has value *only* if it conforms as closely as possible to what is, in fact, outside the mind. Objective truth validates your opinion's claim to be true. Your opinion on a physics question is probably not as good as Steven Hawking's, even if you have a Ph. D. in Elizabethan drama. My opinion on astronomy can't contend with Carl Sagan's. On the other hand, his opinion about the limits of what can be real may not be as good as mine.

A poem isn't a Rorschach test: "What do those words make you think about?" One day early in my teaching, I got a lesson from a student that changed my whole understanding of my task as a seducer of minds. We were doing a poem called "Wind and Silver."

> Greatly shining
> The Autumn moon floats in the thin sky
> And the fishponds shake their backs
> and flash their dragon scales
> As she passes over them.[3]
>
> —Amy Lowell (1874–1925)

I explained that, even with the metaphor comparing the flickering from the wavelets to dragon scales and the personification of the moon, it was just a simple picture; no great probing of the human experience. A hand shot up: "I've got a different interpretation."

I said fine, provided the evidence from the poem backed up the opinion. "It's about a U-2 flight over Red China." I gaped; where's the evidence? "Right there: 'dragon scales.'" You've just taken two words and spun out your own poem, like repainting the *Mona Lisa*. "That's *your* opinion." I tried sarcasm: why couldn't it be a U-2 flight over medieval England; they apparently had dragons too. "That's *your* opinion." My teeth fused, but I knew I had him: "Look at the *bottom* of the poem!" I sort of shouted. "She was *dead!* There *were* no U-2s! There *was* no Red China!" But his face was smug as marble: "That's *your* opinion." The last I recall of the incident, before the white coats arrived, was two stout football players trying to pry my thumbs from that kid's windpipe.

As inquiring reporter columns prove, every person on any street in America has an opinion on any subject at all: welfare, abortion, homosexuality, the president, the coach of the Knicks, the guilt or innocence of the latest tabloid murderer. But you wouldn't go broke offering a dollar to any one of them who had read a book on any of those topics. Like free choices, opinions seem self-justifying simply because one holds them, bedamned the evidence. "Don't bother me with facts. My mind's made up."

How, then, do we establish that human beings deserve to be treated better, more fairly, and with greater dignity than we treat whales? Simple: You look at the objective facts.

The rock comes to me; it tells me what it is and how I can legitimately use it. It has mass, weight, electrical charge, and it just sits there, unfeeling. I can use it as a weapon, kick it, mortar it into a wall. The objective facts tell me that.

The carrot comes to me; it tells me what it is and how I can legitimately use it. It has all the qualities of the rock, BUT it can also take in nourishment, grow, reproduce other carrots— which no rock can do. That's one quantum leap upward.

Because, like the rock, it has no feelings, I can cut a carrot up, boil it, and use it to stay alive. Conversely, that inherent quality in the carrot which empowers it to feed makes it objectively unfitting to throw it around in a cafeteria food war as if it had no more value than snowballs. The objective facts tell me that.

The bunny comes to me; it tells me what it is and how I can legitimately use it. It has all the qualities of the rock and carrot, BUT it can move around, sense danger, feel pain— which no rock or carrot can do. Another quantum leap upward. Because of that objective sensitivity to pain, it is objectively unfitting to torture a live rabbit as if it had no feelings like the rock and carrot. Conversely, because a rabbit is of a lower species than humanity (which still has to be proved), it is legitimate to use the rabbit's flesh to sustain my family.

Human beings come to me; they tell me what they are and how I can legitimately use them. They have all the qualities of the rock, the carrot, and the bunny, BUT they are self-aware, able to encompass the not-yet-real, canny enough to improvise, to invent ways to outwit unexpected cataclysms and to fabricate machines that will give them powers programmed into other animals but denied humans. If a new Ice Age looms, we needn't struggle as far as we can, like animals, then die; we can take the skins of other animals, we can make fire. No other animal can do that. If nature has denied us the wings it gave birds or the gills to swim underwater it gave fish, we can make machines that allow us to transcend our limitations. No other animal can do that.

Dolphins and whales communicate at great distances underwater, but so far we're unable to decipher it, nor are they yet able to communicate with us. Chimps seem able to fathom certain simple symbolic communications, but so far that ability is like an infant's ability to point things out, call them by name, express basic needs. But the capper is that, at least as far as we can determine, not even the cleverest animal is troubled by *conscience.* There is no such thing as a "bad dog"; mad perhaps, but not bad. If a dog wets the rug, it's only "doin' what comes natcherly." Not bad dog, lazy owner.

As far as we can tell, no lioness lumbers out of the jungle, gobbles a villager, and lurches back moaning, "Oh, God! I did it *again! I've got to get counseling!"* Humans do. At least good humans do; bad humans don't. That's how you tell the difference.

Humans come in widely varying colors, sizes, shapes, sexual proclivities, and habits, but any medical examiner can tell whether this tissue is from an animal or a human. The Declaration of Independence says each of us has inalienable rights to life, liberty, and the pursuit of happiness—not because we are American but because we are human. And those rights are "self-evident," based on inescapable objective fact.

Nor is this an insight restricted to our own society or to this particular era. Thomas Traherne asks: "Can you be righteous unless you be just in rendering to things their due esteem? All things were made to be yours and you were made to price them according to their value."[4] And Aristotle says, since every "is" implies an "ought," the aim of education is to make pupils like and dislike what they ought to like and dislike.[5] In early Hinduism, righteousness is identified with *satya,* the truth: correspondence to reality. The Chinese Tao is the Way, that is, the way the universe goes on, the laws written into the natures of things. It is a belief in *objective value,* the conviction certain attitudes are true to things as they are and others are false.

This is called Natural Law. As C. S. Lewis writes:

> This thing which I have called for convenience the *Tao,* and which others may call Natural Law or Traditional Morality or the First Principles of Practical Reason or the First Platitudes, is not one

among a series of possible systems of value. It is the
sole source of all value judgments.[6]

Those values within the ascending stages of the entities we
encounter are objective facts, and therefore, any subjective
opinions about their value and the legitimate ways we can treat
them must be grounded in those objective facts.

In a futuristic novel called *Stranger in a Strange Land,* the
society has enlisted Fair Witnesses, functionaries whose sole
purpose is to tell the truth only insofar as they have objective
evidence to substantiate what they claim. To demonstrate, a
man asks a Fair Witness the color of the house on yonder hill.
Her response is: "The two sides I can see appear to be a shade
of white." However, if one were allowed to speak only on those
conditions, our society would be mute.

But at least one's best attempt to do that would make the
world a bit less angry and frustrated, a bit more honest and
trusting. At the very least, we would be honest with ourselves,
not telling ourselves comforting lies—and, worse, believing
them. "I want a good education; I'm an honest person; I've
done nothing to feel guilty about; it certainly wasn't *my* fault."
The greatest enemy of narcissistic self-absorption is the truth.

They tell a story (perhaps too good to be true) of George
Bernard Shaw sitting at dinner next to a beautiful woman. He
leans over and inquires, "I say, would you sleep with me for
100,000 pounds?" She blushes and says, "I rather think I would."
Shaw twists his mustache and asks, "Would you sleep with me
for five pounds?" The lady stretches her neck and arches her
brows, "*What* do you think I *am?*" Shaw snorts, "We've already
settled that part. Now we're just haggling over prices."

Such honesty and refusal to deceive oneself is not a popular
sport. But then it never has been. In *Pilgrim's Progress,* Christian
and his companion showed up at Vanity Fair to buy truth. They
were thrown into prison for nonconformity.

Reductionism

In order to understand things better, we set them off against their opposites and contrast them *as if* they really were completely independent of one another:

—masculine/feminine

—autonomy/community

—left brain/right brain

—scientism/fundamentalism

—black/white

—positivism/existentialism

—good/evil

—denotation/connotation

—flesh/spirit

—absolutism/relativism

—reason/intuition

—cerebral/visceral

—sacred/secular

—justice/mercy

But in concrete reality, they're not as easily separable. Male/female, for instance, is an objective fact, instantly clear; lift the diaper, case closed. "Masculine/feminine," not so. If by "masculine" (as opposed to "male") we mean qualities associated with the left brain—logic, calculation, decisiveness, etc., then Margaret Thatcher is more "masculine" than June Cleaver, yet both are females. If by "feminine" we mean qualities associated with the right brain—intuition, inclusiveness, ability to see a problem in context rather than in isolation, Alan Alda is more "feminine" than Norman Mailer, though both are male.

Reductionism is uncomfortable with more/less; it prefers everything either/or. It is a result most often of the tyranny of the strictly analytical, unemotional, objective left brain over the mistier but nonetheless real apprehensions of the empathic, intuitive, let's-see-this-in-*context* right brain. The left brain deals in strict definitions, but look up the word *love* in a dictionary, and after forty-plus lines ask yourself if that "captures" what love really means. Definitions are like cookie-cutters, sharp and clean, but they leave out a lot.

Reductionism is dear to propagandists, ignoring any evidence contrary to their convictions. For instance, you may believe, unflinchingly, a fetus is nothing more than a part of a woman's body, like her appendix. The objective fact, however, is half the fetus's DNA is completely different from the mother's.

Conversely, you may believe, unflinchingly, that an ovum becomes human the instant it's penetrated by a sperm cell. The objective fact, however, is most fertilized zygotes never implant themselves in the uterine wall; thus most human beings die before they are born. This tendency to simplism led me to O'Malley's Law: "The less you know, the more certain you can be."

Literalism is reductionist too. It removes all overtones, connotations, suggestiveness. To the reductionist Gradgrind, a horse is an "equine quadruped." Surely, that is what a horse *is,* but is that all a horse *means?* If we go beyond strict definitions, we can, at least in some degree, understand friendship, love, loyalty even though we can't "dissect" them.

Credulous literalism (fundamentalism) believes every word in (their) scripture is the univocal voice of God, even when it contradicts objective reality and common sense: God created light before there were planets and finished creation in seven literal days; prophets lived a millennium; those who look with lust should literally blind themselves; heaven is a real golden city and hell is endless fire—even outside physical space. Such simplism requires we keep all we know about physics, biology, chemistry, psychology in one brain lobe and all we know about spiritual realities in the other, and never the twain shall meet.

Skeptical literalism (scientism) will admit nothing as real (or at least pertinent) which is not verifiable through physical instruments and mathematical logic. Thus, it asserts humans are merely more highly skilled and complex animals, and the daily newspapers offer plenty of evidence that far too many at least *act as if* they were little better (or in fact worse) than animals.

Even more reductionist is the assertion that humans are no more than more complicated machines, products *solely* of heredity, environment, physics, and chemistry, which can be manipulated by using the proper stimuli to effect a desired purpose. Surely, the advertising industry offers a great deal of evidence of success in *acting as if* that were true.

But some of the best minds studying the brain today seem to give unquestionable testimony that we are nothing more than a superior tangle of electrochemical interactions. Remember: Your children hear their biology teachers more credulously than they hear you or any agent of religion. This is what many hear:

> Despite our every instinct to the contrary, there is one thing that consciousness is not: some entity deep inside the brain that corresponds to the "self," some kernel of awareness that runs the show, as the "man behind the curtain" manipulated the illusion of a powerful magician in "The Wizard of Oz." After more than a century of looking for it, brain researchers have long since concluded that there is no conceivable place for such a self to be located in the physical brain, and that it simply doesn't exist.[7]

The inescapable conclusion from such research is that *I* simply don't *exist*. I am no more than a self-delusion. Which I naively accept. But what is left out?

Rationalist Reductionism

Psychiatrist Gerald May questions equating brain and soul:

> Paradoxically, as we discover more about the brain, we are increasingly tempted to try to reduce our spiritual realities to matters of chemistry. Perhaps the most obvious example was the great psychedelic craze of the 1960s. Discovering certain chemicals could alter awareness through their effects upon the brain, many entertained the notion drugs might be a vehicle for greater realization of God. Psychedelic drugs affect brain chemistry directly, thereby sometimes producing states . . . very similar to naturally occurring spiritual experience.[8]

One might draw the same conclusion from the use of hypnosis or from outbursts in charismatic sessions or from emotional stimulation at a rock concert. The critical question is whether such experiences have any permanent effect, whether they are true spiritual nourishment or merely momentary stimulation of the nerves. When people smoke marijuana, for instance, they sometimes giggle helplessly—even though there is nothing funny, and they are not laughing sociably but entirely alone. It is like being tickled, which few adults enjoy, but they nonetheless laugh helplessly because a nerve is being stimulated.

No doubt our emotions are *dependent* on electrochemical functioning of nerve cells. But which triggers which? Surely anxiety triggers ulcers—and whatever in the brain makes ulcers happen, not the other way around. Am I anxious because some unknowable transactions in my brain "tell" me to be anxious, or is the whole process triggered by something outside myself?

> Just as certain concentrations and combinations of brain chemicals can trigger thoughts, feelings, memories, and behavior so also can thoughts feelings, and the like trigger changes in chemicals.[9]

Romantic Reductionism

Such reduction of humanity to mechanics is challenged by an opposite but equally reductionist romanticism: existentialism, flower children, beatniks, Burroughs, Shelby, *Pulp Fiction*. Nickles, the character in Archibald MacLeish's J.B. who assumes the role of Satan, is typical of this life-stance. He is painfully aware of the world's wickedness, agonizingly focused in the sufferings of Job and his family. But he is self-blinded to the smiles of children, the glory of sunsets, the vastness of stars, "the little green leaves in the wood and the wind on the water." All life is for him unrelieved misery, then you die.

Sydney Hook characterized existentialism as a philosophy of the absurd which appeals to those "who are terribly excited by ideas but resent the discipline necessary to analyze them." Here we have two radically contrasting mind-sets: scientism's study of humanity using an objectivity as cold and rarefied as an unrooted calculus; existentialism's study of humanity through an utterly subjective focus on the self in meaningless angst. For either, questioning the purpose and meaning of human life is itself meaningless. It just is. But if you subscribe to either mind-set's common initial premise—that the reality of the spirit must be a delusion—their conclusions are inescapable.

Absolutism / Relativism

Another pervasive apparent dichotomy is between absolutism and relativism, "Anything not compulsory is forbidden," or "Anything goes."

The absolutism of the Grand Inquisitor, Napoleon, Hitler, Stalin, white supremacists, fundamentalist Islam, and B. F. Skinner is a tempting outlook, especially when the streets are crime-ridden, unemployment is crushing, and the railroads don't run on time. As the Grand Inquisitor suggested, if you give them bread and circuses, miracles of productivity and healing, and the power to coerce rectitude, they will put their freedom in your hands as quickly as they can. Yet most of us are not quite ready to go to the extreme of contented slavery. As someone once said, whoever would surrender freedom for security deserves neither.

By far the most prevalent simplism today is the opposite, relativism. It is difficult to avoid. In colleges and even in high schools, students ingest radically different life views from differing professors, and of course they all have to be right. After all, each has a terminal degree. Since students were children, they have been barraged by contradictory voices: on the one side, parents, clergy, some teachers; on the other, the media, the commercials, rock lyrics, *Playboy,* plus a grasp of cookbook science just sufficient for them to misunderstand it entirely. And the latter voices are far more compelling.

For today's relativist, the basic justifications for human choices are: "Everybody does it" and "Can we get away with it?" In effect, relativism justifies and absolves everything. But if everything is right when it is expedient, then "right" has no meaning. A neutrality regarding values is absurd once one acknowledges that all human (moral) relationships are two-way streets. Easy enough when injustice lands on someone else, but not when it's aimed at me. What's more, it's the rules which leave us free to play the game. We want an umpire who is consistent and impartial; we want a game with rules.

Immanent / Transcendent

A final apparent dichotomy that pertains to a study of evolving a soul is rooted (as all the others probably are) in the age-old conflict between immanent/transcendent, flesh/spirit, good/evil: that is, the view of humanity as radically corrupt or humanity as radically good. It is a conflict that torments King Arthur in T. H. White's *The Once and Future King,* but it is probably seen most clearly in contrasting the two books students for thirty-five years have said "tell it like it is": *Catcher in the Rye* and *The Lord of the Flies.* They never seem to have realized or been told that the two books completely contradict one another.

The premise of *Catcher:* humanity is radically innocent, like Holden's sister, Phoebe: society turns them into "goddam phonies" like Stradlater and Ackley. On the contrary, the premise of *The Lord of the Flies:* humanity is radically corrupt and only a veneer of civilization keeps us from savagery.

Which are we?

Both.

Each of the apparent dichotomies we have seen has legitimate and worthwhile insights into what it means to be human, but each needs the corrective of the other, just as the extreme liberal needs the corrective of the extreme conservative, and vice versa. Any virtue without the balance of its opposite becomes a vice: justice without compassion becomes cruelty; compassion without justice becomes maudlin sentimentality.

We have an itch to reduce things to their least common denominator, which is a perfectly natural function of the human mind. Unfortunately, reality—especially the human reality—eludes our cookie-cutter definitions and theories. Humans are not merely rational animals, males are not all swagger and females merely yielding, love is not just physical and emotional. Too much is left out which is not only pertinent but essential to a genuine (if tentative) grasp of the real truth. Therefore, we will be speaking often about *polarities.* To understand the human soul—or anything else—we need a tolerance for ambiguity.

In *The Abolition of Man,* C. S. Lewis castigates a system of education that produces "men without chests," with no connection between instinct and intellect, *mens sana in corpore sano,* rational animals.

What is left out of that definition and its resultant education of human beings is all that is associated with the heart, magnanimity, the right brain, the "feminine."

What is left out is the soul.

Happiness

What do we all want? What will make us wag our tails even when we're exhausted? That's simple: happiness. No matter with what images a particular society might embody that desire, all societies are looking for the Garden of Eden, the Workers' Paradise, the American Dream, a Gauguin lagoon, the Kingdom of God, the womb, kindergarten, over Jordan. Not in some future (and perhaps nonexistent) heaven: *Now.* As one perceptive high school senior asked, "Why is fulfillment always in the future?"

But has anybody ever sat down and figured out what the hell "happiness" *means?* If we set off in pursuit of happiness, what are we really looking for? How will we know we haven't blundered right past the road to it? The most basic question is the one Dionne Warwick posed to Alfie: "What's it all about?"

Trouble is, few of us have had time (till now) to ponder just what "success" and "the good life" and "fulfillment" really mean. Strange, isn't it? The whole purpose of human life—and nobody has time to figure out what it is. Surely our education is too busy with such profound matters as the tangent of angle AOC and the law of supply and demand to help us find it.

But you can't achieve a vague goal: Where are you going? "Oh, uh, . . . *some*where, that's for sure!" Which is one of the reasons so many of us feel a continual, indefinable malaise, like the hero in a Kafka story: because, by our very nature, we're sent on a quest. But we haven't the slightest idea what we're looking for.

Although relatively few have taken on the arduous task of puzzling what happiness means, we all have a gut feeling what it is: feeling good. And the ad makers, the rock lyricists, and the soaps are more than willing to share their insights on what will bring that about. But if feeling good is the criterion for happiness, as William James wrote, "drunkenness would be the supremely valid human experience." And reality being what it is, the quest for uninterrupted gratification inevitably gives rise to "I Can't Get No Satisfaction." We can find no satisfactory answer to the question of human happiness unless we factor inevitable suffering into our definition.

Happiness is not an *emotional* condition, any more than love is. We want not just to feel happy but to have a *reason* to be happy. Pleasure is not the goal of our aspirations but the result of attaining them. As Viktor Frankl says, "Pleasure is, and must remain, a side-effect or a by-product, and is destroyed or spoiled to the degree to which it is made an end in itself."[10]

One way of looking at the meaning of human happiness is to consider what we want for our children, which again brings forth an instinctive, why-of-course, and too simple answer: to give them "the best" and shield them from harm; maximum security and minimum suffering. But that is too simplistic.

What does such care to "provide and protect" keep our children from, at least after puberty has kicked in? Adulthood. Every society that ever existed has known that once a child has achieved physical adulthood, he or she must *begin* to take on a completely different role in the community, to become one of the ones who provide-and-protect.

At puberty, girls' bodies give them painful evidence of that, but the men had to take pubescent boys out into the woods, scare them to adulthood, circumcise them with stone knives, in order to inflict on them the same bloody realization nature had inflicted on their sisters. Again, no answer to the question of what human fulfillment means is complete without factoring in pain.

In Walter Miller's *A Canticle for Liebowitz* a futuristic abbot mulls what he should have said to a Doctor Cors, who runs an assisted suicide parlor at the outset of an atomic war:

> "Really, Doctor Cors, the evil to which even you should have referred was not suffering, but the unreasoning fear of suffering. *Metus doloris.* Take it together with its positive equivalent, the craving for worldly security, for Eden, and you might have your 'root of evil,' Doctor Cors. To minimize suffering and to maximize security were natural and proper ends of society and Caesar. But then they became the *only* ends, somehow, and the only basis of law—a perversion. Inevitably, in seeking only them, we found only their opposites: maximum suffering and minimum security."[11]

When most of us think of "peace" (which is usually somewhat short of "happiness"), we probably think of it in terms of "being unbothered," the urge most travel ads play on: Come to Tahiti or Curaçao or Aruba, and get away from it all. Peace is all that's promised by est, Rolfing, New Age crystals: "Eat this and you'll become like God."

But if our idea of peace is being unbothered, then we landed in the wrong galaxy. The least bothered people are in cemeteries or solitary confinement. What good is a story without surprises; how exhilarating is a game you can't lose?

If what we want most out of life is security, then we have a wrong notion of what genuine, lasting security requires. If we are dependent on anything *outside* our selves—money, fame, power—we can never be secure, because all those are subject to chance. Only when we possess and are content with our selves, confident enough to face whatever comes, will we be secure.

The Greeks had a similar idea of the meaning of happiness. Their word for it was *eudaimonia,* having a good soul; not feeling good but being good. It had nothing to do with emotions. Rather it was a sense of being "at home" within oneself and within society and within the world. Self-possessed yet open to all. In that sense of "happiness," victims at Auschwitz stumbling toward the gas chambers with their chins high and their souls in their own hands were happy. Hitler capering at Napoleon's tomb over the humiliation of France was merely feeling good.

Toward the end of his life, Freud evolved an insight into human fulfillment called "The Pleasure Principle," which uses the word *pleasure* far differently from feeling good. He said that within each of our souls (and he did use that word, as we will see later) there are two antagonistic polarities: *Eros,* the life wish, and *Thanatos,* the death wish. Eros is a drive toward challenge; Thanatos is a drive toward being unbothered.

It is Eros in our souls that impels us to take the risk of marrying, committing ourselves to children we will not see for nine months, setting sail for home from Troy not knowing what the winds and waves portend, giving up something comfortable in the hope of something better.

Thanatos impels us back to the womb, where we were closer to Eden than we will ever be again: warm, fed, floating, untroubled by doubts because we couldn't think. Eros is willing to strive, even if one doesn't achieve; in the going, I'm already there. Thanatos settles for the maximum return from the minimum input. The Eastern concept of Nirvana is in a real sense the fulfillment of Thanatos: liberation not only from all unpleasant sensation but from any sensation whatever, even from being an individual.

If Freud is right, the best in us does not crave the happiness, fulfillment, and peace of feeling good or being unbothered. The best in us craves the serenity of tightrope walkers, fighter pilots, people who defuse bombs to save others: knowing you're doing the right thing and at least have a chance.

Chapter Four

Myth: The Will
to Meaning

Long before there were philosophers to think systematically about the question, men with matted hair and bodies daubed with mud realized that this humanity of theirs was somehow something that could be lost, something fragile, to be guarded with offering and sacrifice and taboo, to be cherished by each succeeding generation. "What must we do to be human" is a question as old as humanity itself.

Margaret Mead—*Male and Female*[1]

The Need to Feel "At Home"

When a child wakes up in the night after a bad dream and finds herself alone in the dark, reality is all askew; she's lost in a dark

89

landscape where there are no reassuring landmarks. So she cries out in terror for her mother, and her mother is there, turning on the light, holding the child in her arms, rocking her, and saying, "It's okay, honey. Everything's just fine." At that moment, the mother is the high priestess of meaning. Wordlessly the child feels harmony restored to her world, and things are "as they should be." All of us, no matter what our age, need some sense that "It's okay, honey."

In the womb and for the first year or so, the infant feels at one with the mother. But when the mother goes back to work within a few months or weeks, what effect does that have on a child? A century of child psychology has taught us that the child feels "disconnected." Throughout the first two years of life, a child has a deep need for continuous contact with one sensorily identifiable human being. Going back to work may seem essential to keep up "a certain standard of living." But what do those words mean? For whom are we keeping it up?

This is true also of the human race in modern times. Once, we were at-one with nature, the soil, animals, plants. When that connection is lost, as a people we feel "disconnected." We can see it in the history of Native Americans, dragged into "civilization" and finding themselves lost, aimless, and disenchanted. That pervasive sense of rootlessness can be assuaged, momentarily, by drugs or sex or by absorption in a family, group, team, work. At least we're not wandering, alone.

Home is a "sacred" place, even for the nonreligious. Just as religious people believe that at the church doorsill, they step from secular into sacred space, all of us believe there is a special space beyond our own doorsills which simply cannot be violated. This is my place, where I can close the door on chaos and find some kind of cosmos, peace, belonging. "Home is," as Frost said, "the place where, when you have to go there, they have to take you in." Objects in that home are also "holy": a box of letters, an old photograph album, objects and pictures on your desk that say, "This is mine; here is a place I *belong.*"

Christmas is a "sacred" time even for those who do not practice or believe in religion. It is "a time to go home," to recapture a meaningful past where family made everything more or less "make sense." Thanksgiving and Christmas are the busiest times of the year for airlines: "Gotta get home! It's Christmas!" And without family, Christmas can be the most soul-harrowing time of the year; Christmas is also the busiest time for suicides—who die of "homesickness." We remember. And we want to go back to when things were "right."

There are three basic human drives: to pleasure, to power, and to meaning. Our present society offers us ample (often spurious) means to achieve the first and second, but little, if any, help in achieving a sense of meaning or wholeness. We still feel haunted by nostalgia for the sense of "rightness" a child feels before being differentiated from its mother. We want life and self to be an organic unity of parts, whose boundaries are nonetheless open-ended and fluid. The idea is captured in such terms as *wholehearted, whole-minded, wholesome.*

But home is also the place we must *leave.* In folktales— stories that societies have told for thousands of years to explain growing up—the heroine or hero is forced to leave home on a perilous journey, or some displacement in the home (like a new wicked stepmother) has made "home" not the same source of reassurance it had always been. We find it in the great myths and parables: *The Odyssey* and *The Aeneid,* the uprootings of Adam and Eve, Abraham and Sarah, Noah, Rachel, the missions of Buddha, Jesus, Paul, and Mohammed, *The Divine Comedy, Pilgrim's Progress.*

"Hansel and Gretel," for instance, says children sooner or later must leave the nest and discover how to make their own way using their wits. And that need is true of the great folktales of our own day, as we will see. They mirror the polar tension each of us feels in our souls (not minds or bodies) between wanting to belong and wanting to become an independent self.

Yet even if the journey lies away from home, the goal is always to return home. As Dorothy says when she clicks her red slippers, "There's *no* place like home." But she returns not the dismissable girl she was; she is now becoming a woman. The goal of the evolving soul is to bring cosmos out of chaos again, but it will not be the old order but a new, different, better one.

The quest of an evolving soul is to become one's *own* mother and father, the true mother who knows no misdeed is beyond forgiveness, the true father who knows every misdeed demands amends.

Myths: Symbolic Stories

> I don't know Who—or what—put the question. I don't know when it was put. I don't even remember answering. But at some moment I did answer Yes to Someone—or Something—and from that hour I was certain that existence is meaningful and that, therefore, my life, in self-surrender, had a goal.[2]

The first step toward a meaningful life story is affirming the world *as it is:* good and bad, darkness and light, rather than hoping it might yield to your expectations. Every natural human impulse—sexuality, aggression, sensitivity, doubt—must not be denied or subjugated or suppressed but sublimated, integrated, made fruitful. As Hammarjsköld said, we must say "Thanks" for all that has been and "Yes" to all that is to come. The only alternative is neurosis.

We must forgive the past and face the future with serenity and confidence. But for that we need a map. Without one, we are as adrift as Updike's Rabbit Angstrom or Kerouac's Dharma Bums. It may be a chart as primitive as a Renaissance sea captain's, but you can constantly update it. That's what a personal philosophy of life—a myth—is for.

The word *myth* has two valid but contradictory meanings, as different as "false" and "true." Its more common usage means a widely held delusion, as in "The Vietnam War dispelled the myth America could never lose a war." The other, opposite meaning—as in the myths of Sisyphus, the Grail, Holden Caulfield—is a story that acts like a symbol, trying to capture a truth of human life in a right-brain metaphorical way rather than in a left-brain philosophical way.

These systems of stories have been retold for thousands of years, passing from one culture to another so often that the details which individuate them to a particular culture erode and what is left is a scheme embodying a *universal* truth, applicable to any human being of whatever time or culture.

A myth in this sense has many functions. First, mystical: attempting to capture the wonder of the universe and ourselves; second, cosmic (science): explaining how the universe and human beings work; third, societal: seeking to ground the humanizing customs of the tribe in an archetypal story; fourth, pedagogical: showing the young how to live humanly under any circumstances.

Do I matter? Am I useful? Have I value? We need some context against which to justify the struggle and assuage our horror of futility. We need a *pattern* to life in the disparate elements of our experience, anchored in trust with a basis for hope, so our very being is not haphazard. We need to feel that our selves and our toil have significance. (The activity of a beehive or an assembly line may be purposeful, but it is not meaningful.)

As Nietzsche said, anyone with a "why" to live for can put up with just about any "how"—if there is some felt context in which the hardships make *sense*. Frankl and others have shown this movingly in their studies of human behavior in the un-reality of the Nazi camps. Without a sense of purpose, life "is a tale told by an idiot, full of sound and fury, signifying nothing."

Meaning, purpose, commitment are inseparable. And without them, there is no hope of fulfillment. For those who "keep their options open," life is merely something that happens to them.

Symbols

Rational definitions are essential if we are to understand the world and ourselves, but they simply can't go far enough when we try to understand realities peculiar to human beings. A dictionary can box in any reality from aardvark to zymurgy, but in no case does it help us grasp anything's *meaning*, especially the prickly realities specifically human: love, hope, pride, integrity, trust, etc.—even meaning itself. For that, we need symbols. My dictionary takes forty tightly printed lines to define love, and when I come to the end of them, I'm still befuddled. But a little girl with meticulously cornrowed hair "says" love, too, and a great deal more satisfyingly than Noah Webster.

A symbol is an inadequate way to physicalize a human reality that actually exists but is not of itself physical: death (skull), achievement (diplomas), freedom (wings). As Saint-Exupéry saw, "The essential is always invisible." A symbol, then, is like the clothes the Invisible Man had to don in order to be seen. The symbol is inadequate because it is only an approximation, not experience of the actual reality, but rather like describing green to a blind person as "chewing mint leaves and sucking the juice." Not the reality, but better than nothing. Problems arise in considering fundamentalism and scientism from taking the symbol literally and either making it into an idol or poo-poohing it as childish.

Some symbols are universal, exuding the same connotations no matter what the time or culture: natural symbols. Other symbols have meaning only within the framework of a particular time and society: culturally conditioned symbols.

Fire, for instance, is a natural symbol of light, energy, zeal, enthusiasm. Unchecked, it is rapacious; harnessed, it gives power. From ancient Druid pyres to modern beach bonfires, fire focuses those assembled, a challenge to the darkness. Thus, any person, in any culture, can resonate to the connotations of the fiery phoenix resurrecting from its own ashes.

Other symbols are culture-bound, and in order for them to be revelatory, one has to be "in on" the symbol matrix of a people. A pinch of incense on coals at the foot of an emperor's statue is a trivial act, except when some believe the emperor divine. An American flag is just a piece of cloth, but it is unwise to burn it at a construction site. A name on a document is simply a configuration of ink, but it takes on a different meaning when one reads "I do so swear" above it; that pictograph is the physicalization of my name, my word; it puts my *self* on the line.

In some symbolic stories—Shakespeare's, for instance—the culturally conditioned classical symbols are so thicketed we have to resort to footnotes. But most myths have passed through centuries from culture to culture, so most culture-bound symbols have been rubbed off or changed to some reality more universally understandable. (We can guess *Cinderella* began in China since it hinges on a woman's tiny foot.) But these stories were composed for simple people.

Still, they do take some pondering. Some are surprised, for instance, that the three little pigs are really one pig who finally learned his lesson, and when he boils and eats the wolf (the Id) rather than burying it, he is assimilating and sublimating Id power rather than repressing it.

You can't be in a literalist frame of mind when you read folktales and myths. Why did Jack risk going up the beanstalk the third time when the golden goose guaranteed him lifetime solvency? (Because money isn't enough in human life; Jack needed the enrichment of his "feminine" soul: the music of the golden harp who turned out to be an enchanted princess.)

Why did Hansel trick the witch with a bone while Gretel tricked her with an oven? (The Freudian symbolism obviates explanation.) Why would Little Red Riding Hood be dumb enough to get into *bed* with a wolf, who looked no more like her grandmother, even in a nightcap, than Boris Karloff? (Because girls Little Red's age have gotten into bed with "wolves" for centuries and regretted it.)[3]

Archetypes

Cro-Magnons thirty thousand years ago had the same bodies we do today, which put the same demands on those primitives as they do on us: food, sleep, disease, warmth, shelter. Everywhere and always, the primary human concern is to stay alive. But food, clothing, and shelter are not enough. We also live by being *related* to what is *beyond* the limits of our own skins: parents, siblings, neighbors, the environment, the mysterious Beyond-the-Beyond—none of which relationships can be captured in definitions but only in evocative symbols.

What's more, those earliest humans went through the same predictable but challenging physical and psychological stages as we do today: birth, infancy, childhood, learning the skills to survive and the customs of the tribe, puberty, parenthood, aging, and death. And the people of every culture between Cro-Magnons and people today have had the same human bodies and the same stages of human growth: Egyptians, Aztecs, Polynesians, Zulus, Iroquois.

Whether we lived in a cave in southern France or live in an apartment in Chicago, no matter how brutal or sophisticated our surroundings, we still have the same bodies and the same stages of human growth and challenge.

Therefore, we respond to the same images, symbols, and stories human beings for thirty millennia have found helpful to understand those physical and psychological changes: what Carl Jung called archetypes—universal ideas grounded in the changes of the human body. Despite differences in hairiness, posture, food, weapons, shelters, every human story is the same story: birth, infancy, childhood, play years, learning years, adolescence, marriage, parenthood, aging, and death.

As Joseph Campbell says, it's the same play but translated into different languages by different players. And if we are amnesiac about history, we just improvise. Then we die. The story hasn't changed since the first *homines sapientes* lifted themselves off their knuckles, looked around at the world, and asked "Why?"

Very often at the outset of the story the hero or heroine is lost, or summoned, or sent away. He or she embarks on a journey, encountering helpful folk or animals as well as disconcerting dragons, griffins, orcs, and other unpleasantnesses, and in such uninviting locales as fire pits, sealed rooms filling up with water, spacecrafts without propulsion but plenty of suspicious creaks and alien grunts. If the hero or heroine doesn't actually descend into the underworld (and often they do), he or she at least contends with fearsome approximations of it.

The ages have discovered, again and again, that the only place one takes ownership of one's soul is on a journey through hell. Concentration camp survivors will validate that. We think we know ourselves, possess ourselves, until we plunge to rock bottom. Then, as with Lear, our eyes are truly opened.

The Wizard of Oz

The story of that journey to selfhood is told from a girl's perspective in the undyingly popular film *The Wizard of Oz,* which came out at the end of the Great Depression, when Europe was already at war and America was teetering on the brink of it. It came on us at a time when people needed to see in recognizable images the clash of good and evil, a need for hope—and friends—in the midst of despair.

Hollywood—The Dream Factory—has always been able to reflect America's daydreams, and a myth is for a society what a dream is for an individual: a way of symbolically explaining what troubles us. Most of *The Wizard of Oz* is, in fact, a dream, and like all dreams it contains the residue of Dorothy's day before the cyclone hit: Miss Gulch who has taken Toto reappears as the Wicked Witch; the three farmhands as the Tin Man, Lion, and Scarecrow; and Dr. Marvel as the Wizard.

The story is a myth of a young girl forced (by the cyclone) to leave home and go out on her own, and it deals with the two questions that have bedeviled every adolescent for the last thirty thousand years: Who am I? and Where do I fit in? Before, Dorothy had moped around the farm, getting in everybody's way, dreaming of an ideal world somewhere "over the rainbow."

She's an orphan (no explanation why), and the strongest figure in her life is Auntie Em, a no-nonsense hardworking lady. Most of the males in the black-and-white story which bookends the dream are nice but ineffectual: Uncle Henry, the three farmhands, Dr. Marvel. In order to be a woman, does Dorothy have to be like Auntie Em?

Then as the technicolor dream begins and Dorothy finds herself "over the rainbow" in Munchkin Land, she's immediately hailed as a heroine for inadvertently killing a wicked witch. As a reward, Glinda, the good witch, gives her the dead witch's red slippers. But why doesn't Glinda send her back to

Kansas right away? The "power" is in the slippers, and she already has them. But Dorothy has to find her power for herself, *in* herself.

On her way, she falls in with three friends, who—as Toto is a symbol for Dorothy's own frisky spunk—are symbols of her own lack of self-esteem based on not being intelligent enough, loving enough, courageous enough. During their many adventures, it becomes clear that however beautiful over the rainbow might be, it is just like this world. The difference is that, in this dreamworld, it is very clear where the good and the evil are, not, as in this world, all deceptively "smeared together."

It is Toto (Dorothy's inquisitiveness and pluck) who causes Dorothy to throw water on the witch when she is trying to burn the dog, and it is Toto who unmasks the Wizard. Unlike the roaring projection who terrified the foursome before, he is just a fussy old man manipulating levers. But he is entirely unlike the wicked witches. "Oh," says Dorothy, "you're a very bad man!" But the Wizard answers, "Oh, no, my dear. I'm a very good man. I'm just a very bad wizard."

The answer is not magic, but kindness and wits. By the time they arrive back at Emerald City with the witch's broomstick, the friends have already proven that they had more than enough heart and brain and courage; all they lacked was belief in themselves. So the Wizard merely makes it official by giving them symbols that capture those inner realities: a heart-shaped watch, a diploma, a medal. And the Wizard promises to take Dorothy back to Kansas in a big bag of hot air. But it's not a man, however wise or kind, who can get Dorothy "home." It is Glinda the Good who tells her she must get back to Kansas by clicking her red heels and saying three times, "There's no place like home."

The magic in the slippers is Dorothy.

When she returns—just as Psyche and Odysseus on their return from the underworld, she is changed. She has brought home a self she can be proud of—a soul—energized by her adventures.

Star Wars

The same journey to evolve a soul is told in the modern myth of the *Star Wars* films. In discussing the film, Joseph Campbell told Bill Moyers that the success of the films was not merely the exciting production values but that they posed for people who needed it (especially the young) an uncluttered and unsanitized image of the clash between good and evil. "They needed to be reminded of idealism, to see a romance based upon selflessness rather than selfishness."

The fact that the evil power was nameless (only The Empire) allowed it to stand for *any* monstrous, heartless, totally rationalistic force in the modern world. When Darth Vader's mask is removed, we see an unformed man who has never developed a soul, as unaccountable as the faceless generals who sent William Calley into My Lai or the godfathers who order mass slaughter during their grandchildren's baptisms or the terrorists who approve the booby-trapping of school busses and later receive the Nobel Peace Prize. Men who have bypassed their own souls.

Moyers said that when he asked his son why he saw the *Star Wars* films so often, his son replied, "The same reason you read the Bible all the time." To which Campbell replied:

> Well, you see, that movie communicates. It is in a language that talks to young people, and that's what counts. It asks, Are you going to be a person of heart and humanity—because that's where the life is, from the heart—or are you going to do whatever seems to be required of you by what

might be called "intentional power"? When Ben Kenobi says, "May the Force be with you," he's speaking of the power and energy of life, not of programmed political intentions . . . The Force moves from within. But the force of the Empire is based on an intention to overcome and master. *Star Wars* is not a simple morality play; it has to do with the powers of life as they are either fulfilled or broken and suppressed by the action of man.[4]

Quick-Fix Myths

As the above typical myths show, the gods emancipate our souls only at the price of considerable effort. But in a time when, as Carrie Fisher says, "instant gratification takes too long," we blithely bamboozle ourselves into thinking that one weekend of this or that placebo drill will set our whole lives to rights.

These quick-fix myths were catalogued as well as I have seen by Sam Keen:

> In the milieu of what has been variously called "the New Age movement" or humanistic psychology, I found an uncorseted spirituality that abandoned the classical effort to open a path between faith and reason that had been so important to me. No one in the Age of Aquarius seemed concerned to offer reasons for what they believed, much less to gather evidence to support their conclusions. The New Age was credulity gone wild—belief in healing crystals, channeling of entities, out-of-body experiences, pyramid power, sorcery and prosperity for all. LSD visions were assumed to be true. est offered enlightenment in two weekends. Swamis, enlightened masters, and neoshamans spoke knowingly of the being of

One and *the* Truth . . . and you can tune your Body, Mind, and Spirit to the Universe with the fabulous Cosmic OM Tuning Fork ($34.95 plus shipping and handling).[5]

With a smug, gnostic certitude that would have embarrassed even a '50s monsignor, unsubstantiated "authorities" offer universal blueprints and suppress all different opinions or even honest questioning. At their most pernicious, you have Jones of Jonestown and Koresh of Waco. At their best, they seem merely silly. But as Barnum opined, "There's one born every minute."

Perhaps one acid test of any philosophy (or religion) is whether its adherents are able to laugh at themselves—and even at the ways they sincerely express their beliefs. But certainly the fundamental criterion is whether any worldview generally and genuinely produces believers who are more openhearted, more open-minded, more openhanded than any nebbish off the street.

Leaving Home to Find Home

You will find the same basic themes in the myths of Egypt, Greece, Buddhism, Judaism, Christianity, Islam, Native American religion, the Arthurian legends, and all the myth systems the world over since the rise of human beings on this planet. At the bottom of the dark abyss (hell, underworld, forest, depths of the sea) is the light of salvation (one's hard-won soul, meaning, purpose, justification). It is only at the bleakest moment that transformation—conversion—comes.

There must be some reason for the basic similarity despite the different symbols chosen; for instance, the Tree of Knowledge of Good and Evil and the legend of the Fountain of Youth are both embodying the same human truth, but with different symbols. The key is that myths are clues to the spiritual potentialities of human life, no matter in what time or what culture. They serve not so much to give an understanding of life as to embody the *experience* of being truly, humanly alive! They give inner sustenance in crises, making them bearable. They give models of endurance, like Luke and Dorothy.

Stories of the call to leave home on a questing journey are so constant in the myths of every culture in human history that such a call must be a universal in human spiritual growth. The hero or heroine is one who gives his or her life to a struggle bigger than themselves and is ennobled by it. The journey is always a "death" and a rebirth, as it is embodied in the heroic act of a mother's labor and giving birth: risking her own life that a new life might emerge. The Chinese *Tao Te Ching* says the same: "When you have been hollowed out, you will be full."

It is a journey that—to find a soul—we all must undergo.

Chapter Five

DISCOVERING A SELF

Spirit, like wind, is visible only in the movement that results from its presence. We see trees swaying, the breath moving through the cycle of inspiration and expiration, but we do not see the thing itself. Soul, like light, can be detected only by what it illuminates. We must creep up on the intangible quarry, and when we are in its vicinity we can detect its presence or absence.

Sam Keen—*Hymns to an Unknown God*[1]

"Soul" reflects the core of one's personal existence: the whole living being of an individual. But there are aspects of that reality which are often used as synonyms yet at least can be considered separate facets of the one reality: spirit (a unifying vitality) and character (conscience).

"Spirit" reflects a *quality* of soul: the soul awakened (as Buddha means "the fully awakened one"). It is an aliveness of the soul-self, as in "spirited," like the relation of the flame to the candle. Spirit is an energy that fuses the contrary facets within our selves as well as connecting our selves with those around us and with the universe. It is this spirit that has never ignited in "so many dead-ended eyes."

"Character" is the moral aspect of the soul-self, the principles by which one deals with self and others; character is in the conscious Ego, reasoned and chosen. We can see the difference between "character" and "personality" in "She's got a lot of personality" and "She's got a lot of character."

Personality (extrovert/introvert, feeling/thinking, etc.) is external to the true self and automatic, formed within the first few years by instinctive reactions to parents and siblings. Our internal self-image forms not just from our experience but from our *interpretation* of the experience.

For instance, if my mother puts me into day care when I'm only an infant, my mother probably loves me less than other mothers love their children. That might not be the truth, but it is my *perception* of the truth, and far more influential than the truth itself. Later, that self-image tells me how I can expect to be treated by everybody.

Character (conscience) is internal and by no means automatic. It feeds on the outer world and digests it to achieve a modicum of wisdom. Each of us has a personality, willy-nilly. Not all of us have genuine character.

Unfortunately, we rarely take time to experience our spirits, even to feel that inner self as a unified entity, much less challenge it to greater aliveness. Rather, our selves are mixtum-gatherums of conflicting desires, values, ideals, pulling us this way, then that. Similarly with conscience. Most of our "principles" are really only the contradictory clutter closeted in the Superego, taped uncritically from all sorts of sources. Character can *alter* personality, but only at great effort.

Paradoxically, we are all alike, as humans, yet each of us is unique, as a self. Each of us has gone through the same stages of growth, in fact the same stages humans have gone through since the caves. Thus, we can learn something about being human from every story in which we immerse ourselves, whether a modern novel or an ancient saga. Yet as individuals, each of us is irreducible, even identical twins who are still two separate psyches, two intertwined but separate stories.

There is a third aspect to the self: not only is each of us human and a self, but each of us is also a *participant*. Except for the few hermits among us, we are part of a family, a community, a workforce, a nation, and the whole human family. Therefore we have not two questions but three: What does it mean to be fulfilled as a human being? Who am I as a unique person? How do I fit into the web of relationships which is society?

In all three senses—human, self, participant—we are forever incomplete, on the way. A humanly fulfilled soul is not a destination, but a process. We want not a static definition of self but an ongoing *sense* of self. Each of us is not only a fact but an opportunity.

Humanity

Being human doesn't guarantee we will *act* humanly. Humanity is a potential which we needn't activate, an invitation we can refuse. We are the only species forced to choices and decisions. Thus, all education should be empowering us to decide honestly and wisely; anything less is merely Gradgrind job certification.

All other natures are programmed and inescapable: no wolf refuses to be vulpine, no cabbage refuses nourishment, no rock tries to reproduce itself. But humans can act like beasts, vegetate, use others as stepping-stones. It's what a simpler age called "original sin," the only religious doctrine that can be established irrefutably from the daily newspapers. It is a human state we now reduce to neurosis or, as we have seen, victimhood.

Neurosis means literally "nerve sickness," but such a reduction of understanding puts soul-sickness into the same category as ulcers and tumors. Physically healthy children whose basic needs have been more than amply fulfilled nonetheless commit suicide. What afflicts most neurotics, misfits, troublemakers is a warped and unfulfilled humanity, a refusal to knuckle under to things as they are and move on from there. It is a dis-ease of the soul: loss of meaning, doubts about life's values, loss of courage or hope, self-hatred, alienation from others, conviction of the impossibility of love.

The Greek word for "soul" is *psyche,* which means literally "butterfly." It is an apt metaphor. By rights, the soul should emerge from the fusion of body and mind as naturally, effortlessly, and irresistibly as a butterfly easing bright-winged from within the ugly cocoon. But that is the human difference. We can refuse to emerge from the state of being merely rational animals. We can stay within the cocoon and die as human beings.

Baby : Cub = Acorn : Marble

At first glance, an infant and a bear cub look and act quite alike (except the baby has less hair); they spend their days eating, sleeping, excreting, prowling, romping. So, too, the acorn and the marble seem alike. But there is a vast difference in the pairs. Plant the acorn and the marble, and the marble is just going to lie there inert; it hasn't the potential to be anything other than what it is.

But the acorn has the *potential* to be vastly different from what it is: an enormous oak, unrecognizable from its tiny source. But that potential needn't be activated; the acorn can fall into a swamp or onto concrete, where it will rot or shrivel. Similarly with the baby and the cub; both will grow physically, but unlike the cub the infant has the *potential* to become Abraham Lincoln or Helen Keller. Or not.

Therefore, there is a whole spectrum of meanings to the word *human,* depending on the extent to which the individual has activated the potential soul. It ranges from mobsters, pimps, pushers, and terrorists at one end, through most of the rest of us, to truly inspired souls like Leonardo da Vinci, Florence Nightingale, Albert Schweitzer at the opposite end. The only limit to the evolution of the soul is death—and our own unwillingness to evolve it, which is in itself death-as-human.

> What is it, then, to be natural, or to be human? Perhaps we must say that the truly natural man is one who strives for an unnatural end which is beyond, not below, the natural.[2]

The human invitation is to surpass ourselves.

Individuality

> In the eyes of the world, I am an average man. But to my heart I am not an average man. To my heart I am of great moment. The challenge I face is how to actualize, how to concretize the quiet eminence of my being.[3]

Each self goes through the same process of natural growth, but each uniquely. Therefore, if you want a book that explores who you are as a unique individual, you'll have to write it yourself. All I can do is describe the stages each of us went though and ask you to reflect on your singular experience of each stage.

Psychiatrist Erik Erikson shows that our whole life is a predictable series of painful crises, or disequilibriums, which can be catalysts that draw our characters down into deeper and richer levels of our humanity and widen the radius of our lives. But if we evade these crises, they can strand us in a labyrinth of games and self-delusions and pitiful imitations of life.

—Birth: The first painful crisis or shock is birth itself. For nine months you lived as a fetus in the mindless bliss of the womb; then suddenly you were ejected into the cold and noise, ripped from paradise, and your first birthday present was a slap. But without that disruption of your former equilibrium, you would never learn to breathe on your own. Then the first task of those around your birth was to clean you and get you as quickly as possible back next to that heartbeat, which for nine months had made you feel "at home."

—Infancy: For the next year and a half or so, you were unconditionally loved; whatever you needed, Mommy and Daddy provided; if you were hungry or cold or sick, they took care of that; if you dirtied yourself or spit up, they took care of that too. For those first months, you were little more than the bear cub we saw before: the Id, with little comprehension or concern or even awareness of anything but self. The natural purpose of this stage is to establish trust once more, to reassure a child still unable to think that he or she is still "at home."

—Childhood: But then, again suddenly and confusingly, the all-providing parents "rejected" you again: weaned you and potty-trained you. It was not your fault, but a natural result of a growing body capable of muscle control. The all-loving Fairy Godmother suddenly metamorphosed into the Wicked Stepmother. This can be a traumatic time for a child. If it is brought on too early, the child can end up fretful and anxious for the rest of its life (one wonders if Woody Allen might have been weaned too soon); if it is withheld out of "love" for the child, the child can end up petulant and demanding for the rest of its life (one wonders if John McEnroe was weaned too late).

At that time, the child begins to hear two words she has never heard before but will continue to hear for the rest of her life in one form or another: *good* and *bad*. Incapable of reflection or seeing a cause-effect relationship, the child has no inkling why throwing the ball to Daddy gets a "Yes" and throwing the spaghetti to Daddy gets a "No." It's all right to bite the breadstick but not the cat's tail. But it's the parents' ballgame, and they control the food supply. What's more, they are the only assurance of the child's *self*-worth.

What the parents are doing is imposing a Superego on the child as a temporary conscience, a sort of survival manual until the child can develop her own conscience. If she ever does.

Remember that these unfathomable strictures are taped uncritically in the child's mind, and they can never be erased—perhaps critiqued and found wanting later on, but never expunged. And they are taped with all the force felt by a two-foot person looking up at a six-foot person (which is why many villains in folktales are giants).

Further, achieving a sense of rightness of behavior was much easier up to the '50s, when all the voices crooning do's and don'ts into the child's Superego still sang more or less the same song, in harmony: fairness, thrift, honesty—all the Scout virtues.

Today, however, there are other voices sending the child's Superego discordant messages through TV ads and programs, magazines, videos, and especially rock lyrics: self-absorption, rebellion, greed, winning-at-all-costs. The child is incapable of sorting the good "goods-and-bads" from the bad "goods-and-bads," and the people whispering the desirability of the bad "goods-and-bads" permeate the child's experience more often, more subtly, and more slickly than their parents can.

One major problem, from childhood through the rest of a person's life, is a sense of inferiority—to parents, to siblings, to the athletically more skillful, to teachers, to the "brains" in the class, to the opposite sex, to the boss. When children begin to believe the color of their skin or the backgrounds of their parents or the cost of their clothes determines the limits of their hopes, they suffer a lasting blow to their sense of identity and therefore can become convinced all their efforts are in vain. Then they drop out, run away, stay out all night, withdraw into inaccessible moods.

Each of us, no matter where we came from, had and has a need to be *recognized,* a need for accomplishment. You see it even in the chronic candidate for detention. The suicide. At least someone might notice me. Contrast that with infancy when that recognition was unquestioned. From childhood through old age, that need to be more than merely "there" is pressing. There is always that need to feel "at home."

But the natural purpose of this stage is to begin slowly to achieve some measure of independence from the parents, who can no longer be hovering all the time, especially if another new child has begun the whole process over again for them.

—Play Years: Then your mother again "rejected" you, forced you outside to play with the other fractious children, even in the cold! It would be far pleasanter to sit inside the warm house and watch cartoons all day, but if the Cruel Stepmother kept you clinging to her apron strings, you'd have been tied to them for the rest of your life, if not to hers at least to some "mother substitute's."

What's more, sooner or later you had to learn to deal with other people without a parent around to arbitrate your disputes.

Perhaps you learned Nietzsche's approach to such difficulties, before you could even pronounce his name: might makes right, and you have to be either king of the hill or some shade of loser. In the best of cases, you learned how to compromise, a skill girls seem more naturally adept at than boys.

The natural purpose of this separation and disequilibrium is to learn initiative without your parents ("Mom, it's raining out, and there's nothing to do!") and to learn to deal with interpersonal difficulties without their intervention ("All right, I landed on Park Place. So how much do I owe?")

—School Years: Then came that awful betrayal at the kindergarten doorway, when the former Fairy Godmother stranded you with all those strangers! The terror! The screams! The tantrums! People have told me they thought their parents had brought them there to put them up for adoption. Hansel and Gretel time! In a very real sense, yes. You had to continue learning how to handle problems on your own in ever wider and more challenging circles. There are some intelligent parents who opt instead for home schooling, one set of parents teaching a group of same-age children math, another reading, etc. It is quite likely such children (usually of better educated parents to begin with) will get superior, less traumatic, more long-lasting instruction. But academic instruction is not all schooling is about.

The natural purpose of this disequilibrium is to develop not only the skills needed to support yourself, give you a sense of achievement, and gradually prepare you to take your place as a breadwinner, but also the skills needed to deal with other people—who are all not from well-educated families, white, well-mannered, or fair.

—Adolescence: By the time you got to seventh or eighth grade, everything more or less had become settled and acceptable once again. You'd learned not only to cope with this broader challenge but to accept it and become at ease with it. Then, out of nowhere, secret distilleries in your body began to send out magic potions into your bloodstream. Your limbs elongated and went gangly. Like Wolfman at full moon, hair began to sprout in embarrassing places, which in turn seemed to be developing an unsettling will of their own. You thought you'd known all about S-E-X from kids sniggering in the locker room and the powder room, but . . . WOW!

Physical growth happened through no fault of your own, but you had to cope psychologically with that new and surprising and at times painful challenge—or remain a little kid.

It was a radical change of perspective, and not too many kids got much help in absorbing and dealing with it, except (again) a sheerly Gradgrind factual approach which left the far more important *psychological* confusions. Answers to those soul problems coming from the media had far more appeal to a hormone-charged teenager than the authoritarian or altruistic (and therefore unintelligible) answer of parents, church, or some teachers.

When condoms become readily available, free, right in school, abstinence becomes more or less unthinkable. Sometimes even parents seem to side with the prevailing ethos. One boy told me his parents came home and found him and his girlfriend naked on the living room floor. The kids got dressed, and they all sat around and had a good laugh over it. One father, pillar of the church, told me, "If my sons are still virgins at eighteen, I'll be very worried."

Unlike physical maturity, psychological maturity doesn't happen without your cooperation and a lot of painful reassessing of what "everybody says." The story of Snow White in her crystal coffin says she was physically able to be a wife and mother, but psychologically unable to be either. If you don't take on the painful task of reining in your own animal Id, if you balk at pawing over all the commands on your Superego, testing them one by one against the objective facts, if you don't assume responsibility for your own self, someone will do it for you. And you'll be a victim of your moody Id and/or your tyrannical and self-contradictory Superego for the rest of your life.

In 1991, there were 1,213,700 births to unmarried women, including 11,000 to those under fifteen years of age and 797,000 to those fifteen to nineteen, and a million and a half abortions, most of them to younger women.[4] Doubling that figure (since it takes two to tango), it seems that well over 5 million young people every year (and there are only 20 million from ages five to twenty) have not been taught how to treat the challenge of adolescence as responsible becoming-adults, nor does it show promise they ever will.

Nonetheless, the natural purpose of adolescence is to develop a sense of identity, an Ego, a personally validated self, free of the dictates of the Id and Superego. Autonomous. Only then will a young man or a young woman be adequately prepared for the next natural stage: marriage.

—Young Adulthood: Although we will treat marriage in a separate chapter, joining the self to another self requires a great deal of adjustment, reorienting priorities, surrendering one's original family to set out together on a quest without a map. What's more, in settling conflicts, which are inevitable, each no longer brings a single autonomous self to bear on the problem; each one, in every case, has to come at the problem as an equal *partner,* with neither one at an advantage because of sex or family clout or higher salary. If either "wins," both lose.

As we shall see, the blending of two selves in marriage has to negotiate the tricky challenge of being one while at the same time each partner maintains an authentic self. Each must have separate "space," separate interests, separate friends. Otherwise, he or she becomes less and less interesting, intriguing, challenging, especially after the sex is not as heady and healing as it was in the honeymoon years.

The natural purpose of this stage is to develop a broader self through intimacy and partnership. Of course, if the partners never really developed authentic selves in adolescence, the union is like joining hands with a stranger and jumping off a cliff. It is a very weak basis for the next stage: parenthood.

—Adulthood: We will also devote a complete chapter to the effect of family on the evolving soul. Suffice it to say here that if a couple would disdain owning a dog, they would be far better advised to consider the convent or monastery than to have a child. Each child is going to bring a whole *host* of disequilibriums, day after day, for at least twenty years if not more.

For the first year or so, an infant's schedule dominates the family's schedule. Its every wish is your command, no matter how inconvenient, no matter how exhausting, which is why today we have so many more stories about child abuse than ever before: because two children got married, and two children had children. Blame lies not just with the media but also with the educational system, failing both these childish parents and the nation.

The natural purpose of this crisis is to wean the parents from self-absorption or even absorption with one another to selfless love, but they are capable of that growth only if each has achieved that sense of an autonomous self in adolescence, surrendered it in intimacy and partnership—yet still maintaining an authentic, autonomous self.

No one said the truth would make you happy, just set you free to be a fulfilled human being.

Freud and the Human Soul

It is amazing—and tragic—how a seemingly trivial mistranslation, an apparently minor violation of semantic nicety, can
harrow souls, generation after generation. Translating the Greek
hubris, for instance, as "pride" instead of "arrogance" has led
countless thousands to fear any genuine sense of pride at a job
well done, since "Those whom the gods would smite, they first
make proud."

Also translating the Hebrew word *tamim* (blameless) into
the Greek *teleios* (perfect) has led countless others to an impossible (and ultimately blasphemous) struggle for perfectionism,
since Scripture enjoins them to "be perfect, therefore, as your
heavenly Father is perfect"[5]—when to a Hebrew "perfect"
meant "whole, all-together."

In a 1982 *New Yorker* article, Bruno Bettelheim pointed out
that students of Freud, especially Americans intolerant of
ambiguity and hell-bent on validating psychiatry as a "real
science," purposely mistranslated the key terms Freud used,
effectively turning an introspective psychology into a behav-
ioral one. Purely left-brain psychology not only clung to
objectivity but succumbed to it, making the person an object
ruled by "mechanisms" and a therapist a sophisticated
mechanic—or at best a personal trainer. On the contrary, I do
not *have* a self, as I have a computer or a toaster; I *am* a self.

Bettelheim writes:

> It became apparent to me that the English transla-
> tions of Freud's writing distort much of the essential
> humanism that permeates the originals. . . . [It]
> makes Freud's direct and always deeply personal
> appeals to our common humanity appear to
> readers of English as abstract, depersonalized,

highly theoretical, erudite, and mechanized—in
short, "scientific." . . . Psychoanalysis, Freud
wrote in a letter to Jung in 1906, "is in essence a
cure through love."[6]

Freud wrote in "Postscript to 'The Question of Lay Analysis'":

"Psychoanalysis is not a medical specialty . . . I
want to entrust it to a profession that doesn't yet
exist, a profession of secular ministers of souls."[7]

Freud shunned arcane technical terms whenever he could, not
just because using them was bad style but also because the
essence of psychoanalysis is to make the unknown known, to
make hidden ideas accessible to common understanding. . . .
Freud chose words that are among the first words used by every
German child: "I" and "it."[8]

Freud wrote in "The Question of Lay Analysis" that it was
his express purpose to *avoid* classical jargon:

You will probably object to our having chosen simple
pronouns to denote our two institutions or provinces of
the soul instead of introducing for them sonorous
Greek names. . . . We must proceed in this way
because our teachings ought to be comprehensible to
our patients who are often very intelligent but not
always learned.[9]

The words Bettelheim primarily takes mistranslators to task for
are the following: *instincts, erotic, Id-Superego-Ego,* and *mind* or
mental. Freud was a meticulous stylist.

The word that the translators substitute for "of the
soul"—*mental*—has an exact German equivalent;
namely, *geistig,* which means "of the mind" or "of

the intellect." If Freud had meant *geistig,* he would have written *geistig.*[10]

Instinct

English translations render Freud's use both of *Instinkt* (instinct) and *Treibe* (drive) with the same word: *instinct.* But Freud carefully used *Instinkt* to mean only the inborn instincts of animals, which are irresistible and unchangeable. He used *Treibe* to indicate only the power or energy to get things done, aggressive vigor, impulse, as in basic urges such as self-preservation, hunger, and sex.

Unlike animal instincts, drives can be changed, suppressed, or sublimated. Unlike animals, if "I" am driven by fear or ambition or greed, "I" can do something about that. We can create a life in which our hardships are not allowed to swamp us in despair and our dark impulses do not draw us into chaos. But most consider sex "just an animal instinct."

Erotic

> To view Eros or anything connected with him as grossly sexual or monstrous is an error that, according to the myth, can lead to catastrophe. . . .
> In order for sexual love to be an experience of true erotic pleasure, it must be imbued with beauty (symbolized by Eros) and express the longings of the soul (symbolized by Psyche). . . . Devoid of such connotations, these words not only lose much of the meaning [Freud] wished them to evoke but may even be invested with meanings opposite to those he intended.[11]

Most likely Hugh Hefner read Freud in translation.

Id, Superego, Ego

Das Ich, das Es, and *das Überich* become *Ego, Id,* and *Superego,* Latin terms substituted for words that have easily accessible

English equivalents. On the contrary, French translators render them *le moi, le ça, le surmoi.* Therefore, to Freud's mind, the Id is "the It," the Superego is "the Over-Me," and the Ego is simply "the Me."

Translating *das Es* (the It) into the Id and *das Ich* (the Me) into the Ego—into Latin rather than into English equivalents—rendered them cold, and technical rather than associative. Moreover, *Ego* becomes pejorative: "egotistical, egoism, ego trip." Freud himself said:

> The impersonal "It" is immediately connected with certain expressions used by normal persons. One is apt to say, "It came to me in a flash; there was something in me which, at that moment, was stronger than me."[12]

The most misleading mistranslation is the use of *mind* where Freud used *die Seele,* "soul." When he conceptualizes the workings of the psyche, he uses *soul* as the overarching entity which encapsulates all the other functions: Me, It, Over-Me, conscious, and unconscious. He is not talking merely of mind, the intellect, but the whole *self.*

In standard editions of Freud, "treatment of the soul" is rendered "mental treatment." But as early as 1905 in *Psychical Treatment,* Freud wrote:

> "Psyche" is a Greek word and its German transla-
> tion is "soul." Psychical treatment hence means
> "treatment of the soul." One could thus think that
> what is meant is: treatment of morbid phenomena
> in the life of the soul. But this is not the meaning
> of this term. Psychical treatment wishes to signify
> much more; namely, treatment originating in the
> soul, treatment—of psychic and bodily disorders—

by measures which influence above all and immediately the human soul.[13]

Yet in the standard translations of that passage, each occurrence
of *soul* is rendered *mind*. They make us believe Freud is talking
about our intellect, when his actual goal is to integrate the
emotional life into the intellectual life—which is precisely what
his strictly analytical interpreters want to shun, turning what its
discoverer intended to be a "science of humanity" into one
more mechanistic "natural science."

The Me (Ego) is only our conscious mental life. The soul
(psyche) is the seat of both the mind and the passions, conscious
and unconscious. It is what makes us human. The purpose of
soul-therapy is to strengthen the Me, to make it more independent of the Over-Me and to appropriate into itself the
power of the It.

Id (the It) holds all that is irrational, infantile, and entirely
selfish in ourselves, and yet also many of the dynamic powers
of the child: creativity, curiosity, the desire to explore, the
urge to touch and experience. The main purpose of therapy is
that the Me can bring more and more of the It into conscious understanding.

The distinction between the "I" and the "It" is clear in "I
went there" as opposed to "'Something' (It) pulled me there."
The Id wants immediate satisfaction: instant coffee, relief from
indigestion, service with a smile. But it is also a profound source
of creative power if it is harnessed.

The civilizing process, not only in the human story but in
the individual story, often turns off not only the antisocial
behavior of the Id but also its ability to create and have fun!

For this reason Freud so frequently depended on imagination, metaphor, and symbols. Though psychoanalysis faces hard,
objective facts, it doesn't deal with them that way but rather

with the imaginative interpretation of hidden causes. Often, too, because of the repressive censorship of the Superego and Ego, the unconscious can reveal itself only in symbols and metaphors. Finally, metaphors are more likely to touch a human chord and rouse emotional responses than purely intellectual statements, just as at a wake reasoned words are powerless and gestures are the only way to convey compassion.

Freud himself often used the metaphor of a midwife to explain the analyst's function. She neither creates the child nor decides what he or she will be but only helps the mother to give the child safe birth. So the analyst does not shape the person or try to make him or her over. Only the soul can.

Evolving a soul is a process of *liberation,* but liberation depends on a felt realization of enslavement: to the If Onlys, to the moody Id, and to the tyrannical Superego. As Twelve-Step programs insist, the very first step is to admit one has a problem he or she can't handle alone. Then comes the establishment of trust in oneself and others, then a sense of autonomy, and finally a sense of initiative.

Self-esteem v. Narcissism

> True self-esteem rests on qualities which a person actually possesses, while self-inflation implies presenting to the self and to others qualities or achievements for which there is no adequate foundation. . . . Narcissism is an expression not of self-love but of alienation from the [true] self.[14]

Narcissism: Arrogant Self-absorption

Genuine pride is rooted in genuine achievement; arrogance is firmly rooted in illusion. Narcissism is self-infatuation which overlooks all flaws and overestimates all virtues—just as someone head over heels in love with another does. Narcissism is not honest self-love; it is being-*in*-love with the self; not a person but a personality; not an individual but an individualist, who substitutes the admiration of others for love. People we saw earlier "who had it all" yet killed themselves—Elvis, Marilyn, et al.—are prime examples.

This omnivorous egotism runs the spectrum from the rhapsodic self-infatuation of Walt Whitman ("The scent of these armpits' aroma finer than prayer") to the self-flagellant but immobile egotism of Hamlet ("Oh, what a rogue and peasant slave am I!"). Whether they stand hypnotized at the mirror by their flawless beauty or by their limitless shortcomings, they are locked in a cramped autistic world in which self looms way out of proportion. Narcissists may be manic or depressed, but they are never unaware of the intoxicating—and self-justifying—self.

> I have been drunk more than once, my passions were never far from madness, and for neither do I feel remorse, for I have learned in my own measure to understand that all men above the ordinary who have done anything great or seemingly impossible have invariably been decried as drunkards or madmen.[15]

Narcissists are capable of being admired or envied but incapable of real human relationship. They at least seem tough-hearted, walling off their vulnerabilities to escape the pain it takes to be a genuine person. Perhaps the key to narcissists is that they are not reciprocal; all the streets are one-way.

Interestingly, the Greek root of *narcissism* is *narkoun,* the same as the root of *narcotic;* it means "to benumb."

Narcissists find it completely impossible to admit even making a mistake, much less owning it and making amends. Thus they become experts at subterfuge, using all kinds of defense mechanisms: *repression*—pushing the gaffe into the unconscious ("If I forget about it, it'll go away); *denial*—convincing the self that an experience or demand simply doesn't exist ("I surely *can* make her love me more than she says I can"); *projection*—making oneself the victim rather than the perpetrator ("My sisters are jealous of *me*"); *displacement*—satisfying the more demanding hungers of the soul into some less threatening activity (work, drink, overeating, drugs, noise, meaningless copulation); *scapegoating*—taking out the anger at oneself on someone else ("I cheat because of my parents' pressure for grades"); *rationalization*—discharging uneasiness indirectly (possessiveness is really love, overweening ambition is really devotion to a cause, the need to counter the felt condescension of others is productivity). One must justify the self at *any* cost. They wear themselves out keeping up their defenses, like a juggler trying to keep plates spinning on top of spindles, because they feel the effort to keep up a flawless front is less painful than facing the objective truth and becoming a genuine person. Narcissism is, in brief, an abdication of personal responsibility.

Nor are all narcissists on the *Tonight Show.* Shoving in front of people who are too sheepish to complain isn't in the same league as the Mob selling "protection" to small shop owners. But it's the same game. Calling someone "spick" or "nigger" isn't in the same league with the Klan; shredding someone's reputation is not in the same league as assassinating a head of state; quicksanding oneself in "the sulks" is not in the same league as suicide; handing in the first draft a week late, saying, "Could I have it back by three, because the final draft's tomorrow?" isn't in the same league with enslaving others. They may be Little League, but they're all the same games.

There are even pettier versions which seem self-justifying:

—parking in a handicapped parking space because it's closer to the door;

—spitting gum into the drinking fountain because the trash basket is down the hall;

—nudging into the line because the movie's about to start;

—snapping at customers because they're faceless nothings in a long line of them;

—scrawling graffiti to let everyone know I was there;

—cheating for a few points on a quiz I'll forget in a week that I even took;

—double-parking to avoid a quarter—and I'm in a rush;

—arguing long after I know I'm wrong because everybody will think I'm a coward—or stupid;

—leaving the toilet roll empty because I've got better things to do.

Without our realizing, such seemingly insignificant acts say: *I'm more important than they are.* However petty, every one of them is an act of narcissism that contributes to the ugly quicksand of narcissism our society is becoming. And their very pettiness seems to absolve us, rather than embarrass us.

In *The Screwtape Letters* by C.S. Lewis, an archfiend is sending advice to his nephew, a novice tempter. He tells him there is no need to make his clients ax-murderers or potentates of porn; all he has to do is give them a mirror. And in another

Lewis novel, *The Great Divorce,* one character says to another who would rather reign in hell than serve in heaven: "Friend, could you, only for a moment, fix your mind on something not yourself?"

Self-esteem: Character

> Few and mean as my gifts may be, I actually am, and do not need for my own assurance or the assurance of my fellows any secondary testimony. . . . It is easy in the world to live after the world's opinion; it is easy in solitude to live after our own; but the great man is he who in the midst of the crowd keeps with perfect sweetness the independence of solitude.[16]

Unlike the narcissism that is natural in children and that must be challenged in adolescents, adult character says, with conviction, "*I* am responsible for what I do, for what I say, for who I am. I appreciate the support of my friends; I honestly entertain their criticisms; but even without the support of those I honestly love, I can stand alone if I must." There surely are scars left on my soul by too strict or too lenient parents, by siblings, betrayals of trust, my own stupid mistakes and cowardice, but from this moment on *I* take responsibility for what happens to the rest of my life. There are no more "If Onlys."

I am responsible to the truth, without illusions or clinging to my own vested interests. I am as rigorously honest with myself as I can be; I refuse to tell myself lies and allow myself to believe them. I have searched out my defenses against the truth, and I have given them up. What I "must" do has become what I "want" to do.

I am also responsible to myself, with no dependence on anything or anyone outside to validate my worth. I am capable of questioning assumptions everybody else accepts, free of "What will people say?" and "Everybody's doing it." I am unafraid to be "different" and willing to accept the probability of criticism. If I must or I choose to, I can go to bed alone.

The very first step toward character, the sine qua non, is "the serenity to accept the things that can't be changed." People of confident character are content with "the rules of the game," not the rules imposed by society or peers or government or a church or its scripture: the rules in things as they are. They are flexible, with a wide-open perspective, able to roll with the punches, ready to experience whatever comes with confidence.

Ironically, such confidence takes both humility and vulnerability. We have to be humble before the reality of our own limitations and content to settle with the best we can do for *now*. To become more and more humanized, we have to be vulnerable to the truth, wherever it leads, and vulnerable to others who can open deeper and deeper levels of themselves to us—and in so doing open deeper and deeper levels of our own souls. The web that binds us together is made of trust, and trusting involves a risk which is unappealing in a world of low-grade paranoia.

Character also requires "the courage to change the things that *can* be changed, and the wisdom to know the difference." It requires the effort to reason to a personal opinion, not just mull it over, but gather the data, sift, line it up logically, draw a conclusion, and have someone wiser critique it. (A skill to reason which writing courses are really intended to teach but seldom do.) Then you have to stand up and defend it, no matter what anyone else says. If someone offers substantial and justified criticism, you go back and work it over and try it again.

If you're willing to accept everything, then you stand for nothing. Yet, especially today when things and opinions and the vox populi change day to day, most of us balk at commitment, preferring to "keep an open mind" in case something better comes along, not realizing that the most open mind is an empty head. Chesterton said, "Art, like morality, consists in drawing a line somewhere." Unless you say, "Thus far, no further," you become a walking reaction to other people's choices.

People of character seem always devoted to some task *outside* themselves; their careers are really "callings:" Martin Luther King Jr., Eleanor Roosevelt, Dag Hammarskjöld, Anne Morrow Lindbergh. They seem able to balance the polarity between autonomy and community which we too often treat as an either/or dichotomy. On the one hand, they have a self-possession and self-sufficiency to develop a unique identity; on the other, they have the confidence to surrender themselves, to identify themselves with others and with the world.

Once you grasp the basics, the rest is all improvisation.

Chapter Six

BUILDING YOUR
OWN CONSCIENCE

---

*They talk of a man betraying his country, his friends, his
sweetheart. There must be a moral bond first. All a man
can betray is his conscience.*

Joseph Conrad—*Under Western Eyes*[1]

When I was a boy back in the irretrievable '30s and '40s, "soul"
had nothing to do with coming alive as a human being. It was
a repository of sin and worthlessness. In our catechism, the soul
was pictured as three milk bottles. (It came in bottles then,
cream popping the cap in winter and craning out like the neck
of a Strasbourg goose.) The first bottle was squeaky-clean and
sparkly: utterly blameless. The middle bottle was all smudgy,
defaced by pardonable sins: not too serious (but watch your

step). The third looked filled with Mississippi river bottom: a soul in mortal, deadly sin, scarcely salvageable.

But that wasn't at all enough for my Pelagian soul, not by a long shot. I sat down and pictured my soul as an old Brillo pad, blackened, tangled, soggy, wasted.

It might not be a bad idea to pause and reflect on what object you would say best physicalized your sense of your own soul as a youngster. It's instructive.

> There is a limit to a child's and an adult's individual endurance in the face of demands which force him to consider himself, his body, his needs, and his wishes as evil and dirty, and to believe in the infal- libility of those who pass such judgment.[2]

And so in the '60s our mind-set changed regarding pangs of conscience. Now hell is apparently (and mercifully) no longer in session, or at least no longer an effective deterrent. "Salvation" no longer means to "save us from sin" or some Dantean Inferno. Rather, some of us look to save ourselves from atrophy here and now, from dull, dead-ended, nine-to-five lives. Unless we do, we "lose our souls," our selves; under the carapace of surface personality, there is a void. We surrender our souls not to some Faustian Mephistopheles but to obses- sions, addictions, loss of meaning, moods. We live not in hell but in an emotional vacuum: emptiness, meaninglessness, vague depression, disillusionment, loss of values, yearning for fulfill- ment—whatever that means. Our souls starve to death on the junk food of television, gossip, and ball scores. Cock an ear in the lunchroom someday.

What Conscience Is Not

In every class, I give a survey, statements to which students agree or disagree, no comments from me, just to find what my "customers" think. No sense hurling jeremiads either at the saved or at the self-deafened. To "Conscience is the result of socialization: parents, school, media," a third to a half agree; to "Objective morality changes from age to age and culture to culture," nearly all agree, as they do to "Conscience is inborn." To "Conscience is just another name for 'lifestyle,'" about half agree. And most have been victims of from eleven to fourteen years of (obviously ineffective) "religious brainwashing."

A genuine conscience is not merely the result of socialization, the Superego. Conscience is, perhaps, as most people seem automatically to call it, "a small voice whispering in my head." But it is not a *single,* consistent voice. It is rather a jangled chorus. As Pirandello wrote, "Don't you see that blessed conscience of yours is nothing but other people inside you?"

To own a genuine conscience, one has to subject every one of those voices to dispassionate scrutiny and see which check out with the objective facts: "Fights don't settle anything" usually proves right; "Don't trust people with darker skin" fails the test if one is fair-minded. At the end of the process, you have a conscience you can call your own.

Nor is genuine conscience the result of scrupulous adherence to the laws of one's country or religion. A law does not *make* an action reprehensible or righteous. Rather, wise lawmakers discern that a particular action is objectively dehumanizing both to the victim and to the perpetrator and form a law for those too busy or lazy or dumb to figure that out for themselves. There should be no need for a law against battering your own children or driving sixty miles an hour in a school zone.

Also there are bad laws. Was it wicked to hide Jews in Nazi Germany? Was it salutary to abandon female infants in China? Was it good Tevye denied his beloved daughter because she married a Gentile? Was Augustine right in saying slavery is merely part of the natural order? A law is valid not because of the person enjoining it but because it coheres with the objective facts.

"My country, right or wrong" is not the claim of an exemplary citizen. If there's something objectively wrong about my country, I have an obligation in loyalty to speak out against it. A real conscience is not a series of military commands or a categorical imperative like the instincts of beasts: "You must because you *must*" or "Because I *said* so!" A bee or a cell in the body feels no obligation because it has no choice. Humans do.

Nor is genuine conscience inborn. If it were, we wouldn't have such tangled feelings trying to make prickly decisions, and we would never have had Hitler or hit men. Like humanity itself, only the *potential* for conscience is inborn. We aren't driven by instinct to moral behavior; quite the opposite. We have to *decide* to act morally. Nor do we set out to "have a good conscience." If we did, we would be self-righteous pharisees. As Viktor Frankl says, "I doubt [saints] ever had it in mind to become saints. If that were the case, they would have become only perfectionists rather than saints."[3]

What Conscience Is

True conscience (the Ego) is, in brief, a sense of personal responsibility and *self*-discipline. It is a *reasoned* ethic, grounded in the objective natures of things, especially the nature of human beings as opposed to high-level animals. It is a set of longtime, habitual modes of behavior and responses to moral problems, just as the rules of driving get into your conditioned reflexes. It is a set of principles reasoned out beforehand and ready when we're faced with a quick decision, with neither the time nor the clearheadedness—or even the inclination—to check the rule book.

Conscience is like the system of triage we see on *M*A*S*H*. During battles, whom do you help first? The officers? The people you know? Start from the left and work to the right? To simplify (if that's the right word) those choices for medics caught up in the terror of combat, often blinded by fatigue, doctors and nurses devised a system called "triage," dividing victims into three groups, independent of any other factor: those certain to survive, those certain to die, those with at least a chance. The only rational—if seemingly heartless—choice is to work for those with a chance and not spend precious time, medicine, and skill on the almost surely dying or the sure survivors.

True conscience requires that same clear-eyed common sense. However, such a true conscience is completely rational, left-brain, "masculine." It is essential for a humanized person to have such a set of personally validated principles *before* the fact. *After* the fact, we must call into play the empathic, right-brain, "feminine" qualities of the mind in judging the perpetrator, even when the perpetrator is oneself.

The hierarchical, vertical priorities of the left brain are essential to justice; the inclusive, horizontal qualities of the right brain are essential to compassion. Justice without compassion is heartless and therefore less than human; compassion without justice is unfair to both victim and perpetrator and therefore less than human.

Motivation for Moral Behavior

The two bases for moral judgments are utilitarian ("What works?") and altruist ("What's right?"). The utilitarian motive is enlightened self-interest. At bottom, utilitarians want to minimize pain and maximize profit. When they say "It wouldn't be right," they don't mean "It would be objectively wrong" but "We couldn't get away with it" or "We'd make more by coming clean."

The altruist's motive is unselfishness based on principle and the welfare of others. When altruists say "It wouldn't be right," they mean "It would be objectively wrong, no matter how much I profit or lose" and "If I did it, I couldn't live with myself."

Say you've had a dog named Rags for years. She follows you around like a shadow, senses your moods, curls up on your feet. Suppose a zillionaire offered a cool million if you toss Rags off a cliff. Don't be too emotional or hasty. A million smackers is not small change. You'd be set for the rest of your life and your children's lives. And Rags is getting pretty old.

That separates the utilitarians from the altruists.

Actually, for anyone with a larger perspective than moment-to-moment, moral behavior is always in your *self*-interest. If for instance you are honest when the chips are down, people will tend to believe you the next time, when it seems you've been dishonest but haven't been. Further, moral or immoral behavior not only affects yourself, your soul, but affects the web of human relationships you have to live in: society.

There need be no hell for drunkards; when they've emptied the bottle, they've already ingested their own punishment. The very real effect of consistent unethical behavior on the soul is far less obvious than bleary bloodshot eyes, unkempt clothing, and the staggers, but it is no less real. As Carson McCullers said, the heart of a mean-spirited person shrivels up until it is hard and pitted, "like the seed of a peach."

Oscar Wilde's *The Picture of Dorian Gray* captures this shriveling of soul well. A handsome, captivating young man betrays his friends, debauches women, lives a hedonistic life of unprincipled charm. One day he happens to catch sight of his portrait over the fireplace. It seems somewhat changed, but he puts it out of mind. Later, though, he sees the portrait has become more twisted, sullen, ugly, until finally he has to hide it in the attic, where it continues to mirror the decaying soul within the enviably handsome man. Even if you pay no penalties, even if you suffer no shame or guilt, your misbehavior punishes you. You carry your hell inside you, unseen, but real.

Like all denizens of Earth, you are subject to the laws of physics, chemistry, and biology. Those laws are objective and inescapable. You are free to violate them, but not without consequences. You can walk off a tall building in defiance of the law of gravity, but only once. You can drink a cyanide cocktail, play with scorpions, poison your liver. But sooner or later the natures of things will prove you wrong.

So, too, with the law of humanity, which is just as objective and inescapable. You are free to violate it, but not without consequences. Even without your realizing, you become no better than a swine; a jackal; a sheep; a snake; or like Gregor Samsa, a cockroach.

Though many say, "Society be damned; I take care of Number One," they still ultimately pay for their narcissism, titanic or trifling, especially if their self-justification is "Everybody does it." If everybody lies, everybody backs down on promises, everybody cheats, and everybody cons the telephone company, the government, the insurance company, we all ultimately pay, not only higher taxes and premiums but living in a paranoid world where no one can trust anybody else.

What's more, just as morality is a two-way street, so is immorality. If you lie to me, don't expect me to be honest with you. If I seduce your daughter, I have no legitimate claim to anger if you seduce mine. If we've agreed that this affair has "no strings," you give up the right to feel jealous or ill-used. A boss who bills her Bermuda vacation as a business expense has no right to be upset if her secretary calls in sick, when the boss knows she's going to the Poconos with her live-in love.

There are not only human "sins" of commission but also "sins" of omission: failing to do your fair share, to stand up and be counted, to decry injustice, to confront the surly and the demeaning. As Edmund Burke said: "All that is needed for the triumph of evil is that good people be silent." We are as responsible for the evil we allow as for the evil we commit.

Moral Evil and Sin

As we saw in the introduction, there is a real difference between moral evil and sin. Any human being—atheist, agnostic, theist, or indifferent—is capable of moral evil, acting less than humanly and treating others less than humanly. Strictly speaking, however, only one who believes in a Higher Power is capable of sin, violating not only the horizontal web of human relationships, but also violating a vertical relationship with that Higher Power to whom the individual feels indebted. Any human being has a legitimate right to be irreligious; no human being has a right to be inhuman, that is, immoral.

Similarly, there is a real difference between guilt and shame and between guilt and responsibility. Shame is unfocused, a sense that nothing can be done about one's inadequacy. Guilt (when the objective facts justify it) is a very salutary and human hunger to set things right, but it is either dismissable, or corrosive, or paralyzing unless it turns into responsibility. I've done something wrong, and I can and will do something to make amends, perhaps not to a God or to society, but at the very least to my own conscience, so that I can go on living with my self. That is painful, because it means one has to go back to the first wrong turn and start over again.

More credulous times attributed this penchant for botching up our lives and its concomitant shame or guilt—which apparently only human beings suffer—to "original sin," or what Jews call *Yetzer Harah*, "the evil inclination." Now I have strong doubts that this proclivity is traceable back to a not-overly-bright pair of nudists who fell prey to a slick-talking snake. But I haven't the slightest doubt about its effects. One has only to check the daily newspapers for evidence beyond rebuttal.

But if an insufficiently evolved tribe of apes were given—or achieved—the intelligence to choose and the freedom that comes from it, moral evil was inevitable—not from the human element but from the residual ape element. At the root of the cerebral cortex there is still a reptilian brain stem. Stand in front of an old ape's cage and ponder what you see. Unless he is disturbed by some stimulus outside his smallish brain—fleas, hunger, intrusion, the pheromones wafting from the damsel next door—he will just lie there, dozing, totally self-absorbed. Behold, our ancestor. We may have left our animal limitations behind, but unless we evolve souls we remain little better than animals with an undeveloped potential.

There is the root of "original sin": the narcissism and inertia we inherited from our simian progenitors. Narcissism is the unwillingness to admit one has made a mistake. The law of inertia declares that any body at rest will remain at rest until affected by an exterior force. Inertia of the soul is the unwillingness to expend the effort to undo the mistake, unless forced to by a parent, spouse, teacher, cop, judge.

One needn't go to a zoo; visit just about any classroom. The only difference, again, is that the clientele has less hair. Depending on the style of the moment.

Evolving Consciences

As we saw above, there are two complementary polarities involved in evolving a real conscience: the left-brain analytical approach of Lawrence Kohlberg and the right-brain empathic approach evolved by his student, Carol Gilligan, and others. As always, each needs the corrective of the other.

Lawrence Kohlberg[4]

Using such moral dilemmas as deciding whether a poor farmer could legitimately steal an exorbitantly priced drug for his dying wife, Kohlberg developed three separate levels of moral motivation, depending on the scope of the respondent's human concern: from completely self-centered, to group-centered, to principle-centered, each level further divided into two stages. I will lay it out schematically first.

LEVEL I: PRE-CONVENTIONAL—Id—Child—Self Centered

Stage 1:   Fear of Punishment: If I'm bad, I'll suffer.

Stage 2:   Hope of Reward: I can gain more by cooperating.

LEVEL II: CONVENTIONAL—Superego—Parent—Loyalty Centered

Stage 3:   Group Loyalty: This group deserves my sacrifices.

Stage 4:   Law and Order: Society depends on our cooperation.

LEVEL III: POST-CONVENTIONAL—Ego—Adult—Principle Centered

Stage 5:   The Human Family: *All* humans are equal.

Stage 6:   Integrity: I will not violate my principles.

Level I, the Pre-Conventional, is basically focused on the Id, what Transactional Analysis calls "The Child." Stage 1 of this self-centered level is motivated almost solely by fear of punishment. Stage 2, one step upward, is motivated primarily by hope of reward, no matter whether the profit is licit or not.

Level II, the Conventional, is a quantum leap upward, spreading beyond the self to a convinced loyalty to the Superego, what Transactional Analysis calls "The Parent." The individual's awareness and concern reaches beyond the level of self-interest—at Stage 3, to small groups like a family, a team, a platoon, and at Stage 4 to a larger collectivity such as the nation or the church. It is a personally held belief in law and order.

Level III, the Post-Conventional, is another quantum leap upward, basically focused on the rightness of an action in itself, rather than on what is good for oneself or one's group. It is the stage of the personally validated moral Ego, what Transactional Analysis calls "The Adult." The individual's concern moves beyond parochial concerns—at Stage 5 to the whole human family and at Stage 6 to the primacy of personal integrity.

The levels and stages have nothing to do with educational attainment or age. Kohlberg and his colleagues found morally decent youngsters and illiterates and morally cramped educated middle-aged people. Consider Forrest Gump and G. Gordon Liddy.

The difference in the levels is that, at Level I, the person says, "My parents would kill me." At Level II, the person says, "This would kill my parents." At Level III, "It would kill me to do that, even if my parents asked me to." Moving from Level I to Level II frees the person from the tyranny of the Id; moving from Level II to Level III frees the person from the domination of the Superego. Such people would opt for the objectively better moral choice even if all the police in the world went on strike.

The difference in the stages is, on the one hand, a broader and broader moral awareness and basis for human decisions and, on the other hand, a greater self-confidence and moral autonomy.

Stage 1, Fear of Punishment, bases all moral choices on the chances of getting caught and the proportionality of the punishment. Such people, in a predominantly white neighborhood, would decide whether to sell their house to Orientals or Blacks based solely on whether their former neighbors or the disappointed newcomers could cause them more damage. If they worship, they do so out of fear of damnation. When there are no authority figures around to catch them, they might try something they would never dream of otherwise. But eating broccoli beats Mommy being mad.

Stage 2, Hope of Reward, bases all moral choices on the chances of getting away with it, of getting the maximum return from the minimum input. Faced with the dilemma of selling their home to "outsiders," they would have not the slightest qualm about their former neighbors if the price were high enough. If they worship, they are buying celestial insurance or trying to impress their neighbors. They haven't the slightest compunction if the kickback is high enough. If the broccoli is the price of dessert, so be it.

Once you cross into Level II, you find people whom those in the lower stages are going to consider saps. Sacrificing for others fails to compute.

Stage 3, Group Loyalty, bases all moral choices on fidelity to a tested group. When asked if they would protect their drug-dealing brother rather than his victims, almost all respondents choose the brother. In the dilemma of selling the house, they would probably defer to their longtime neighbors, making what people at higher stages would consider the wrong moral choice for a not-unlaudable reason. If they worship, they do so because it's good for the family. Eating the broccoli keeps the peace.

Stage 4, Law and Order, bases all moral choices on what is morally acceptable to the community and its leaders. The country has been good to us, and we ought to contribute our fair share, even if it means our lives. In the house dilemma, they would sell to whoever offered the fairest price because that's the law. If they worship (and they usually do), it is out of felt gratitude to the Divinity and the denomination that supports them through thick and thin. Dietitians say you should eat broccoli.

Once you cross into Level III, you discover people willing to be unpopular. Thinking for yourself usually assures it.

Stage 5, the Human Family, bases moral choices on human equality, no matter where they live or the color of their skin or the way they worship or don't. To such people, selling the house would not be a dilemma; the "difference" would be no difference at all. If they worship, they do so not because there is a "law," but because it is the right thing to do. If all the constitutions and commandments were abrogated, they would still do the right thing. Eat the broccoli or not; it's not important.

Stage 6, Integrity, bases moral choices on carefully reasoned principle, and such people are willing literally to die rather than violate their consciences. For that reason, their numbers are not manifold. Socrates was one, surely; Jesus; Joan of Arc (who was unlettered); Thomas More; those who carried their souls, head high, into the gas chambers.

Kohlberg and his colleagues also made several other discoveries about moral awareness. Perhaps most important is that persons at a given stage cannot even *comprehend* the motivations in moral dilemmas of persons two stages above them. Thus, someone at Stage 2 would find the law-and-order motives of someone at Stage 4 ludicrous. "For a *law?* When you can get *away* with it?"

Therefore, attempts by those in charge of moral development in the young to motivate moral behavior by an appeal to the authority of Level II—much less the altruism of Level III—are spinning their wheels. According to the research, the very best one can hope for even as late as senior high school is Stage 4 motivation.

Kohlberg's conclusions are satisfying, rational, easily schematized. They offer a clear outline of developmental growth and a check on educators' expectations of what is possible. (Though most teachers I know who have read Kohlberg still expect to graduate altruists.) But they are one-sided, incomplete. They need the corrective of the right-brain, empathic, feminine.

Carol Gilligan[5]

Gilligan, a student of Kohlberg's, called her mentor to task for being overly rationalistic and "masculine," citing the fact that a disproportionate number of his respondents of all ages were male. One telling incident she reports sums up her objection perfectly. After a session on a moral dilemma, one young boy said, "These dilemmas are just like math problems, only with people."

But people are not numbers, and ethics is not calculus.

As we saw considering reductionism, cold-eyed (and cold-hearted) analysis is not enough—essential, but only partway. It is helpful to understand before the fact that some acts are objectively supremely inhuman, others serious, some trivial.

Yet each inhumanity has to be judged in context, with inclusive, "feminine," right-brain insight. Murder, for instance, is objectively evil, depriving another human being of the supreme right: the right to life. But most philosophers would agree that if you were set upon by someone with a lethal weapon and you had one yourself, you could deprive your assailant of life because, in attempting to deny you of life, he or she had surrendered his or her own right to it.

Contrary to the total impartiality one expects from law courts and empirical science, in judging *human* (i.e., moral) problems, one has to include not only the objective moral evil but the specific, unique situation and the perpetrator's context as well—even when the perpetrator is oneself. As Gilligan insists, too often moralists and church folk encourage us unselfishly to factor our own selves out of the moral equation, which is manifestly lopsided in favor of the law. What she suggests is not a regression to relativism but an admission of ambiguity.

Certainly moral education should provide a hierarchical understanding of moral evils rooted in objective facts in order to equip us with an understanding of those evils *before* the fact of committing one. *After* the fact, if we are to be truly human and not vindictive vultures, we have to temper justice with compassion, no matter what our religious beliefs or lack of them.

All of which leads us to the next chapter.

Chapter Seven

⟋⟍ ·•· ⟋⟍

THE ANDROGYNOUS SOUL

Relations between the sexes are very largely determined by the relation between masculinity and femininity within each person, male or female.

Abraham Maslow—*The Farther Reaches of Human Nature*[1]

Later, we will explore the areas of sexuality and specifically male and female spirituality, but here I would like to focus solely on *gender*, which has very little to do with sexuality. Sex is a matter of objective fact: either/or, internal or external genitals.

Gender is a judgment call: more/less, a spectrum from Conan the Barbarian and Diana Christiansen at one end to Casper Milquetoast and Edith Bunker at the other. I base that distinction on the work of Carl Gustav Jung and on the fact languages have no sex but three genders: masculine, feminine, and neuter. If William Safire wrote an oracular article on the difference between sex and gender, there might be greater clarity in the often obfuscated battles for political correctness, which have a worthy purpose but often devolve into squabbles between Big Endians and Little Endians.

At least within these pages, I'd like to confine *sex* to the ways our bodies work as males and females and *gender* to the ways our souls work, no matter what our sex.

If by *masculine* (as opposed to *male*) we mean those qualities associated with the left brain—logic, calculation, decisiveness, etc., Hillary Rodham Clinton is far more "masculine" than Mother Teresa, yet both are females. If by *feminine* we mean those qualities associated with the right brain—intuition, inclusiveness, the ability to see a problem in context rather than in left-brain isolation, Dag Hammarskjöld was far more "feminine" than Senator Joseph McCarthy, though both were male.

Every society creates artificial divisions and personality expectations for each sex which limit the humanity of *both* sexes. For instance, the unspoken—but pervasive and unchallenged—feeling that all men should be taller than women, which inferiorizes very short men and very tall women like Charlie Chaplin and Eleanor Roosevelt. And there are thousands of other baseless expectations, tangled up in our refusal to recognize the nearly infinite variety of human beings of both sexes: a man with a scanty beard, a woman with a faint mustache. One needn't be "all *man!*" like Stephen Seagal nor "all *woman!*" like Madonna. "Me Tarzan, you Jane" isn't a very healthy basis for communication between the sexes—or within the sexes.

The left-brain characteristics both sexes share—like logic, analysis, tough-mindedness, decisiveness, competition—and the right-brain characteristics—like intuition, synthesis, openness, patience, cooperation—are not physical (sexual) but rather attitudes and preferences (psychological).

"Isn't That Just Like a Woman (Man)?"

In simpler stories, the male is the clear-eyed and clear-thinking, noble, muscular knight, and the female is the muddleheaded, helpless damsel-in-distress who always twists her ankle when they're running away. Despite the solely left-brain (therefore half-witted) assertions of such eminences as Luther, Hegel, Freud, and Henry Higgins, males are not all singularly sterling chaps while all females are merely brood-sows, their heads "filled with cotton, hay, and rags."

Far too easy (therefore the usual procedure) to stereotype males as muscular, competitive, autonomous, and analytical, and females as pliant, cooperative, dependent, and intuitive. "Everybody knows" males make good business leaders and scientists; females make good homemakers and nurses. Males think; females feel.

As so often, a single- (therefore simple-) minded theory blinds us to the observable truth. There have been some crack-erjack female heads of state, astronauts, and surgeons, and most of the world's composers, artists, and chefs have been male. Nonetheless, most fathers would blanch if their sons asked for ballet lessons, and most mothers would swoon if their daughters came home with a tattoo. If you go to buy your friend's child a birthday present, you hardly consider a tea set for the boy and a plastic Luger for the girl. It's not . . . normal.

But the mere use of the word *normal* or *unseemly* implies a kind of *standard* of what males and females are allowed to be. The question is whether it is an objective standard based on the unchangeable *natures* of males and females, and therefore a moral question. Or is it merely a subjective preference based on no more than the changeable whims of a particular individual or society or century, and therefore morally completely indifferent.

On the one hand, male priests hurled female virgins off temples to placate the gods, fathers sold or drowned less desirable female babies, officials noted for fervent religious practice neutered males to do guard duty in harems and have more beautiful singing voices for papal choirs.

On the other hand, French kings who were remarkably fecund wore weird hairdos, Joan of Arc led an army, Madame Curie discovered radium, Scotsmen wear skirts, contemporary males wear earrings, and more than half the physicians in the former Soviet Union are women.

No matter what the source of the unfounded stereotypes, the image of the aggressive male and the nurturant female will probably be with us for the rest of our lives. Courageous ignorance will outlive cockroaches.

But the stereotyping is psychologically corrosive: boys thinking men don't cry and any genuine affection for another male is a hint of homosexuality; girls believing women are by nature homemakers and any urge to stand up and challenge is a threat to their femininity. It *is* a challenge to their femininity, but not to their womanhood.

On the contrary, although empathy with "The Elephant Man," even to tears, may be a "feminine" quality in a man, it does not make him *effeminate,* and although rigid analysis may be "masculine" in a woman, it doesn't make her "butch." Any unspoken strictures against a boy playing the flute or a girl being a mechanic are strictly subjective, societally induced.

Nature / Nurture

The nature/nurture controversy has been around about as long as the chicken/egg controversy. Whether you believe boys are aggressive and girls are adaptive because of the way they are made (nature) or because of the way they've been brought up (nurture) depends pretty much on which psychologist you read last. But whichever is the cause of the characteristics we expect of males and females—or if both are, until the definitive answer arrives from Delphi and the appropriate changes are made, we have to take people as we find them.

Nature

Even little kids playing doctor in the garage discover that although males and females are equal, they are not the same. But the sole *objective* difference between males and females is their reproductive organs; males external, females internal.

Yet there is also a difference in the psyche *resulting* from the physical genital difference. Each of us is a self but also an *embodied* self. Our bodies have an effect—sometimes justified, sometimes not—on our psychology, our way of looking at life and at ourselves. Those differences affect—not objective morality (humanity)—but our *viewpoints* on morality. Skin color, disfigurement, wasting disease, or loss of limbs have a stunning impact on the mind and soul, but they do not make us less than human. Often, in fact, they have precisely the opposite effect. They make us more human. But they do change a person's viewpoint.

As the philosopher Rousseau wrote, "The male is only a male now and again, the female is always a female, at least in her younger years." A male experiences his sexual difference only in arousal, but a woman experiences her sexual difference also in menstruation, conception, pregnancy, labor, and nursing. Males may feel more sexual, but females *are* more sexual.

If any inequity exists between the sexes, it is precisely there: Although the sexual act may be pleasurable to both males and females, events leading up to and following the act of intercourse are in no way equal. But since that inequity antedated the caves, no one can blame it on a male-dominated society or culturally imposed custom or tradition. It is a natural, objective fact blamable only on the gods or the quirks of evolution. An unsat-isfying explanation, but inescapable.

Another psychological difference which might arise from the physical difference, at least in females after puberty, is that women by their very nature have to accustom themselves to pain simply because of the way their bodies are made. Therefore, one might guess a woman would have at least the potential for a greater compassion for others who undergo pain. This does not mean that only females should be nurses; it does imply they might be naturally better at it than males—and perhaps also better physicians and clergy.

Even more so, a woman who has conceived, carried, nursed, cared for, cleaned, fed, and tried to comprehend the needs of an infant who can't speak must be profoundly sensi-tized, in a way no male, no matter how well-intentioned, could ever be. All women don't react to the burdens of femaleness in the same way. But no man ever had even the opportunity.

In general, women also have by nature smaller body size than men, but that difference is less and less significant in a mech-anized age. Any woman can drive an 18-wheeler, operate a crane, fly a jet. The question of whether women should fly in combat seems as nugatory as whether a homosexual of either sex should be allowed in the services. Ah, but a woman could be captured and raped. So could a man, as witness Lawrence of Arabia.

Unlike male/female, *masculine/feminine* is a polarity, not a dichotomy. Gender is not a definition, as sex is, but a matter of *connotations,* resonances a word sets up in a listener—as *home* is warmer than *house,* and *steed* is more romantic than *nag.* Unfortunately, slovenly thinking constricts the words *masculine* and *feminine* into synonyms for male and female, equating sex and gender. So if you say a female's writing has a strong, masculine bite, or a male's reaction to someone in need is feminine, you'd better be armed.

Outside of physical, sexual matters, males and females are equal and should be treated equally. Women are as (or more) intelligent, as (or more) resilient, as (or more) decisive. But despite that equality a woman's sex still works against her, particularly in the marketplace, especially in situations where the style has already long been set by the opposite sex: truckers' bars, police, military. The newcomer of the opposite sex is a definite minority, like a newly arrived immigrant. Does a woman have to become an "emasculated male" in order to make it or even survive in "that jungle out there"? If she does (like Faye Dunaway in *Network*), she thereby loses precisely the contribution she could make *as* female.

Psychologists assert there is at least some ground on which to claim that "masculine" and "feminine" attitudes and preferences are based on nature. A male child most often spends most of his early formative years with a mother of the opposite sex (or a grandmother, female day-care personnel, or teachers), especially since the Industrial Revolution when the father stopped working on the farm or in a shop connected to the home. The boy develops his individuality by separation from the mother.

A girl, however, experiences herself as like her mother and therefore doesn't feel that need for separation. As Deborah Tannen writes, a brother and sister grow up "in two different cultures." Thus, psychologists say, the female self develops by vulnerability, by connections with other people, while the male self develops invulnerability, by establishing more defensive ego boundaries.

Further, psychologists claim girls' internal worlds are more continuous with the external world, with fewer boundaries. Girls want to yield to the world in order to understand it; boys want to dominate it. That is true in adult life. Tannen's study, *You Just Don't Understand,* shows men talk twice as long and often as women in public meetings. Any teacher knows boys will object before they even grasp what she is saying, while girls usually wait. Therefore, since masculinity is defined through separation and femininity through union, male identity is threatened by intimacy, while female identity is threatened by separation.

However, I would think a little boy, just as a little girl, feels the same maternal abandonment at weaning or the kindergarten door, nor would a woman suffer from solitary confinement more than a man. Similarly, I find it difficult to believe a boy, by his *nature,* brushes away maternal (or especially paternal) caressing as "sissy." Sissiness, like all prejudice, has to be taught. If older males consider physical forms of affection "unmanly," I have to suspect it is based not on nature but on nurture, since in most societies outside Anglo-Saxon influence males kiss one another on meeting as a matter of course.

In a world where television affects children's attitudes about sex-gender expectations at such an early age, the line between the influence of nature and nurture becomes blurred. But psychologists like Janet Lever find boys play outdoors more than girls, in larger groups, more competitively, and for longer periods—not because the games require more skill but because disputes arise more often among boys, who enjoy the debates as much as the games.

In contrast, girls are more tolerant in their attitudes to rules, more willing to make exceptions to include the clumsy and unskilled (if they like her), and more easily adaptable to innovations. Rather than elaborating rules for resolving disputes, girls would rather change the game because they find the game less important than the friendships.

Girls want to play together; boys want to win. As a result, girls use relationships as weapons; boys use fists. Both boys and girls want their own way, but by different means: boys by one-upmanship, girls by persuasion (cf. Samson and Delilah). After about age two, boys continue hitting others to get their way, but most girls stop, preferring to get their way more by fear of exclusion than by force. Boys judge their place in a group by who calls the shots; girls judge by how alliances shift.

Again, how much those preferences are rooted in objective sexual differences and how much is induced by spoken and wordless expectations from parents and from the inescapable TV is difficult to say. Whatever the cause, according to the experts, that is the case: boys are (more) defensive-aggressive, girls are (more) inclusive-adaptable.

For two years, Erik Erikson studied 150 boys and 150 girls at play constructing a scene with toys as if they were setting up a shot for a movie. He found girls emphasized "inner" space while boys emphasized "outer" space. Girls' scenes were most often interiors, sheltering people and animals, with low walls and inviting doorways. Boys' scenes were almost exclusively exteriors: high walls and turrets, more moving parts, more accidents, more policemen. Ruins, in fact, were exclusively boys' constructs. Erikson concluded that, by nature, children's games in some way subconsciously reflect their genital structure: the boys with external, the girls with internal genitals.

Such studies suggesting gender choices rooted in sexuality are reliable only when children are very young, after which the expectations of parents, peers, and especially the media smother the evidence. The Fisher-Price toy-testing center in East Aurora, New York, found kids of either sex will play with just about any toy, from train sets to tiny vacuum cleaners—until about age three or four. After that, it's strictly the stereotypes.

Nurture

Because parents know "most" female children grow up to be mothers, creating protective, civilizing space, and "most" male children grow up to be breadwinners climbing the beanstalk to

bring home the golden goose and acting as last-resort discipli-
narians, parents assign gender roles, along with the "proper"
toys and games—dolls and jump ropes for girls, video games
and ray guns for boys—long before the genital differences are
even activated. Again, the word *proper* implies that the standard
(i.e., normal) little girl "ought" to aspire to be a good little
homebody and the standard (i.e., normal) little boy "ought" to
aspire to be an aggressive go-getter.

Most often mothers don't differentiate between boy and girl,
but fathers tend to roughhouse with boys and treat girls like little
princesses. Boys usually sense that their acceptability depends on
performance: taking spills good-naturedly, winning the game—
with an underlying fear of being unloved if they fail. Fathers are
ordinarily soft to their daughters, while mothers try to be sure
they are not spoiled. A girl manipulates her father and resents
the mother's intrusions—which carries over to her resentment
of her mother's interference in adolescence over boys.

The stereotypes are reinforced even more strongly by the
child's peers. Few children are strong enough to bear the burden
of being "different," and most respond "Yes" to the statement:
"There are very few prices too high to pay for acceptance by
at least some of your peers." The boy who can't spiral a football
(and the girl who can do it better than her brothers) takes the
great risk of being ostracized, even though carrying an inflated
pig bladder through eleven boys on a striped lawn has little if
anything to do with being manly, and more than a few skilled
NFL players are practicing homosexuals.

Once the children go to school, one would expect, they
would be treated the same, but that is not concretely true.
Teachers simply expect girls to be more "ladylike," and any girl
who is not is a "tough." They also expect boys to be more
rowdy than girls. Ironically, though academic education seems
squarely in the stereotypically "male," left-brain arena, most

teachers are females. Thus many boys are left to think education is "girl stuff," while a girl who stereotypically should be taking nothing but home economics, health, and infant communication, is forced to take trigonometry and physics.

Surveys show that the one thing girls will not tell their boyfriends is their grades, if the grades are good. Subconsciously, that skewed conviction lasts. Researchers have discovered women about to get doctoral degrees often find themselves oddly losing interest, missing assignments, delaying completion of the dissertation. In most cases the women felt subconsciously that the degree would somehow impair their femininity and desirability.[2]

Also, both the media treatment of sex and gender roles and the women's movement have altered the way both boys and girls consider not only sexuality but themselves. Up to the '50s, any boy who was sexually active at least didn't talk much about it, and any girl who was "easy" was considered a tramp. Now, any boy who is a virgin at eighteen must be queer, and girls have become as sexually competitive as boys were "supposed" to be. It's sad at a boys' school to see how many girls from all-girls' schools show up each afternoon, like Lili Marlene, pining outside the prison gate.

The Androgynous Soul: Anima / Anima

Carl Jung has made a strong case that the human self is *androgynous*; that is, whether male or female, each of us has both masculine and feminine qualities—just as men secrete recessive female hormones and women secrete recessive male hormones. Half each person's DNA comes from a person of the opposite sex.

Jung called the (potential) masculine characteristics in the female the *animus*, the (potential) feminine characteristics in the

male the *anima*. Most readers have seen the Chinese pictograph
of the Yin and Yang, a circle cut by a wavy line separating two
principles, the Yin richly dark and feminine, the Yang bright
and masculine—but each having within it a small circle of the
other color. The interaction of the two influences one's destiny.

Thus, both the female's animus and the male's anima have
real, positive power. In order to be fully human, each sex must
evolve the spiritual power the other has in greater preponder-
ance, by nature or nurture. But the animus and anima are
sources not only of animation of the soul but also of animosity,
what Jung called "the shadow." Lack of development or active
repression of them makes them primal, dark, threatening,
tangled in the Id-roots of either. "What the devil's gotten into
you?" The stymied animus leads to unbudging opinions in a
woman, the frustrated anima to irrational moods in a man. If a
male can make peace with his inner feminine side, and a
woman can harness the power of her inner masculine side, each
of the sexes will be better empowered to deal with the males
and females outside.

Another effect of leaving either animus or anima undeveloped or of actually repressing it entirely is "projection," laying
off the development of animus-anima on someone else or
ascribing the suppressed potential onto someone else.
Projection is caught well in the old "Well, s'r, the little woman
purty much takes care o' all them things like birthday cards 'n
religion" and "Oh, I could *never* wrap my silly little head around
a *budget*."

Girls with a suppressed animus go gaga over omnicompe-
tent types like Mel Gibson; boys with a suppressed anima deify
Marilyn Monroe. (Joe DiMaggio and Arthur Miller married
her; Norman Mailer wrote a book about her.) Women, especially in the United States, often see males as cynical
dominators; homophobes, with a completely repressed anima,

project their own unnerving (therefore inadmissible) inner feelings on gay men and beat hell out of them. They "blame the mirror for what it reflects."

Animus

The animus is the man-within a woman, a source of initiative, courage, objectivity, confidence, savvy, usually (but not always) shaped by her father. One thinks of such fictional women as Kristen Lavransdatter, Scarlett O'Hara, Princess Leia, Shug in *The Color Purple,* and such real women as Indira Gandhi, Claire Booth Luce, Katherine Hepburn, Linda Ellerbee, Anna Quindlan, who exerted their intelligence and their rights without ever losing their femininity.

Authors have traced this journey to full womanhood in sources as disparate as the Psyche myth[3] and *The Wizard of Oz.*[4] When Psyche tries to see (understand) her husband, Eros, who will never let her see him as he is, she lights a lamp and tries to look at him. As punishment, Aphrodite gives her the tasks she needs to become a woman, as opposed to a desirable, lovely, but empty-headed girl. She sorts seeds, discriminating; she comes back with the wool of the Sun Rams not by aggression but by cunning, pulling the wool off the brambles; she gets through Hades by saying "No" to other people's needs.

If a woman fails to develop her animus, she becomes like Miss Celie at the outset of *The Color Purple.* If she overdevelops it, she becomes a strident virago like Kate in *Taming of the Shrew.*

Once she has taken hold of masculine ability to make decisions and be heard, she has to go back and access her own inner feminine. Otherwise, she is an emasculated male.

Anima

Most civilizing of the soul has come from the feminine side of males, prodded by females: mothers and spouses. *Lysistrata* is a good example of women showing more common sense and long-range perspective than their dominant males. It is the feminine qualities that bring meaning to life: relatedness to others and to the environment; controlling the masculine pursuit of power, prestige, and accomplishment with compassion; and the introspective quest for wisdom. It is not a forced sense of spontaneity but an inner at-homeness with one's true, inner, bipolar self.

Most societies, including our own, do not suffer from a surfeit of empathy, altruism, or nurturance.

Anima is the woman-within a man: vague feelings, hunches, receptivity to the nonrational, capacity for personal love, relation to the unconscious—the Sibyl, the gods. The anima is right brain, feminine: receptive rather than trying to "master" the subject. Men who have accessed their anima find that loving involvement with the subject (person, topic, animal, work) actually *enriches* perception. The uneducated mother knows her baby better than some harried doctor in a clinic. Any judgment that is totally objective and value-free is nonhuman.

One thinks of such literary figures as Teiresias, Merlin, Santiago in *The Old Man and the Sea,* Atticus Finch, and such real men as Socrates, Mark Twain, Pope John XXIII, Leonard Bernstein.

Not only every woman but every man has within the "shadow" Aphrodite characteristics: vanity, conniving, tyranny, the goddess whose slave walks before her carrying a mirror so she can always reassure herself she is "the fairest of them all."

Since childhood, a man gets most of his sense of self-worth from a woman—his mother, his wife. Ideally, however, he must ultimately get it from his own anima. In the story of Jack and the Beanstalk, Jack went up three times: once for a transient bit of solvency in the bag of gold, the second time for definitive security in the goose that laid the golden eggs. But he went up a third time, for the singing harp, not because it was gold, but because it sang to his soul.

Thanks to the women's movement, sensitivity is not so hateful to many men. They cook, diaper, dust, sometimes even becoming "Mister Moms," while their wives do most of the breadwinning. Still, as Abraham Maslow says, the fear of poetic feeling, of fantasy, of dreaminess, of emotional thinking is stronger in men than in women, in adults than in children, in engineers than in artists.

If a man fails to develop his anima, he becomes like Rambo; if he overdevelops it, he becomes a lapdog. Just as a woman must access and own her masculine but then return to her femininity, a man must access and own his feminine and then return to what Robert Bly calls his "wildman." Otherwise, he is domesticated.

In the most ideal cases, there must be a "marriage" within each man and woman of the contrary factors involved in gender. That marriage is well embodied in the union of Raskolnikov and Sonia Marmeladov in *Crime and Punishment*. Raskolnikov has murdered an old woman moneylender, meaninglessly, only to "prove" himself. Sonia, his prostitute lover, will not turn him in to the police, even though she loathes his crime.

Because she loves him, Sonia persuades Raskolnikov to turn himself in, not because a crime has been committed and must be "paid for"—the masculine demand that the books be balanced. The masculine judge in Sonia sees the crime; the feminine lover in her sees beyond that to the criminal. She convinces Raskolnikov to turn himself in to redeem *himself*. Mere punishment does not change the victim or the perpetrator. Freely accepted, legitimate suffering does.

Sonia's judgment is not better than a judge's because she is a woman. It is better because she is a fully human being.

Maturity begins when we finally take over from our moods, assuming the tiller of our own souls: responsibility—and the root of that word is "respond." One of the goals in evolving a soul is to become "at home" with one's sexuality and gender, at home with members of one's own and opposite sex, at home with those of one's own sex whose fantasies are vastly different from one's own. The goal is "the serenity to accept the things that can't be changed, the courage to change the things that can be changed, and the wisdom to know the difference."

Chapter Eight

Making Sense
of Suffering

If there is a purpose in life at all, there must be a purpose in suffering and in dying. But no one can tell another what this purpose is. Each must find out for himself, and must accept the responsibility that his answer prescribes.

Viktor Frankl—*Man's Search for Meaning*[1]

In blocking out the sequence of this book, I hesitated whether to consider freedom before suffering or vice versa. On the one hand, suffering puts a crimp on our freedom, capsizing "the best laid plans of mice and men." On the other hand, misuse of freedom always leads ultimately to suffering. We want what we really ought not to want, and we suffer even when we succeed in getting it. Lear wants flattery, and Goneril and Regan give it to him, full measure and overflowing. What Lear needs is the honest truth, and when Cordelia and Kent give it to him, he banishes them. But Lear can't escape the results of his choices, and the gods send him freedom *through* suffering, reflected upon.

Every philosopher from Buddha to Karl Marx began with suffering; if you don't start there, you don't start. So I begin with suffering. The core question is: What *legitimates* it? What purpose and meaning does inevitable suffering have in human life?

There are basically two sources of suffering: physical evils (hurricanes, misborn children, death itself) and moral evils (war, rape, dishonesty). Physical evils are in no way humanly blamable, and their cause lies either in a Deity who has reasons for them our minds are too time-space bound to fathom or in the absurdity of evolution's stumbling one step too far and coming up with a species that knows its every trial and triumph is ultimately futile. Moral evils seem attributable solely to human inability to rise above the beast, but that ability freely to choose evil rather than good ultimately devolves, again, either on a God who gave that freedom to apes or on sheer blind chance.

But I'm not quite ready to take on that most profound of questions, not yet. For the purposes of this chapter, I restrict the scope of the question to the following: Prescinding from the existence of a provident God and prescinding from whatever *pre*historical event caused us to suffer and question ("original sin") and from any *post*historical experience that might justify it ("heaven"), is there any value to suffering *here and now*?

The definitive dogmatic answers we yearn for don't exist, otherwise philosophers could stop pestering the question (and vice versa). All I can offer are "clues," taking the lead of Peter Kreeft, from whose book I purloined this chapter's title, the best work I know on this bleak but inescapable subject.

Questioning is equally far removed from both dogmatism (thinking you have all the answers) and skepticism (believing there are no answers). Neither the dogmatist nor the skeptic questions. Dogmatism is intellectual pride and skepticism is intellectual despair.[2]

Suffering and Value

"Suffering" here covers the whole spectrum, not only major catastrophes from flood to cancer, nor the sudden, shocking jolts of accidents, betrayal, heartbreak, but also the less dramatic but nonetheless real distress provoked by Erikson's natural crises or disequilibriums by which our bodies invite us to live larger lives than we'd planned to and even disappointments with others and with ourselves. How can we find *value* in them?

Legitimate Suffering

Before I face the task of validating the unmerited suffering that comes from physical and moral evils, I would like to consider a third source of suffering, not rooted in physical evil or moral evil, but a source within the self: the inability to deal with *legitimate* (as opposed to unmerited) distress arising simply from being an as-yet-incomplete human being in a world where the law is evolution and the lure is entropy.

One can pretend to "solve" the question either by evading legitimate suffering or by suppressing knowledge of it.

As Carl Jung insists, evading legitimate suffering that comes simply from dealing with the world we were dealt (the objective facts) always ends in neurosis—anxiety, obsessions, compulsions without objective cause, narcissism, blaming our faults on our personalities rather than blaming our personalities on our faults. "I'm a procrastinator" seems self-justifying, as if it were an incurable disease of which I am a victim.

But living an illusion, lying to oneself and believing the lies, is very hard work. Thus, what we accept as a substitute for the truth becomes more painful than facing the truth. What's more, denying the suffering that comes from facing the truth, flat on, avoids growth as a human being, since growth is by definition leaving behind something good to become something better, leaving the comfortable security of the cocoon to fly.

Suppressing suffering involved in facing the truth is equally self-destructive—drowning it in booze or drugs or witless busyness, settling for "coping with" what is objectively change-able. Perhaps the most widespread and debilitating neurosis is "minding one's own business," sticking the thumb in the mouth and letting the rest of the world go by, stingy with one's attention, affection, time, and money.

As we saw before when considering Freud's Pleasure Principle, each individual, each culture, makes a fundamental choice between two options, *Eros,* the life wish, or *Thanatos,* the death wish. Now our culture seems at first glance head over heels in pursuit of *Eros* and pleasure, yet it is not in the sense Freud intended *"Eros."* Quite clearly, our society is not in pursuit of heroism but in pursuit of anesthesia: the passive paradise of the womb, the painless, brainless utopias of *1984* and *Brave New World.* Even sex is too often not a quest for love but a quest for Lethe.

As Burger, the psychiatrist in *Ordinary People,* tells the anguished Conrad: "If you don't let yourself feel pain, you don't let yourself feel *anything.* "

Unmerited Suffering: Attitude–Responsibility–Value
Wisdom is making peace with the unchangeable. We do have the freedom to face the unavoidable with dignity, to understand

the transformational value that *attitude* works on suffering. Frankl writes that in the concentration camps, "What alone remains is 'the last of human freedoms'—the ability to choose one's attitude in a given set of circumstances."[3] What Frankl asks is not optimism in the face of pessimism but hope in the face of hopelessness.

> The way in which a man accepts his fate and all the suffering it entails, the way in which he takes up his cross, gives him ample opportunity—even under the most difficult circumstances—to add a deeper meaning to his life. It may remain brave, dignified, and unselfish. Or in the bitter fight for self-preservation he may forget his human dignity, and become no more than an animal. Here lies the chance for a man either to make use of or to forego the opportunities of attaining the moral values that a difficult situation may afford him. And this decides whether he is worthy of his sufferings or not.[4]

Are we responsible for our unmerited sufferings? The answer is no. And yes. We are not responsible for our predicament as its cause—whether it be cancer or job loss or the death of a child or spouse. But we are responsible for what we do with the effects, with the rubble Fate has made of our lives.

> Consider [the prisoner's] behavior—is he still spiritually responsible for what is happening to him psychically, for what the concentration camp has "made" of him? Our answer is: he is. For even in this socially limited environment, in spite of this societal restriction upon his personal freedom, the ultimate freedom remains his: the freedom even in the camp to give some shape to his existence.[5]

The only hand we have to play is the hand Fate deals us. We need not be victims of our *biological* fate. Stephen Hawking is a good example of a phoenix risen from ashes. One night the evening news reported a young man receiving his Eagle Scout Award. Nothing newsworthy in that, except he was twenty-two and couldn't give an acceptance speech. Instead, his father spoke it as the young man pointed to letters on a board atop his wheelchair. He had cerebral palsy: for his merit badge in hiking, he had wheeled his chair for nine miles, then crawled the rest of the way.

We need not be victims of our *psychological* fate. We are, to be sure, driven by the winds, but a skillful sailor can *use* the wind, whereas "I'm doomed" or "I'm nobody" become self-fulfilling prophecies. "My mother made me a homosexual." (If I give her the yarn, can she make me one too?)

As Frankl starkly and firmly asserts: "A faulty upbringing exonerates nobody." Those with callous upbringings in shoddy circumstances with few opportunities are in truth victims of others' mistakes, but it is the inescapable burden they were delivered, and they are no more hamstrung by it than the boy with cerebral palsy. Each of our stories is unique, with its own demons and dragons. Accept that and get on with what you have left: you.

We need not be victims of our *situational* fate, immured in its "laws," living a provisional existence, settling for mere "survival." People who went down on the *Titanic* went down singing. People have gotten off third-generation welfare. Women and men survived Dachau, Auschwitz, the Gulag, Teheran, Beirut. And they came through battered but unbowed, with their own souls clasped firmly in their own hands. If such heroism is possible for so many ordinary people, surely it is possible to say "No" to the soulless societies and soulless selves, to Gradgrind, to the naysayers and nobodies we're surrounded by. Surely it is possible to say "No" to the values purveyed incessantly by the media.

There is a meaning to *value* here totally unfamiliar in a utilitarian society where "dignity, integrity, altruism" simply don't compute. How much do they pay? But would someone who jumped into icy water to rescue someone else, unsuccessfully, be "wasted," less heroic because he tried and failed? Frankl says, "One who fought heroically but vainly died heroically but not vainly." In a life view where one's soul is more indicative than one's bank balance, the fighting alone counts. There is no lost cause if the cause is just. In the going, I'm already there.

As Dr. Martin Luther King Jr. wrote:

> The value of unmerited suffering [calls us] either to react with bitterness or seek to transform the suffering into a creative force. If only to save myself from bitterness, I have attempted to see my personal ordeals as an opportunity to transfigure myself and heal the people involved in the tragic situation which now obtains. I have lived these last few years with the conviction that unearned suffering is redemptive.[6]

Death and Value

Now no matter, child, the name:
Sorrow's springs are the same.
Nor mouth had, no nor mind, expressed
What heart heard of, ghost guessed:
It is the blight man was born for,
It is Margaret you mourn for.[7]

Until we wrap our minds around the reality of death—not in the abstract, but as the only infallibly predictable event in each of our futures, we live in the illusion we have plenty of time. We can ask ourselves will my marriage last, will my children turn out well, will I be happy with my life and job when I reach my middle years? To all those questions one can answer only: Do your best, and after that, *que sera, sera*. Nothing is really predictable. Except one thing. You will die.

Your death isn't an unpleasant possibility. Your death is an unpleasant fact. Some find it so morbid or even grisly they refuse to acknowledge it. But it doesn't go away. The number of breakfasts you will eat is finite.

Today, death is both obscene and trivialized. On the one hand, we hide it away; it always happens somewhere else, to someone else. On the other hand, before they graduate from grade school, most children have seen more deaths, real and fictionalized, than a veteran in the army of Genghis Khan. But ignoring or disparaging death is living in an unreal world, and death is inexorably going to intrude on our lives in the deaths of many we love, before death shatters our own illusions about it.

There are three inescapable facts about death: (1) it is inevitable, (2) with the exception of suicides, it is unpredictable, and (3) it is the ultimate test by which you gauge the value of your life, because it renders everything that has gone before unchangeable. Whether we go on after it or not, death writes an ineradicable "*Finis*" to everything here.

Afterlife or Nothing: Transcendent or Immanent

And after death, what? Over 8 million ordinary people in America alone have had out-of-body experiences. They describe hovering over the doctors surrounding them in bed, hearing themselves declared dead, then turning and seeing some familiar figure like a loved one or a saint or a guru blazing with light, reaching out a kindly hand. Then they come to a boundary and know if they pass that point they can never return. Often they awake and find a meaning to life and a sense of continuity they'd never felt before. But those experiences could be self-induced, wish-fulfillment, hallucination.

People have believed that heroes like Hercules, Psyche, Orpheus, Jesus have come back from death and appeared to still-living people. But at least to our technological, this-world mind-set, people who testify to such experiences end up classified with people who claim to have been abducted by alien spaceships.

But there is one certitude about the afterlife that brooks no argument: either we go on, or we don't; that is a true and iron dichotomy. Either our souls are capable of transcending the physical limits of our bodies (in *some* way), or we are limited in an immanent life here on Earth for as long as we can manage. Either the souls in us are immortal, here and now, independently of their time-bound flesh, or we are just so much potential refuse waiting to be picked up, and we have no idea of the collection date. We're all on the *Titanic,* and we're all headed in only one direction. Either/or; no other alternatives.

There are many—more than a few of them brilliant—who opt for the latter angst-ridden alternative as the only honest one: we are solely immanent. Surely any continued reality beyond the reach of space and time must be either nonexistent or impermeable to the rational mind. Therefore, it is as fatuous to ponder the possibility of an afterlife as to ponder whether unicorns might gambol on Alpha Centauri. It is a reasonable argument and not to be gainsaid by simplistic fundamentalist assertions.

But if death is the final moment of our existence, don't say at a wake, "She's in a better life now." She no longer *is;* she's stopped being real. If all each of us is and all we've struggled to achieve as human beings is simply snuffed out—Phfft!—when we have a flat EKG, then Mother Teresa and a Times Square pimp get exactly the same reward for a life: annihilation.

That may be an insight more horrifying than the realization of death itself. But if the immanentist option is correct, then its conclusion is inescapable. And it has a radical effect on what we think our lives are worth and on all our so-called moral choices. Nietzsche has had the answers all along.

If we are this-world limited, then the only templates by which we judge our temporary value are time, space, and what we see as our human accomplishments.

Time: Draw a time line four and a half inches long (or if you have a chalkboard, four and a half feet). Each inch or foot stands for a billion years, and the whole line represents the time the solar system has existed—not the whole universe, just this somewhat cozy corner containing us. About 65 percent of us will have about seventy years of life (a third of us will have less). Find your seventy years against that background. Maybe a single dot? Then you cease to be real anymore, like the wake of a ship.

In *The Dragons of Eden*, Carl Sagan has drawn a calendar that takes an even wider perspective. He compresses all the events in the history of the universe into a single year, with the Big Bang occurring on January 1 at 00:00:01:

January 1
Big Bang

September 14
Formation of Earth

December 16
First worms

December 24
First dinosaurs

December 28
First flowers; dinosaurs extinct

December 31, 11:00 P.M.
First humans

11:59 P.M.
Cave paintings in Europe

11:59:51 P.M.
Invention of an alphabet

11:59:59 P.M.
Renaissance in Europe [16th century][8]

Against that background, 400 years = 1/60 of a second. Then your seventy years (if you have that many) begin at 11:59:59:50. Then the ball, Cinderella, is over at midnight. For you.

Space

Some of us are six feet five inches, some five feet even. Inside a small room, there's a recognizable difference. Standing next to the Sears Tower, there's not. Big Daddy's ranch looks very big when you ride the perimeter, but not when you try to pick it out from a photograph of Earth from space. Imagine you could get even further out, to the edge of the Milky Way galaxy (920 quintillion miles away). You spot this little solar system with, surprisingly, only one sun and only nine or ten planets orbiting around it.

Draw a circle, say, 3 3/4 inches in diameter, the radius going from the sun to Pluto, about 3,680,000,000 miles from the sun. On that map, 1/16 inch = 62,500,000 miles. Find me the Americas, find me your city, find me you. If what Hitler was able to accumulate is contrasted with what you can accumulate, find me the difference. A burp in a hurricane.

Cocooned in the here-and-now, we are like the Lilliputians, some of them really big guys. Then, of a sudden, Gulliver shows up. And in our case, Gulliver is Death.

Perspective vaporizes our pretensions to importance.

Human Accomplishments

In each of our seventy years (if we have them), we will love a lot of people, accomplish "things," leave a legacy. But take a best-case scenario: You've won two Nobel Prizes, one for medicine for curing the common cold, one for literature. You've published twenty-five books, each of them well received, and you've had ten exemplary children: a research chemist, a historian, a ballerina, an Academy Award director, and so forth. Better than any life could hope to produce.

But put your accomplishments against the accumulated accomplishments of human history: the discovery of fire, the invention of the wheel, the *Dialogues* of Plato, Caesar's conquests, Michelangelo's Sistine Ceiling alone, Shakespeare's plays. Put your twenty-five books into the Library of Congress. Place your ten talented children against the 100,000 human beings snuffed out in one earthquake alone—each of them somebody's child, chemists, historians, ballerinas. Perhaps you will live on in your children, but in the immanentist reality, you'll be unaware of it.

Your contributions may give you a good feeling, temporarily. But it is the opinion of so much refuse awaiting collection.

Archibald MacLeish captured the immanentist truth as well as I've ever seen it captured in a sonnet called "The End of the World." In the octave, he describes a bizarre circus filled with freaks. Then just before the sestet, he writes:

> Quite unexpectedly the top blew off:
> And there, there overhead, there, there hung over
> Those thousands of white faces, those dazed eyes,
> There in the starless dark the poise, the hover,
> There with vast wings across the cancelled skies,
> There in the sudden blackness the black pall
> Of nothing, nothing, nothing—nothing at all.[9]

Blaise Pascal (d. 1662), a mathematician and philosopher, faced that ultimate dilemma. Confronted, he said, with two utterly irreducible options—one of which had to be true, one of which had to be false, one of which was appealing (we go on), one of which was appalling (we are erased)—and having no certain way of knowing which was true, the only sane option was to go with the appealing choice and base one's life on that conviction.

I go toward the doorway of death, skipping. "I'm going to a wonderful, endless party!" If I'm wrong, Friedrich Nietzsche is not going to be on the other side, thumbing his nose: "I *told* you so, *dummkopf!*" If I'm wrong, and reality does not transcend this life, I'll never find out I was wrong!

One can argue for the transcendent also from an inner hunger we humans have which, as far as we can see, no animal shares: we want to survive—not just battering at the waves to stay alive as an animal would, but yearning to survive long before we face death. Perhaps, as the immanentists claim, that hope is self-delusive. But why are we the only species *cursed*— by our very human nature—with a hunger for which there is no food? No sow, snoozing in her ring of piglets, has her dreams disturbed by the understanding they will all one day die. We do. If in fact we will not go on, better to have been born a pig.

Life makes sense only if this is not the only reality but the *foreground* of another dimension where love is not annihilated by death. Again, there are only two starkly irreconcilable options: Either life is an instantaneous flash in a sea of endless darkness or a smudge of darkness on an infinite light.

We haven't yet argued for or against—much less estab- lished—the need for an Ultimate Mind. We have only debated the durability of the human soul.

The Effect of Death on Perspective

Negative as death is, making peace with it has very positive effects in our lives and souls. For one thing, before the reality of death, every other value lines up in proper priority, which is why the Roman senate decreed that each time a victorious general was accorded a triumph through the streets at the head of his captured booty and slaves, a boy stood behind his back, holding a golden laurel wreath over the great man's head, whispering in his ear, "*Memento, mori!* Remember, you will die!"

Death shows us the value of our days. Diamonds are precious; dirt is not, because diamonds are scarce and we have a seemingly endless supply of dirt. Time is precious because it is finite. At the end of *Our Town,* Emily is allowed to come back from the grave for just one day, and she moves among the people she loved, who just "walk through" life, and she asks the Stage Manager if anybody really, really looks at anything while they're alive. He says, "Saints and poets, maybe. They do, some." For most, I suspect, life washes over us, like the sea over stones.

What matters is not the number of our days but the way we use them.

Death shows us what's important. It's an infallible touchstone of all the propaganda. In the face of death, assaults on our easily bruised egos shrivel to their true triviality. Wise folk who have made peace with death try never to go to bed holding a grudge, even when they were right and the other was wrong, because there will come a time when it's too late to say, "I'm sorry." For them, the friendship, however tenuous, is more important than the sick-warm feeling of the grudge.

One time, just as my parents were leaving from a visit when I was studying philosophy, my dad came up to me behind the car, tears in his eyes, and said, "Pray for us, Bill. This last year's been hell." It was the first time, ever, he had shared his weakness with me. He had always been reassuring and unbreakable. Now I had bought the "unwritten rule" for a long time, but at that moment I didn't give a damn if everybody in that school was glued to the windows watching us. I kissed my father. I'm so glad I broke the rule. It was the last time I ever saw my father alive. How lucky I was to be set free.

With an endless supply of days, without death, *nothing* has any felt value. But accepting death, we see that the values we have been *told* are values—long life, accumulation of goods, human accomplishments—are indeed values, but not the most real values. As Frankl says, "The heroic death of one who died young certainly has more content and meaning than the existence of some long-lived dullard." If death is a doorway and not a dead end, the only thing you can take through it is your soul. And if it is a dead end, time is even more precious to the immanentist than to the transcendentalist.

In either case, death is the ultimate criterion. As Carlos Castaneda writes, when you are in a seemingly insolvable quandary, the only sane thing is to "turn to your left and ask advice from your death."

Chapter Nine

FREEDOM

They are the lords and owners of their faces.

William Shakespeare—*Sonnet XCIV*[1]

Freedom is a reality riddled with ironies and paradox. First, you can define freedom (which is very positive) only by negatives: not bound, not coerced, not restricted. Second, freedom works only when you stop having it; it's like money in your pocket—nice to know you have, but of no real value at all until you spend it on something you want more. As soon as you choose one of the two roads in a yellow wood, you give up the freedom to take the other, at least for now. Third, freedom costs: the painful effort of finding out what your options really are, before you can begin the even more burdensome process of deciding which is best. There, too, you confront still another challenge: Does *best* mean most appealing or right?

Nor (despite Elsa the lioness) are we "Born Free." Just as she is, we are born shackled to an animal Id which wants what it wants when it wants it. Then we become even less free than Elsa (unless she's in a circus) when we gradually succumb to the whip of the Superego. Our greatest achievement as human beings is to emancipate our souls from that bipolar servitude and secure a spiritual freedom unassailable by fire, threat, imprisonment, or rape, able to face down poverty, defeat, sickness, torture. At its freest, our soul is impervious to the siren songs of pride, covetousness, lust, anger, gluttony, envy, and sloth. Such a freedom of soul can be surrendered, but it can never be taken away. You can never be degraded without your cooperation.

Genuine freedom means that the soul is unchecked in its choices either by illegitimate forces outside, which try to make you choose an option against your will, or by forces within you which urge you to take the subjectively easier rather than the objectively better choice. ("The tree comes to me.") Note I say "illegitimate forces," since there *are* external forces that have every right and obligation to check your choices.

Somehow, the young (and terminal adolescents like the denizens of *Cheers)* have an unquestioned conviction life is unfair, and that it surely is. But to their mind there must be some Oz up ahead where freedom will be unlimited, without the need for discipline, without the burden of tests, without the obligation to measure up to objective standards, without having to submit to external constraints, without the onus of others' expectations.

Whoever wants total freedom landed in the wrong galaxy.

If there is no objective standard by which to judge rightful and wrongful uses of freedom, then Nietzsche was right, Raskolnikov was right, Lee Harvey Oswald was right. If there is no objective standard, independent of conflicting subjective opinions and desires, there is no way for us to say Joseph Campbell was a better human being than Joseph Goebbels.

Without an objective standard, freedom becomes an end in itself, and any choice is self-justifying so long as it is freely chosen. Dr. Jack Kevorkian, who insists on the freedom to assist self-chosen suicide, puts the issue fairly and squarely:

> In my view the highest principle in medical ethics—in any kind of ethics—is personal autonomy, self-determination. What counts is what the patient wants and judges to be a benefit or a value in his or her own life. That's primary.[2]

Freedom becomes not empowerment to choose between objective right and objective wrong but merely the power to choose.

To the contrary, Robert Bellah and his colleagues argue:

> If the self is defined by its ability to choose its own values, on what grounds are those choices them-selves based? . . . One's own idiosyncratic preferences are their own justifications. . . . Now if selves are defined by their preferences, but those preferences are arbitrary, each self constitutes its own moral universe, and there is no way to reconcile conflicting claims about what is good in itself. . . . All we can appeal to in relationships with others is their self-interest.[3]

Nor is the conflict resolved at the other end of the spectrum from relativism: the absolute finality of the word of the law. Speaking at the awards ceremony of Jewish Theological Seminary, November 1962, Chief Justice Warren Burger said that ethics goes far *beyond* the Law, to human conduct which the Law cannot possibly legislate. It is what he called "the Law beyond the Law," which summons us to be fair, merciful, compassionate, honest. Even if our actions can slide past the letter of civil law, violating that Law-beyond-the-Law puts at peril not only the individual but civilization itself. "Society would collapse almost as completely as though it lacked Law."

Kevorkian's cavils to the contrary, we will never be free of "the things that can't be changed," outside us and inside us.

There are limitations on freedom over which we have no control: outside, the natures of things and the objective obligations imposed by objective human relationships; inside, our DNA, the people who formed us, our own past mistakes.

You'll never be free of the law of gravity as long as you want to stay on Earth. Fire burns, rape savages two souls, all of us will one day die. Not opinion; fact. You will never be free of the fact that, in an intimate relationship, there is not merely a healthy, animal, physical encounter, but two human beings who lay claims on one another stronger than those of strangers. Not opinion; fact. You may be free to get a divorce, but you'll never be free of those years of relationship nor free of your responsibilities to your children. Not opinion; fact. You can never be free of the people you truly love; faced with their helplessness, you will in turn be helpless not to respond to their need. Not opinion. Fact.

Whoever offers total freedom offers a lie.

Of course, you are free to act *as if* total freedom were possible, as Nietzsche asserted and Raskolnikov tried to prove. You are free to do anything you choose. But the limits—the consequences—are there, whether you like them or accept them or even acknowledge them.

You are free to walk off the World Trade Center, but only once; free to withdraw into self-absorption, which negates all unpleasant realities; free to blow the whole planet to smithereens. But you—and all the rest of us—are not free of the consequences. Nor are you ever free of the "cards" dealt to you from the start (family, economic opportunities, education) nor of how you've managed to play those cards so far. You are not free of the society in which you live and its legitimate expectations. You can freely decide, since life is short, to spend what little time you have eating, drinking, and making merry, but you quite likely will spend a large part of that short life nursing cirrhosis of the liver.

We are free, to be sure, to change "the things that can be changed." But are we free? There is a great difference between freedom *from* all outside pressures and the inner freedom *to* make a choice. A student going off to college, for instance, is free of most parental intrusions (even the ones branded on his Superego), free to sleep around with anyone who will have him, drink beer every night so long as his money and liver hold out, shed himself of all the wearying worship services his parents condemned him to. The question is: Is he *free* to be chaste when everybody's "doin' it," sober when he has a test the next day and everyone else on the corridor has a free day, worshipful when the whole dorm is snoring? Or does he have all the freedom of iron filings dropped in front of a magnet?

Are we really free or victims of our moods? When we have a distasteful job, are we free to get the damn thing done? When the family is howling at the TV, are we free to read a book, sculpt, repair the drain, play Monopoly, write letters? Do we make a firm commitment—freely choosing and following through—or do we prefer the comforting indifference of an open mind, even when the situation demands commitment?

There perhaps is the penultimate slavery: Are we free to stand up and be counted, to work for change, to refuse to settle for survival? John Stuart Mill wrote that an individual should be free to do what he (or she) pleases "but he must not make himself a nuisance to other people." Which pretty much condemns such noble souls as Thomas Jefferson, Sojourner Truth, Jane Addams, Susan B. Anthony, Mahatma Gandhi, Dorothy Day, Churchill, and Rosa Parks. Are we free to challenge *illegitimate* incursions on our freedom: the overbearing boss, the facile character assassin, the snotty waiter, the intruder on line? To repeat: whoever would trade freedom for security deserves neither.

Narcissism is very slick at deception and disguise—especially at *self*-deception. It is very easy to convince ourselves that the only infringements on our freedom come from outside. But is that really true? Just because the puppeteers are your *own* Id and Superego doesn't mean *you* act freely.

Unless you consider it worth the time and effort to think for yourself, to reflect on which actions are objectively right and which are wrong, analyze honestly your own internal resistances to those facts, connect acts with their consequences, establish a vertical scale of value-priorities, ride herd on your own Id and Superego—you are a victim.

I have a hunch the ultimate enslavement is the inability to forgive. We are so ego-burned that forgiveness seems unthinkable, perhaps even unjust, or (worse) an apology when we were right. But when we drag our anger around with us all day like a low-grade infection, our rage does nothing to the perpetrator, who is usually oblivious of it, but only to ourselves, collaborating in the corrosion of our own souls. There are some wounds so profound *we* can never heal, unless we forgive, even when the object of our forgiveness is unrepentant and unworthy of it.

— In the 1992 Los Angeles riots, Reginald Denny was pulled from his truck and brutalized. But during the trial of his attackers, he embraced their mothers and understood the agony they must have gone through, seeing their sons acting like brute beasts, captured on television and replayed over and over for millions to gawk at. Even if his attackers maintained a stone-faced indifference to what they had done, he forgave them.

— On May 13, 1981, in Saint Peter's Square, a Bulgarian Muslim named Mehmet Ali Agca shot Pope John Paul II. But as soon as the pope got out of the hospital, he went to the Roman prison where Agca was held, and he prayed with him—to the same God, with different faces for each—and forgave him. *Both* were set free.

— A story tells of two ex-prisoners of the Nazi camps who met one evening by chance in Berlin. The man asked the woman if she had found it within herself to forgive the Nazis. She nodded quietly and said, "Yes, I have. Have you?" He scowled and rasped, "Never!" She looked at him sadly and said, "Then you are still a prisoner."

Chapter Ten

***

IN QUEST OF A VOICE: FEMALE SPIRITUALITY[1]

There is in every true woman's heart a spark of heavenly fire, which lies dormant in the broad daylight of prosperity, but which kindles up and beams and blazes in the dark hour of adversity.

Washington Irving—*"The Wife"*[2]

In *Fire in the Belly,* Sam Keen writes that H. L. Mencken once said the person who coined the term "near beer" was a very poor judge of distance. Keen suspected the same error in judgment in the effort to erase the distance between men and women.

I suspect Keen is right. I'm *certain* Mencken was.

As we saw when considering gender, the only objective difference between females and males rooted in nature is genital—and whatever psychological effects those physical differences cause. But by nurture, females and males are treated differently (though they may respond to that in their own unique ways and even alter it dramatically). Yet children look to their mothers for something different from what they expect from their fathers, and it is difficult to articulate precisely what those different expectations are.

Generally—and very vaguely—the unverbalized expectation of the mother is that she form a protective, civilizing space where all can feel "at home," while the father defends, supports, and protects it. That is too simple by more than half, but for the moment let it stand as a hazy outline.

To begin honestly, I have about as much right to speak about female spirituality as about being Hispanic, Japanese, or Black. At best, I'm a little-league Tocqueville describing a country he understands only from outside, yet a male who may have read more about female psychology than most and can help other males understand, a bit. At the least, the experts out there, women, can correct me where I'm wrong or skewed or shallow. Perhaps my very mistakes will be the occasion for correcting other's mistakes.

What does spirituality mean? I begin with a gimmick: "You don't really see me, do you?" They roll those eyes that say, "Incurable!" But they don't see me; only my body. They study how I move, what comes out of my mouth, what ticks me off, then make educated *guesses* about the Me at the root of all those things. "The essential is always invisible." The Me that gives hints through my body, the Me that will be gone when I have no brain waves, is as invisible as atoms and love. But it's there: my self, my soul. How I nurture that soul is my spirituality.

Further, although I myself can comprehend the philosophical differences between *soul, psyche* (as in *psychology*), *spirit, conscience, character,* and *ego,* I find they confuse the issue when

I'm trying to understand real human beings. My soul is myself—my who-I-am, all the unquantifiable aspects of me: honor, justice, love, faith. I can't separate in myself the Me who feels genuine guilt from the Me who is on a lifetime search for the Grail. I can't separate the Me who stands in awe of mountains in moonlight from the Me who seethes at injustice.

Spirituality is too often restricted to obvious, religious spirituality: prayer and communal worship. But all those words—*soul, psyche, spirit, conscience, character, ego*—mean the same thing: indivisible Me. Thus, for me, the clear rational distinctions between psychology and spirituality blur.

When I use the word *spirituality,* I am talking about that indivisible soul-life in you and me. When I hone the sensitivity of my conscience, I'm enriching my ability to respond to the beauty of art and nature; when I develop a personally validated self, I hope I'm enhancing the lives my life touches.

For reasons I can only fumble around as an outsider, I am convinced that—whether through nature or nurture, through biology or socialization—a woman's psyche-soul-spirit-conscience is quite different from most men's. Not better, just different. And understanding those differences can enrich a woman's self-understanding, character, and dealings with others. And it can also help men better understand the women they live and work with and can help male-dominated institutions deal with women—provided they are willing to drop their preconceptions and listen.

Except for teaching women in summers, one year at two coed universities, and directing twenty parents' shows, I've spent my life teaching adolescent boys, so I pretty well know my way around that particular minefield. But when I was on sabbatical ten years ago, I realized I knew far too little about female psychology, so I set out to remedy that. I was helped enormously by several books. The first was Carol Gilligan's *In a*

Different Voice, recommended by my friend Susan Kennedy. Then *Women's Ways of Knowing,* by four woman psychologists. Plus *She,* a dandy little book by psychiatrist Robert Johnson which explores female psychology through the Greek myth of Psyche.

At the time, I was also searching for a novel to help the males I teach understand the women in their lives, "from the inside," as *A Separate Peace* helps young women understand emergent adult males. And the one I found fits the job perfectly: *The Color Purple,* which starts with a surely worst-case female scenario but rises to a triumphant climax when Miss Celie stands up to her brutish husband. He's just told her she'll go to Memphis over his dead body, and Celie answers, "Your dead body just the welcome mat I need." It's a moment of personal empowerment that makes you want to shout, "Way t' go, Miss *Celie!"*

The premise of *Women's Ways of Knowing* is that, if language and logic are power, most women are "voiceless," since they are at odds with the traditional male model of understanding: that is, establishing truth by objective, *dispassionate* methods. Instead, as Carol Gilligan concurs, women *enhance* objective knowledge with intuition, seeing things in an inclusive *context,* "connecting" with ideas rather than "mastering" them the way most male-dominated graduate schools demand.

In general, men look for cast-iron proof; women look for understanding, to get inside an idea and walk around. Like the little boy who said moral dilemmas were only "math problems, but with people," many moral judgments, alas, have that same dispassionate (and therefore less than fully *human)* mind-set.

If it's not oversimplified, males generally are locked into a left-brain, Greek way of knowing: strict analysis, logic, and definitions. Women are more open to a right-brain, Hebrew way of knowing: inclusion, intuition, and symbols. We can't get along without left-brain definitions, but cookie-cutter definitions leave out important stuff: "rational animal," for instance. What it leaves out is *soul,* what separates us from apes—or savages, mob hit men, Central Park wilding gangs.

I'd far rather unburden my conscience to a female than to a male. Both males and females get an almost exclusively left-brain education, but females are encouraged to develop their right-brain potential, while men are encouraged to suppress it as somehow "womanish" and "sissy." Thus a woman would at least seem more open to see my problems not just on a rigid left-brain scale (like most ethics courses) but also in the *context* of all the other pressures of my life. When I confess the shaming things I've done, I surely want someone smart, but I want someone also with a heart warmer than flint—whether it's a male or a female.

That difference—perhaps rooted in objective nature but certainly rooted in nurture—convinces me that, in the last two years of high school, we should have at least one course where boys and girls, separately, study the assets and liabilities of their different sexual psychologies. I do my best to make my macho boys understand that unless they resolutely open themselves to the "feminine" side of themselves (the anima), they'll end up half-witted chauvinist pigs. On the back wall of my classroom, I have a picture of a shirtless young stud with his naked baby on his knees. The two are staring at one another, in awe. When boys ask why I have that picture displayed so prominently, I say, "You figure it out." We tell them too much.

But I would also hope that in girls' schools—and coed schools—young women would be empowered too; that intelligent-empathic older women would give them a "voice," show them they are as impoverished by not standing up to be counted as a male is impoverished by being afraid to feel any emotion but anger.

In studying thousands of women of all classes, the four women who wrote *Women's Ways of Knowing* isolated six different groups by the ways in which they deal with themselves and with the world, ordering them in stages of development:

1. Silence: passivity and conformity.

2. Received Knowledge: accepting what others say is true.

3. Subjective Knowledge: a gut hunch of what is true.

4. "Separate" Procedural Knowledge: a rational and scientific approach to truth, with the emotions held in strict control.

5. "Connected" Procedural Knowledge: that rational approach enriched by empathy with the subject.

6. Constructed Knowledge: a philosophy of humanity which integrates all the assets a woman possesses.

Silence: In contrast to Kohlberg's hierarchical stages of moral development, *Women's Ways* sees the shallowest moral stance for females is not quite fear but rather silence and passivity, as with Miss Celie at the outset of *The Color Purple*. She's almost literally voiceless, able to communicate her inner self only through letters to God. Blind obedience is essential in order to keep out of trouble; asking for clarification is too embarrassing; trying to know why is impossible. Like a child, such a defeated woman swings wildly between two polarities—despair or bliss, the latter being rare. To develop "inner speech"—to understand the self—anyone (male or female) needs *external* conversation and validation. Teachers can see the strong difference between students who are encouraged to speak out at home and those who have been "seen and not heard."

In schools—for males or females—there is little encouragement of dialogue. Whenever I tell a class I'm going to go up and down the rows and ask, for instance, what the word *success* means to each individual, the voices are barely audible and the words sublimely vague: "To . . . uh . . . achieve your goals." They've not been trained to formulate their own ideas, only to parrot back the ideas of others.

Received Knowledge: This is a stage in which the motivation to understand overcomes the fear of sanctions. At this stage someone at least seems to have confidence in women, makes them see that what they think about is important; what Shug Avery gives Miss Celie.

Think of the equally empowering moment in Henry James's *Washington Square,* when Catherine Sloper, the dowdy spinster, believes she's finally found a man who truly loves her. Her father says, "I can't have you squandering my money, my dear," and she replies, "You'll never know, will you?" He snarls, "You can be very cruel, can't you?" She answers, "I ought to be. I was taught by a master." Another moment to cheer.

But women at this impoverished level equate knowing with receiving, retaining, and returning—equating an authority's word with learning. With such women (and men), anything in print or on TV must be true, even when it contradicts other things they know are true. If there is conflict, go with the majority.

Many good women at this level strengthen their self-esteem by empowering *others,* like so many remarkable grade-school teachers and mothers. But a true sense of self can't come from outside but only from inner *self*-esteem. Such women define themselves by their *role* in the lives of others so that, when the husband dies and the children marry, there's no self.

The nobility of that misapprehension of "a woman's place" was not in any way curtailed by Sigmund Freud:

> The only thing that brings a mother undiluted satisfaction is her relation to a son: the mother can transfer to her son all the ambition which she has had to suppress in herself, and she can hope to get from him the satisfaction of all that has remained to her of her masculinity complex.[3]

As with his emphasis on the Oedipus complex in males, one wonders if what he saw had less to do with objective, culture-eluding facts than with what transpired in nineteenth-century Vienna.

Subjective Knowledge: At this third stage, a woman begins to sense an *inner* voice, a gut feeling of what is tolerable and intolerable. You see it in *The Color Purple* in Sofia, the role Oprah Winfrey played, a woman who stood up to men—even beating up policemen! She refused to be passive; she wasn't taught, but she had a gut realization she had inalienable rights. One woman the authors of *Women's Ways* interviewed said:

> Every person has her own unique body of knowledge that's been given to them through their life's experiences. And realizing that mine is as valid as the next person's, whether or not that person has gone through six or seven years of college, I feel that my knowledge is as important and real and valuable as theirs is.[4]

This subjective knowledge arises usually at a time of choice between a woman's own good and the good of others. Carol Gilligan studied numerous cases of women who had abortions and found it nearly unvarying: each woman mourned her lost baby for the full nine months, at which time she either took up her own selfhood and said, "No one is *ever* going to do that to me again," or slipped further and further into silent despair. At least to me, it makes eminent good sense to include the *self* as an equal claimant in any dilemma. That's when Miss Celie finally says, "Your dead body just the welcome mat I need."

Here, too, in the cusp between the mostly unlettered stage and the more educated women of the next stage, we find the amazing phenomenon and ferocious assertiveness of Roseanne Barr. She dropped out of school in ninth grade, yet can manipulate words and fine-tune a joke like an instinctive magician, even using quite a few words not beginning with *F.* As one of her writers, Lois Bromfield, explains: "She hit that nerve of the woman in the Midwest whom nobody spoke to. They'd had no one to relate to—not for a long time."[5] As Roseanne says to her husband, Dan, when their son's date treats him the way Roseanne treats everyone else:

> But if a girl is pushing a boy around, she's trying to
> elevate herself. Can't you see that? Boys bullying
> girls is a step backwards. But girls bullying boys—
> now, that's the future.[6]

"Separate" Procedural Knowledge: Women at this stage opt for the kind of knowing most males content themselves with—often because women now find themselves competing in areas where men have long been unfairly dominant. This method of accessing the truth is the epitome of the scientific method, where the observer scrupulously keeps herself *out* of the equation.

> Separate knowers try to subtract the personality of
> the perceiver from the perception, because they

see personality as slanting the perception or adding
"noise" that must be filtered out.[7]

According to Freud, women "give in to vanity" to compensate
for a penis. But the wish "to be a man" is perfectly natural:
to access her animus—which society (not biology) has kept
her from.

At this stage, a woman advances to learn how to "fight like
the guys" in debate, build impersonal structures of justice,
discuss not so much to share with others as to see who's got the
"wrong" ideas or is not "politically correct." Here, where very
intelligent women (and men) get stranded and move no
further, a woman has lost a great deal of her major asset: the
empathic right brain, which may not give her a debating edge
but surely makes her a more understanding human being.

Let me tell a story about myself that may shed light on what
these four women psychologists mean by "Separate" Procedural
Knowledge, but which may also sound pretty dismissive
coming from a male. After a lecture on women in Scripture by
a woman biblical scholar, I said I had given a talk myself to a
mixed group and said all that I said above about preferring a
female to a male confessor. After the talk, two women came up
and said my talk had been "so sexist."

I asked if they'd heard what I'd said. And they answered that
I had used the word *bitch* to mean complain. I asked, if I had
said "She *hounded* him out of the room" would that have been
antimale sexist? And they just walked away. The biblical scholar
was irate when I described that dilemma; so were many women
near me. One woman turned, nodding to the woman next to
her, and said, "I can call her *broad*. You *can't*." And I said, rather
helplessly, "I could if we were friends."

In my fallible judgment, those women were at what *Women's
Ways* calls the stage of "Separate" Procedural Knowledge—

separate precisely from their right-brain "feminine" assets. Scrupulously accurate but without empathy. I think at that moment my empathic "feminine" was more active than theirs. But that could be mere self-justification.

But I agree with Camille Paglia that a great deal of militant feminist rhetoric has "descended into dogma." Feminism, she claims, has closed itself against free thought and too often resorts to reductionist propaganda. "It's embarrassing to anyone who is a rigorously trained person."

"Connected" Procedural Knowledge: A woman at this stage has developed her so-called "masculine," left-brain potential ("separate" procedural knowing) but then becomes *re*connected with her major asset: empathy, not only with the subject but with her fellow searchers, no matter what their sex. At this stage, a woman—and a well-rounded man, like Atticus Finch in *To Kill a Mockingbird*—has not only developed intellectual acuity but also found procedures to access *other* people's ways of seeing things. As Atticus tells his tomboy daughter, Scout: "To get inside someone else's skin and walk around in it awhile."

What *Women's Ways* calls "Separate" Procedural Knowledge starts from doubts, sniffing rats. This fifth stage—"Connected" Procedural Knowledge—starts from *believing* in the other, suspending judgment till you've walked together awhile. At that fourth stage of "Separate" Knowledge, the careful woman researcher tries to *subtract* the self from the perception. At this fifth stage of "Connected" Knowledge, the woman realizes the perceiver *adds* to the perception, just as the little girl with the cornrowed hair adds to the forty-line dictionary definition of *love*.

Consider the difference between the "typical" father's and mother's response to the news their unmarried daughter is pregnant. The father might react in any number of instinctive

ways: curse and swear, perhaps even beat her; point at her and
say, "All right, this is what you're going to do, young lady"; put
his head in his hands and moan, "What did *I* do wrong?"; put
his arms around her and share her shame—the latter being the
most rare in a father, yet almost expectable in a good mother.

Constructed knowledge: This approach to questions tries to
integrate all the "voices" a woman has discovered along the way.
Passivity has evolved into forbearance, patience with both the
question and the fellow questioners. The inner voice of the
second stage and the received knowledge of the third are
critiqued now by the sharply honed left brain. But now the
woman realizes—with perfect peace—that the mental
constructions we use to understand the world and ourselves are
always simpler than the complex realities themselves. Unlike
dogmatic institutions, she is content with a high degree of
probability rather than hankering after certitude. She realizes
empathy and compassion not only don't detract from understanding but are essential to a well-rounded view of life and a
well-rounded self. Passion can enliven even the most abstract
thinking, in contrast to most other self-styled learners who
merely pursue a cold knowledge to which they are otherwise
completely indifferent.

In Kohlberg's "Heinz Dilemma," to which I alluded in
passing before, a farmer named Heinz is conflicted over stealing
a drug for his dying wife which a druggist refuses to sell at
anything less than an exorbitant price. The "masculine" response
(in both males and females) would argue that the right to live
takes objective precedence over the right to property, based on
a strict hierarchy of relative values. But the "feminine" mind
asks about the complexities of the situation and offers other
alternatives to stealing: Why is the druggist so unyielding? Can
the mayor or priest persuade him? In the end, most of Carol

Gilligan's female subjects saw it not as an immoral act of Heinz in stealing the drug but of the druggist for withholding it.

You find this kind of exhilarating female mind in such writers as H. F. M. Prescott, Alice Walker, and Toni Morrison, not to mention George Eliot, Sigrid Unset, and Willa Cather.

A woman with a healthy soul-life cannot—for her good or for the common good—be merely the passive doormat of the first stage. Nor can she content herself with the unquestioning acceptance of the second stage. What she needs is not only to feel but to *listen* to that intuitive gut voice of the third step: "I am not *just* a woman. I've got a right to be heard. *And* listened to."

Women who reach the fourth stage have that justified sense of empowerment, but it is painful for those of us who fully embrace that empowerment when they get stranded there, haggling over pronouns when there's so much to be done, unable to open up to the fifth stage and take possession again of their empathy with fallible fellow searchers.

In trying to understand ourselves and the world, the Western mind and the Eastern mind stand as polar opposites: the Western mind, at its extreme, sees the physical world as real and the human soul as an illusion (or at best an intrusive distraction); the Eastern mind, at its extreme, sees the world as an illusion and the soul as the only true reality.

Which is it? Both. In evolving a soul, we withdraw from the world, become detached in order to ponder. But for a fulfilled life, we have to return to attachment again, to bring that enlivened soul back into the web of human relationships. And so we balance, with the serenity of tightrope walkers, back and forth between involvement and withdrawal, each nourishing the other, until after a while there are no longer any clear-and-distinct divisions between the sacred and the secular, between the spiritual and the physical. All are part of the whole.

In Quest of a Voice

In her book *The Dance of the Spirit: The Seven Steps of Women's Spirituality,*[8] Maria Harris suggests five steps to a woman's full possession of her soul: awakening to her self, discovering who that self really is, creating a life that bodies forth that self, consciously dwelling within that self, and nurturing it to further depth and breadth.

Awakening: Meister Eckhart wrote: "This is spirituality: just waking up!" A woman needs simply to call a halt; draw back from the dusting and dishes, from the clients and patients and kids, and ask, "Hey! What am I *doing?*" All the things most women do for others are wonderful, beautiful gifts. But as Miss Celie discovered, the woman can't leave her *self* out of the assessment of her goodness and purposefulness.

Homilists too often equate "repentance" with lists of peccadilloes to dump off at confession, as if to save our souls from some future hell, rather than saving them from withering here and now. *Repent* means rock-bottom conversion, *convertere,* stop and turn around in completely the opposite direction.

Listen to Jesse Jackson: "I am *some*-body!" And to the aging transvestite in *Le Cage au Folles:* "I am what I am, and what I am needs no excuses!" Or to Helen Reddy, "I am woman, hear me roar!" So many women (and men) believe pride is a sin; no, not pride: arrogance, believing I can get along without anybody. Without a sense of pride and self-reliance, a woman becomes a silent slave like Miss Celie.

When Barbara Walters asked Bette Midler where she thought she ranked on the typical "10" scale, she said, "Me? I'm a *40!*" A self-possessed woman isn't going to be enslaved to anorexia or bulimia, the dyes and goos and wrinkle-tucks, the condescending sneers of the size-six models in *Vogue.*

> A first, and perhaps surprising, time to practice this
> receptivity, this hospitality toward ourselves, is
> whenever we get our period. . . . Bleeding is
> blessing. It is not, as too many of us were told *and
> found ourselves believing*, a curse.[9]

Because of their menstrual cycle, women *know* they're women.
They don't have to *prove* it. But for a boy to become a man,
other men must say he's a man; he does indeed have to "prove"
his manhood, often by desperately pressing, but ultimately
foolish, means: duking it out, risking concussion even with a
helmet, smashing a skater into the boards to the screaming
approval of the crowd, swimming the Hellespont.

When a woman finds her pride, she finds a voice: "Your
dead body's just the welcome mat I need." From this moment
on, I take no crap—from my husband, from my kids, from the
pastor, from the checkout girl, and—by God—not from myself.

Discovering: The second step is discovering who that unique
woman is. Granted that any woman (or any man) has been
wounded by others, from the very beginning. Now's the time
to take each one of those wounds and turn it into a weapon—
not a vindictive lash to get back at loveless parents, or the eons
of patriarchal exploitation, or the slings and arrows of outrageous fortune. The woman who has taken possession of herself
will assess her unique assets and liabilities and turn them to
some better use than vengeance or sniffing out political incor-
rectness. There are too many others out there suffering.

Creating: The third step is precisely that: turning the self
outward, questioning, resisting unquestionable dogma (from
whatever source), empowering others—women, men,
children—to shuck off the rat-race mentality, too, and begin to
change the world, if only a little.

Inhabiting: The fourth step—though it is essential from the very beginning of the process—is for a woman to inhabit her self in serenity, to be "at home" within herself. Every woman needs at least a half-hour a day to "be fallow." Whenever I hear mothers' confessions, it's almost axiomatic they confess losing their tempers with the kids. Their penance is: Every day, just before they come home from school, make a cup of tea, kick off your shoes, and be at peace, "at home" within your self. No mother has ever refused that penance. A woman at home within herself can never be "dispossessed" or "deserted."

Nurturing: "Oh, I have no time to read. I can't go to those women's groups; there's just too much to do when I come home from work." Nope. There are very few women whose days and minds are so cluttered they haven't time for a shower. It takes no act of will simply because the need is unquestioned. So ought to be the needs of a woman's soul. It's what a woman serves with, what animates her loving hands and voice.

Every human being—woman or man—goes around only once. Surely it's more important for a woman to find a self, a confident voice, than to fabricate a face, a body, an image.

How do you rate yourself as a woman on the "10" scale? "Me? I'm a *40!*"

Chapter Eleven

⸎

THE GRAIL QUEST: MALE SPIRITUALITY

Yet all experience is an arch wherethrough
Gleams that untraveled world whose margin fades
Forever and forever as I move.
How dull it is to pause, to make an end,
To rust unburnished, not to shine in use!
As though to breathe were life!

Lord Alfred Tennyson— *"Ulysses"*[1]

In John Updike's *Rabbit Run*, the hero simply gets fed up with his humdrum life and just takes off in his car. After a while, he stops for gas and asks if they have maps. When the man asks where he wants to go, Rabbit can't answer. Finally, the old man says, "The only way to get somewhere, you know, is to figure out where you're going before you go there."

The Hero as a Map

I write *SUCCESS* on the board and ask each student what that means to him. The response is invariant. Near whispers, hoping not to be heard. Only one or two dare say, "Money!"—as if money weren't axiomatic in the others' minds too. Except for money, the content of *success* is sublimely vague: "To, uh, achieve your goals. . . . To, uh, have a good life." Which means? Never once in three-thousand-plus replies has one said, "To be a good father and husband"—which pretty much all of them *will* be.

You can't achieve a vague goal. You can't buy a map till you know where you want to go. College seniors I talk to evenings in the dorm are just as vague, even in March.

True enough, when I probe into "success," students find they do have an unfocused, "generic" idea of what they want— not to be, but to have—"when they grow up," and it's usually "the usual": decent (unspecified) job, suburban home, loving (and desolatingly sexy) wife, 1.5 kids, and maybe a pool in the yard. Is that all there is? All you want: to survive seventy years and Phfft!? Or do you want to make a difference? Their faces sag like pizza dough.

No matter the career, a boy certainly is invited to become an adult male. *Invited,* not commanded, not a change that just falls into place if you wait long enough. Becoming a *grown-up* male happens automatically; becoming an *adult* male takes effort, and effort distresses old Narcissism and Inertia. We all know men grown-up but hardly either adult or manly: whiners, grudge-bearers, braggarts, tyrants, terminal adolescents. Men with neither goals nor maps, victims of whatever comes next.

Ancient societies believed a boy became a man only through older men, through ritual, effort, often pain. Only women could civilize a boy, but only men could make him an adult male. Until the Industrial Revolution, boys had fathers working at home, taking as much part in their maturing as mothers. Now, however, most fathers work some distance away, and boys must find adult selves from a person of the opposite sex. Today, many boys don't even have that, since their mothers also work away from home, and of boys born in 1987 about half will grow up in a single-parent home or with a male figure who is not their natural father.

Coping with male life is now left almost entirely to the boy himself, without the help more primitive societies gave boys to accept their adult maleness and new position in society: rituals wherein the males literally scared boys into adulthood. This lack causes a silent malaise Robert Bly calls a "father wound," since most fathers are no longer available to help boys with problems their mothers can't fathom. It is a hunger painfully depicted in Biff and Happy, the soul-dead sons of Willy Loman, who was always on the road, and in Willy himself in hallucinatory conversations with his dead father-figure brother. Not only are sons blighted by "father distance," but fathers are as well.

Women raising sons without a father know the problems when the boy reaches puberty. As one mother put it, her son needed "more hardness" than she could give. If she became tougher, the boy would lose precisely what he needed from a mother.

What's more, it's now very "uncool" to have heroes who might be surrogate father-models—because of the skepticism which set in since the assassinations, Vietnam, Watergate, the hostages, *The National Enquirer*. Sooner or later heroes let you down: use steroids, cheat on their wives, contract AIDS. Many of their own fathers have betrayed boys' trust and left the family behind to "find myself," a challenge most psychologists believe should have been faced before the man left high school—or at least college.

More and more when I ask students who their heroes are, nearly half say, "I don't have any." Others offer some pretty nutty combinations, like Mother Teresa *and* Donald Trump, and they honestly believe they can model their lives on both. The rest are usually rock stars and athletes, whom they admit they admire not for having done anything of substance but for having the smarts to parlay modest talents into megabucks and live enviably in the fast lane. *The World Almanac's* annual poll of kids in malls says the hero of the year is Tom Cruise; the year before, Eddie Murphy—slick, uncommitted, flashy, sexy, but no genuine substance.

Movies like *Die Hard* and *The Terminator* also give a false, shallow idea of an adult male. A *real* man loves football; beats hell out of anyone who gets in his way; never weeps; "scores" as often as possible; keeps his guard up and his feelings hidden; suppresses compassion, fear, and especially guilt. Magazines like *Playboy* offer enough peekaboo titillation to feed adolescent masturbatory fantasies for a lifetime. Even the skinzine ads offer the same message: beer, booze, sportswear and equipment, stereos, sports cars, and cigarettes—all the things that make a real man. A real father and husband.

We're talking about the commonplace acceptance of role models little better than perfumed apes. As Margaret Mead wrote:

> Among our structurally closest analogues—the apes—the male does not feed the female. Heavy with young, making her way laboriously along, she fends for herself. He may fight to protect her or to possess her, but he does not feed her.[2]

Other than anger, there are few feelings a modern male is "allowed," and many male souls settle for The Great Numbness, unable to feel joy, meaning, grief—*anything*. Bland, boring, homogenized. There is no "rush" to being a male today, no sense of greatness; so, many settle for beer and football, *machismo* and horseplay, drugs and casual sex: junk food for the soul.

The wounded male soul is manifest in statistics showing men can expect eight fewer years of life than women, commit suicide three times as often, are more likely victims of alcohol and drugs. Men are the most frequent perpetrators—and victims—of assault and murder and outnumber women in prisons nine to one.

The Detroit police chief remarked that the young men he arrests not only don't have any responsible older man in the house, but they have never met one. Yet each is capable of the *act* of fathering a child, but not of being a father.

For thousands of years young men had heroes like Achilles, Arthur, the Deerslayer, Lindbergh, Tom Dooley, to show them what makes a real man different from a grown-up boy: self-possession, pluck, idealism, responsibility, curiosity, the wits to rise out of sticky situations, the courage to challenge and change, the confidence to make peace, the good grace to laugh at themselves. They served as a map to becoming what a wife and children could look for in a husband and father.

The women's movement made welcome inroads on the Caveman-Viking-Rambo false image. They have been civilizing boys and men since Aristophanes wrote *Lysistrata,* and they've begun to succeed. Many husbands now do chores their own fathers would never have dreamt of doing: cleaning, cooking, diapering. Men have begun unashamedly to contact the "feminine" side of themselves. But though a father needs to learn a great deal about fathering from the mother, the father is *not* the mother.

The men's movement asks us to consider that, granting a woman's equality, a man is not a woman and a woman is not a man, just as a stallion is not a mare. Each of us is an *embodied* psyche. Unlike animals, we can at least attempt to understand our psychosexual differences and use them to enrich our lives.

Nor is any embodied spirit "neuter." A bull is not a cow, but neither is it an ox. Once the aggressive male enriches himself in a healthy relationship with his own anima, he must go back and reestablish relationship with his maleness, what Bly calls his "Wildman." If not, he becomes not just civilized but domesticated, which is quite different.

Perhaps boys are more aggressive by nature, but they surely are by nurture. Most boys have what Walter Ong calls "adversativeness," the need to haggle over rules, duke it out, debate ideas more disputatiously than most girls find comfortable. Again, perhaps as a result of distancing themselves from mothers, most boys treasure personal freedom, resist being told what to do, being bridled and tame. If there is anything true of a fully actualized male, it is a resistance to homogenization.

Ironically, too, the male need to break free, struggle, and take risks also involves vulnerability. Both warlike Achilles and the statue of Ozymandias had fragile ankles. The male who doesn't bow to that fact is a fool. Admitting weakness is not a weakness but a strength; you have to be confident to be humble. The male who does make peace with his own weakness can become a wounded healer, like recovering alcoholics and addicts who reach out to those now weaker than themselves and physicians who treat patients not as specimens but as fellow sufferers.

Also, since the beginning, males developed the need to protect, to be responsible, to be accountable. Women have those same needs to be fully human, but a male "feels" them in a different, more likely proprietorial way—surely by nurture.

Patriarch has become a neuralgic term today, but males can't think of themselves as solely "mothering." There is the need not merely to console but to set things right—which males share with females, but toward which males by nurture feel a compulsion.

What males need to regain is their sense of pilgrimage, of the bloodless crusade: the Grail Quest.

Any male is free to be anything his talent and luck allow him—*but* only once he commits himself, freely, to a goal. Not to choose to be *some*body is automatically to choose to be nobody.

Richard Wilbur has a poem that captures it:

> I read how Quixote in his random ride
> Came to a crossing once, and lest he lose
> The purity of chance, would not decide
> Whither to fare, but wished his horse to choose,
> For glory lay wherever he might turn.
> His head was light with pride, his horse's shoes
> Were heavy, and he headed for the barn.[3]

The Archetypes

Jung discovered male archetypes in the folk stories of all cultures—stripped-down models of the major factors that differentiate a hero from a nobody, a knight from a pawn.

Most societies have expected nine qualities from males: Pilgrim (open to challenge), Patriarch (responsible for others), Warrior (courageously confident), Magician (inventive), Wildman (exuberant), Healer (challenging "sickness"), Prophet (devoted to justice), Mediator (impartial), and Trickster (keeping Lear from taking himself too seriously).

But Jung says each archetype virtue, unchecked by its opposite, runs wild to "the shadow," which takes over when the major assets of the type aren't *balanced* by their opposites. Without purposeful resolve, the Pilgrim is an aimless wanderer;

without father-love, the Patriarch is a tyrant; without a code of honor, the Warrior is a self-serving bully; without humility, the Magician is a manipulator; without a sense of service, the Wildman is a barbarian; without emotional control, the Healer becomes a burnout; without tenacity, the Prophet becomes a whiner; without a sense of self, the Mediator becomes a recluse oblivious of conflict; without reflection, the Trickster becomes a mere fool.[4]

All archetypes—and their shadows—sleep within every male soul, but they won't waken on their own, as puberty did, nor can anyone force a male to swallow them piece by piece, like trigonometry. The choice—and effort—are one's own. Only two options: to be a somebody; to be a nobody. And not to decide is to decide.

Glory? Or the barn?

The Pilgrim: The difference between a pilgrim and a rootless wanderer is that the pilgrim has a goal and a hope, which is quite different from optimism. Optimism can't see the cost with cautious and critical eyes; hope can. The courage of the hopeful man is coward's courage: "I *can't!* . . . But I'll try."

The Pilgrim opens to challenge and change, even to switching careers, willing to risk giving up something good, rewarding, and secure to try for something better, more fulfilling, even though less secure. He is willing to hazard "the road less traveled."

Giving examples of each archetype to clarify its goal takes juggling, since—as well-rounded souls—some could fit as well with another or more. Some with a true sense of Pilgrim are literal explorers: Admiral Byrd, Lewis and Clark, Cousteau, Darwin, Heyerdahl—who are ready like the Enterprise "boldly to go where no man has gone before." But there are other metaphorical explorers, many of them interchangeable with the

Magician: Da Vinci and Galileo; Dante, Kipling, Conrad; Bernstein and Fosse.

Without access to his inner Pilgrim—the *Eros* urge to reach out, risk, learn more, change—a man becomes atrophied inside his defenses. In older men, you see it in burnout (often in men who have never been on fire!), hopelessly dragging on with the job, treading water. In younger men, putting the mind in neutral, doing the minimum, beating the system, getting a diploma without the education the diploma fraudulently testifies to. *Thanatos.* And even they don't realize they're brain-dead and soul-starved.

One question to test a man's Pilgrim is to ask older men: "Do you still find *zest* in your wife, family, job? If not, what would put it back?" Maybe he dreamt of playing ball. Why not coach Little League? Maybe he wanted to act; "foolish." Why not community theater?

Ask younger men "What kind of father do you want your kids to have?" That man starts now. You can't expect to be instantly "ready" the day fatherhood strikes. "What kind of job do you *want*—not something to bring in bucks but something that keeps challenging your spirit?" If you wait till senior year college, you'll surely end up, not with the job you want, but with whatever job you can get, because Welfare will be over.

The Patriarch: Since the women's movement, *patriarch* has gotten a great deal of justified criticism. Government, schools, business, education, and churches have been excessively patriarchal: men giving the orders and women (and other men) submitting, even women smarter than the drill sergeants. Like so many words knowledgeable women find offensive, *patriarch* must be stripped of negative, tyrannical elements offensive to women (and men, who are also its victims) *without* also stripping away its positive elements, which are in fact essential to healthy *males.*

To limit *patriarch* to petty despotism uses only half the word and half the reality. The latter half, *arch,* means "chief": archbishop, archangel, monarch. But the other half, *patri-,* means "father": paternal, patrimony, patriot. The tyrant leads without love. A true Patriarch is a loving man.

A good Patriarch shepherds without corralling, is willing to take a risk—and the heat if he is wrong, refuses to pass the buck to someone else or some agency. Such men go into politics, not primarily to aggrandize themselves (though many don't mind it as a by-product), but to help the helpless, to be agents of change, to care for the abused: De Valera, La Guardia, FDR and Churchill, Truman, Walesa, Tutu, Mandela.

Such men are doctors like Tom Dooley, who could be irascible and demanding, but gave up a lucrative practice to work for the helpless natives of Southeast Asia. Teachers and coaches who chose to give up better-paying jobs in business or professional sports or universities to help young people negotiate the trials of adolescence—usually with little thanks, except seeing at least some become good people. You surely know a few.

A man of such selfless integrity at least does not seem to be the model most leaders today either pursue or present. At best, a lawmaker seems loyal principally to the vested interests of his own constituents, not only because they elected him but because they might again. With such heavy dependence on media to make a candidate known, and thus dependence on big-bucks contributors (with their own vested interests), it's difficult to be sure an official's primary interest is even in his constituents.

The tyrannical shadow side of the Patriarch results from assertiveness unchecked by genuine father-love. We've all known "patriarchal" men—cold, demanding, crushing opposing views, rigidly set against challenge or change: Hitler, the Ayatollah, Hussein, all the way down to petty martinets who strangle us with red tape, puritanism, and "We've always done it this way."

Like the other archetypes, the inner Patriarch in a man is a potential waiting for a challenge, and the question to determine if an inner Patriarch is ready for the lightning is "In your most honest mind, do you genuinely want to lead, or do you prefer the security of following?" If you are in charge, will you care more for profit-and-loss ledgers or for the people who work for you and whom you serve? Will you give bonuses, know who's having a baby and send flowers, know who's bereaved and be at the funeral? Will you be a man whose children believe he is usually right, because he's thought things out for himself?

The Warrior: The Warrior is bred into a male's soul from the days we actually were warriors and hunters. Its urge is to protect and combat: disease, corruption, ignorance, crime. The inner Warrior defends a man's psychic boundaries, gives a sense of self-esteem he simply will *not* allow violated. Often, as with Gandhi and King, the Warrior's weapon is not sword or fists but silence, refusing to turn his rage into a weapon and put it into his oppressor's hand. But there is a difference between silent endurance in a no-win situation and sheepish acquiescence from fear of the cost: embarrassment, rejection, jeers.

Some models of the developed Warrior in the soul actually were or are military men: Colin Powell, Omar Bradley, Jimmy Doolittle, Lawrence of Arabia, Audie Murphy, but there are also others who love to mix it up for a good cause: Lee Iacocca, Tom Dewey, Julian Bond, Lyndon Johnson, William Bennett.

The shadow of the Warrior is a man untouched by his own anima: Hell's Angels, pimps, pushers. We see them also in the corridors of power: military-industrial opportunists, battling emirs of the Middle East, bullyboys on both sides in Northern

Ireland. What differentiates the true Warrior from its shadow is what the man fights for and against. The shadow of the Warrior fights for himself—very often claiming to do it for others. The true Warrior fights for the oppressed. When the Warrior in a man is dead, his usual response is "Oh, what good would it do?"

What saves the true Warrior from the shadow is a *code*. In T. H. White's *The Once and Future* King, Lancelot "tried to have a Word. . . . His Word was valuable to him not only because he was good, but also because he was bad." Devotees of martial arts bow to their own inner weaknesses and thus train not only body but soul, which must control what it allows that well-trained body to do: *never* to act blindly or out of anger or need for revenge; *always* to take full responsibility for whatever they have done.

To find how an inner Warrior fares, ask a man's reaction to an insulting clerk, a sarcastic teacher, intimidating peers. If he stood in a checkout line and saw a mother battering her child, would he speak? If a boy saw sophomores bullying a freshman, would he step in, or walk away staring at the locker numbers?

The Magician: The Magician is a man in full control of his wits, not merely the analytical power of his left brain but also the intuitive power of his right brain. The Magician follows his hunches, his gut intuition. "Maybe," the awakened Magician says, "if we fool around with this bread mold, we can come up with some medicine." And penicillin is born. "What could we finagle out of dumb silicon chips?" The world is changed. The archetypal Magician doesn't work with illusion, but with ideas and machines, words and imagination. Shakespeare was surely a Magician.

There are others with a finely developed Magician: Galileo, Franklin, Howe, Whitney, Pasteur, Edison, Marconi, Heisenberg, Bohr, Einstein, Eastman, Teller, Goddard, Arthur C.

Clarke, and the great Azimov—who all saw possibility in what others saw as "stuff." But scientists are not the only Magicians who stretch the limits of the possible: cummings, Dali, Pollock; Fellini, Hitchcock, Welles, Kubrick; Porter, Hal Prince, and Sondheim; Sendak and Seuss; Bill Robinson and Fred Astaire; Walt Disney alone. Lot of right-brain "feminine" going on in that crowd!

There is a shadow side of a man's Magician. Unchecked by humility—the realization one serves rather than dominates—the Magician begins to believe he is the *source* of power, rather than its servant. You see it in Hitler who, like King, could bring people to their feet with the magic of words and in televangelists who start out, most times, sincerely preaching the word of God, but their success—especially their financial success—goes to their heads, and they disgrace themselves, preaching generosity, chastity, and honesty but practicing something quite different.

How to check a man's Magician? To distrust what is always said, what seems, what "everybody knows." As stunted Warriors walk away from confrontation, stunted Magicians settle for tried and true. Beware books; they will upset your equilibrium. If you've read this far, your Magician has a good chance.

The Wildman: The archetype of the Wildman is not Charles Manson on a rampage, but a man of nature: hunter, trapper, explorer, scout, with a feel for winds and rain, an easiness with open spaces. He is the itchy nomad sleeping in the souls of men since the days we actually were roaming from camp to camp.

Civilization has been a process of "feminizing" the wildness out of cavemen, Vikings, barbarians thundering into Europe and China in the Dark Ages. Civilization gave savages a code, law, discipline. In the Middle Ages, chivalry—all we associate with the Round Table—taught men to harness raw power in the service of justice, honor, and protection of the exploited, especially women and children. In our own time, the women's movement succeeded in convincing males that gentleness, empathy, and inclusiveness are as much qualities of a fulfilled male as of a fulfilled female.

But again, a man is not a woman. He loses something important in his soul when he eliminates his Wildman entirely. He becomes . . . neuter. Chesterton says, when the lion lies down with the lamb, we assume the lion becomes lamblike. That, he says, is rank imperialism on the part of the lamb, the lamb devouring the lion instead of vice versa. Rather, the lion must lie down with the lamb and retain all his leonine ferocity. It is not that a male must *become* the Wildman, but he must always remain *in touch* with his Wildman, or else he becomes nothing but a pussycat.

It is good that a man be disciplined, ordered, predictable. But something within every man—something not entirely suspect—wants to shuck off the shirts and ties, to bust free into the earthy, the carefree, the sloppy, to tell 'em all to go t' hell. It's the Crocodile Dundee in us. Huck Finn. Odysseus.

We are too "civilized" to allow too many Wildmen. There was a time they were commonplace, the roots of legend: Kit Carson, Davy Crockett, Gauguin. Rabelais was also surely one to rip off the civilized corset. But there are still men of Wildman souls: Robin Williams is one, Mel Brooks, the Marx Brothers, Buck Jones, Picasso, Jonathan Winters, Steve Martin. They make us suspect we might be missing something about being human, and male.

But our society, businesses, and churches don't want that surge of power loose. Business wants deodorized men in gray flannel uniforms, noosed in neckties, presentable, predictable. This is a serious enterprise, and we don't want anything wild-eyed or loony. In church, men should be tame as children, while only a few men (in dresses) lead them through their paces. No place for the exuberant, the enthusiastic, the carefree. Rock concerts draw so many because they celebrate the Wildman, yearning to break free of the weeklong spiritual mummy bindings.

The Wildman has a healthy sense of self that—despite full awareness of shortcomings and weaknesses—refuses to be manipulated, degraded, or owned. Where does a man find that sense? It's highly unlikely he will find it in the uptight conformity of the office or parish church or the lockstep day-to-day workings of a school. Most find it in the wilderness, away from the distractions and intrusions of business, school, TV, papers, glaring lights, blaring stereos. Only out in the "desert," alone, a man finds his soul, understands both his vulnerability and his stamina. There he exchanges what he thought was real for the Really Real. The wilderness is a place of empowerment.

Most men—young or old—are too busy, too "tied up," to take time in retreat from the world. So they slog on, one day at a time, making a living, without any sense of what living is for.

The test of the true Wildman—as with all other archetypes—is the purpose toward which his fierce power is directed: his own glorification or the service of others. Why doesn't he—as so many modern men do—just "go along"? Simply because he can't. He is driven, not by the need to succeed, but by the need to help.

The Healer: To our sophisticated world, the idea of some Priest-Magician seems embarrassingly primitive, the belief all sickness is rooted in the spirit. But for years doctors have accepted psychosomatic illnesses, genuine physical distress with no discernible physical cause: rashes, ulcers, migraines. These diseases are not caused by "demons" but by some kink in the soul, which has to be unearthed and unraveled. Now more and more doctors also suspect a healthy spirit—a positive, confident, faith-strengthened soul—can also help heal the body.

There is a difference between "masculine" healing and "feminine" healing (in both males and females). "Feminine" healing is nursing, easing distress, soothing. "Masculine" healing is instead aggressive, combating the disease itself. It often increases pain: cutting the flesh, drilling the tooth, forcing a neurotic to face the abrasive truth. But without it, the victim goes on suffering. The most fortunate patients have doctors and nurses (of no matter what sex) with a healthy combination of both: the knowledge and determination to uproot the causes of the illness but also the sensitivity to regard the patients as not merely biological problems but as fellow human beings in misery.

The best Healer has gone through his own harrowing: the wounded healer whose knowledge—and acceptance—of his own weakness have *empowered* him, as the Wildman's sojourn in the wilderness empowers him with a sense both of his vulnerability and his resourcefulness.

There are obvious Healer-heroes who are literally physicians: Jonas Salk, Louis Braille, Albert Schweitzer, Erik Erikson, Alexander Fleming, Carl Jung, Joseph Lister, the Mayo brothers, William Menninger. But others are less obvious: Frank Capra, John Ford, and most Magicians and Tricksters. The Three Stooges make us heal, at least for a while, by making us forget.

The shadow side to the Healer uses spiritual power to fleece rather than to help: voodoo practitioners, faith healers, tarot readers, televangelists who accept payment for their services.

How can one tell if a man's Healer-soul is alive? It is easy to see when it is not: self-containment, condescension, aloofness from the sordid and involving. The alive Healer can't rest until he has tried. It all comes down to trying. But when the pain is one of "the things that can't be changed," the healthy Healer is willing to submit in serenity.

The Prophet: The Prophet is the sleeping idealist in a man. To all the other archetypes, he adds the element of fearless confrontation: indicting, exhorting, challenging others to stop kidding themselves and be what they were born to be.

The common use of the word *prophet* confines it to one who predicts the future, and that is part of his purpose. But the Greek root of the word is *pro-phemi,* "one who speaks in someone else's place," in this case, for the Truth. He sees the iceberg ahead and suggests we stop dancing. You can buy on credit, play on the rim, dare the odds, but not forever. The Prophet has a passion to keep us from hurting ourselves by our own choice.

No getting away from it: Prophets are hemorrhoids, not only to the people they exhort but often even to people who care for them: "A martyr is someone who lives with a saint." Probably none of the archetypes is more susceptible to its shadow than the Prophet: the frustrated idealist who devolves into the constant crank, the crotchety griper, the yak-yak-yakking voice.

The real Prophet is a man of tough-love, with no illusions, especially not about himself or his chances of changing the world radically. But he has to try, simply because he couldn't live with himself otherwise. We all have pet peeves about things that just shouldn't be that way. But we grit our teeth and anesthetize ourselves to them; grin and bear it. Not the Prophet.

Charles Dickens was a Prophet: Mark Twain, George Orwell, Ed Morrow, Ralph Nader; C. S. Lewis and Paddy Chayevsky; Jesse Jackson and Pete Seeger—all men unwilling to say, "I'm mad as hell, and I'm not going to take it anymore," and leave it at that.

How to judge if a man's inner Prophet is functioning? How does he react to people who cut into line, bosses who treat the help with indiscriminate disdain, all the petty narcissisms we saw before? If a man knuckles under to trivial insults, one ought not to expect him to stand up to major humiliations.

The Mediator: The Mediator is usually an easygoing man. He may have access to his Wildman, but he has him well in check—not suppressed, but on a leash. He doesn't get overly enthusiastic—or too upset—about things. At its best, the Mediator in a man is able to see all sides honestly, without predispositions or personal bias. For that reason, partisans and propagandists hold him in disdain for being wishy-washy. But a man with a developed Mediator is the only one to act the Solomon when two hell-bent sides clash. His task is to make the unyielding yield to the truth that we have to live together and *that* requires compromise.

The Mediator power in a male is a somewhat "feminine" quality not much prized in our society. Therefore, our Solomons are few. "Go in there an' by-God *nuke* 'em! Burn the abortion clinics! (Or shoot the ones who try!) Impeach the bastard!" To the unthinking, thoughtfulness means indecision and gutlessness.

One of the most notable Mediators in our time was Judge John Sirica, who refused to bow to the administration and ordered the Watergate tapes released. Dag Hammarskjöld, Ralph Bunche, Dean Acheson, Thurgood Marshall, Kissinger, Carter—all men whose quiet integrity is unbudgeable in the face of bullying. Kermit the Frog is a helpful (if harried) Mediator.

The shadow of the Mediator arises when making peace— his strongest asset—becomes an obsession, and the weakened Mediator wants peace at any price. Neville Chamberlain comes to mind. He becomes an ostrich, unwilling to acknowledge, much less cope with, unpleasant truths which really ought not to be escapable.

A man's Mediator is in good shape if he is clearheaded enough in the thick of things to say, "Hey, *wait* a minute!" Not so caught up in the confined present moment and its anger that he is unable to see this event in perspective. A man whose Mediator is healthy doesn't ground a child for a month for a missed dentist's appointment. Like Arthur, he can go on loving both Guinevere and Lancelot, even after he knows the truth.

The Trickster: The Trickster has been an archetype from Homer's mischievous Hermes to Shakespeare's wise fools. In the Uncle Remus stories, Br'er Rabbit outfoxes Br'er Fox—and quite often himself. Hobbes lies in wait for Calvin; the Roadrunner beep-beeps by Wile E. Coyote; Hawkeye and B. J. conspire against everyone in the 4077 and often get blown up by their own bombs.

To avoid the iron pomposity of Puritanism, we need Tricksters to keep us laughing at ourselves and make peace with the shadows in our souls. Even (perhaps especially) church folk need the sly distorting mirrors of Fr. Guido Sarducci and the Church Lady. The healthy Trickster who can avoid being merely an excruciating practical joker is a good friend who shakes us up when we wallow in self-pity. Without him, we convince ourselves that our problems really are earth-shattering (because we are the focus of reality). When we swell up with self-importance, we're fortunate if a gentle Trickster sidles up and pops our presumptions.

Chaucer and Jonathan Swift were geniuses at it. Many men have an extraordinary ability to defuse our own petards: Walt Kelly ("We have met the enemy and they are us!"), Gary Trudeau, Gary Larsen; James Thurber and Kurt Vonnegut; Victor Borge, Danny Kaye, Peter Sellers. As soon as Margaret Dumont comes on the screen, you know there's a cream pie somewhere.

The only question to ask of your Trickster: Do you quite often have the good grace to laugh—at yourself?

Hunger for Fulfillment

...edral was the sacred center of a medieval town, now banks and commercial buildings focus our cities. "The Dow," Friederich Franck writes, "has replaced the Tao." But corporations, universities, and government are all suffering burnout. "Stress cannot be dealt with by psychological tricks," Sam Keen says, "because for the most part it is a philosophical rather than a physiological problem, a matter of the wrong worldview." Not sick minds, sick spirits. He says the same of dispirited sex. "We can lose ourselves in loving sexuality only to the degree that we have found the self elsewhere. It takes a very secure person to surrender to another in love."

The soulless marketplace—"the jungle"—is infectious. It is wrenching for a man to keep his guard up all day, then switch gears into the loving father, the sensitive husband, the compassionate friend. If we could convince men of the absolute need of at least a half-hour a week to ponder, we might give men not only a sense of personal meaning and hope but vigor again, not only souls but enspirited souls.

Perhaps men don't realize that what Thoreau called "quiet desperation" arises from a starved spirit, that they truly *need* an active connection to their own souls. That "soullessness" is evident not only in the grinding routine of many adult males but in a great many becoming-adult males as well: the blahs, the spiritlessness of senioritis, aversion to commitment or any incursions on freedom, often trying to prove they even have a self and are "here" through graffiti and boom boxes blasting out territorial claims, and at worst "wilding" sprees and random shootings of strangers. There's a hunger there all right.

Chapter Twelve

LOVING

Of all the worn, smudged, dog-eared words in our vocabulary, "love" is surely the grubbiest, smelliest, slimiest. Bawled from a million pulpits, lasciviously crooned through hundreds of millions of loudspeakers, it has become an outrage to good taste and decent feeling, an obscenity which one hesitates to pronounce. And yet it has to be pronounced, for, after all, love is the last word.

Aldous Huxley—*Tomorrow and Tomorrow and Tomorrow*[1]

Probably no word in any language is as misused and bandied about as *love*. It's trivialized even more than *value*. Every day you hear it misapplied: "I'd *love* a beer right now. . . . I just *love* what you've done to this room. . . . I'd *love* to poke that punk right in the puss!" The same word you use for your attitude toward your mother, spouse, or best friend—used for a mug of suds, a collection of furniture, and hatred.

In TV movies when two people are boiling over with hormones, they gasp, "Let's make love." To give the Rolling Stones their due, they didn't say, "I want to make love"; they said, "I want *it!*" The precise word to differentiate two copulating animals and two loving human beings.

At the inmost core of the web of human relationships is the relationship with one's self, the innermost "at home." Ordinarily, we join that self to a spouse, perhaps the firmest bond in the web. Then most often children attach themselves to that union, binding the parents to them and, one hopes, themselves to the parents; "at home" takes on a greater circumference.

The relationships fan out from the family to friends, in varying degrees of intensity, to coworkers, employers, and clients, to the community in which we live. In most lives, that is about as far as a felt awareness of the web goes, even though—simply by being a fellow passenger on Lifeboat Earth—we each have a real if unconscious moral relationship with the nation and the whole human family.

As one reaches further and further out into the web, the word *love* becomes thinner (if not nonexistent), but the need for it is nonetheless real. "Do unto others as you would have others do unto you" is not the shibboleth of a single religious persuasion. It is a matter of human survival.

Loving

Love is not rational. It's not *ir*rational, but it's not something one sits down, ponders, and decides to "do." Outside a family we didn't choose, why do we hang with these friends rather than others? Why would people in their right minds give up the swinging bachelor-bachelorette life? "Who can explain it, who can tell you why" you picked this particular spouse and stood up before a hundred or so people and vowed to be responsible each other "till death do us part"?

Why would any couple be foolish enough to have a pregnancy they could avoid and commit themselves to a child, nine months before they can even *see* it, much less approve of it, and bind themselves to caring, worrying, prodding, disciplining, and trying to understand this stranger for twenty years or more—not to mention a quarter-million price tag, each? It doesn't "make any sense"! But it does. As Pascal said, "The heart has reasons that reason knows not of."

We need to cut through the confused and confusing burdens we ask the word *love* to carry, to find a touchstone so clear and unquestionable we can use it to test all other relationships we call "love" and see which relationships deserve the word. The prime analogate of loving is surely good parents, and even more unquestionably the love of a good mother for her children. Tested, over and over, yet enduring.

A mother's love reaches out impartially to each of her children. It endures whether the child becomes a saint or a sinner, a world-beater or a beggar, a source of pride or shame. Conversely, children have an ineradicable conviction that they have a claim on their mother's love simply because she is their mother.

For those we truly love, we have the same alertness a mother has for her baby. She wakes up to a child's cry, even though she can snore through a thunderstorm. As with a mother, we love those we love with full awareness of the bumps and blemishes, most of which we come to cherish. Like a mother, our gift to those we care for is evocative: to discern unsuspected potentialities, like a sculptor sensing the statue within the marble.

Mother-love, in fact, goes *beyond* what any other of our loves can claim, since the good mother is helpless *not* to love her child. She may not always *like* the child, but she still loves her. That may be the heart of the touchstone: Genuine love is not a feeling; it is an act of the *will,* which takes over when the feelings fail, when the beloved is no longer even *likable.* Love is, in a word, commitment.

Spurious "Love"

Justice is not love; love goes far further. Justice demands we treat everyone as a human being and better than dogs; as soon as the debt is paid, the liability is over. On the contrary, genuine love forgives even before the debt is paid. Its meaning nestles perfectly into "above and beyond the call of duty." To put the distinction somewhat pithily: justice is washing your own dishes; love is washing someone else's.

Abigail Van Buren had a letter from a young man sleeping with a pretty nurse for three months, even though she had been living with another man for two years—and still was. Leaving the man was "impractical" for her:

> I am very fond of her and want her to devote herself completely to me. Would it be advisable for me to insist on her total loyalty and risk losing her? Or should I knowingly share her and leave things as they are? Please ignore the question of morality and answer me frankly. IN DOUBT.

Ms. Van Buren's answer was not only frank but terse:

> Dear In Doubt: One who is concerned with HUMAN relations cannot "ignore the question of morality." Since morality is what sets us apart from beasts, and you choose to ignore it, I suggest you direct your inquiry to a veterinarian.[2]

Though you can have justice without love, you can't have love without justice. Justice and fairness are intimately bound up in loving—whether it's the pale-as-smoke love of the anonymous neighbor or the deep, vibrant sexual communion of two lifelong spouses. Even if I only share my lunch with you, I have a claim on your courtesy and concern greater than a casual stranger has. If you have any sense of honor, you can't claim we've never met.

Much more have I a claim on someone with whom I've shared my body, the carrier of my self, intimately and secretly. Trouble is, we can share bodies without sharing selves, open our clothes without opening our hearts. But loving goes beyond justice, beyond quid pro quo. In love, you "give yourself away," in both senses of those words.

Far too many people think of love primarily as the assurance of *being* loved; therefore (with the eager connivance of the ad makers), the problem becomes how to become *lovable:* successful, rich, attractive, sexy, too good not to conquer. At least once.

M. Scott Peck writes:

> If being loved is your goal, you will fail to achieve it. The only way to be assured of being loved is to be a person worthy of love, and you cannot be a person worthy of love when your primary goal in life is to passively be loved.[3]

"Unrequited love" is an oxymoron. You can't make someone love you more than he or she is *able.* For someone who honestly loves, as with the good mother, the question of a kickback is simply unthinkable. Put the contrast concretely: A young man is head over heels in love with a young woman, but she says she thinks things are moving too fast; they ought to meet other people, open their options, test if this really is "the real thing." He goes along, fuming, but he finds from her friends who's taking her out and where—and he arranges to have the next table. He does that, he tells himself, out of love.

Another young man is also head over heels in love with another young woman, but, as will happen, she begins to take an interest in one of his friends. He says to her, "If you honestly think he can make you happier than I can . . . that's what I want." The contrast between those two cases makes it slightly more difficult to confuse spurious, self-absorbed love with the real thing. "Unrequited love" is most often self-pity in the face of the unchangeable.

Nor does genuine love brook jealousy, what Frankl calls "erotic materialism," treating the other not like a masterpiece before which one stands in awe but a masterpiece one insists on owning. The honest word for jealousy is not *love* but *enslavement*. Either jealousy is unfounded because the beloved is faithful—and therefore it is an insult undermining the putative relationship, or it has a genuine basis in fact because the beloved is unfaithful—and therefore jealousy is pointless because the relationship is a delusion.

After Tristan and Iseult gave up their addiction to the love potion and settled down to become worthy of their respective spouses, there was a chance for "happily ever after." But as soon as each found the other was *happy(!)*—without *them(!)*—it became intolerable. If he had truly loved her and she him, wouldn't they rather have the other happy, fulfilled, with a future, than be together out in the forest, freezing and eating grubs? But millions of otherwise intelligent people have wept at their plight, having endured the same corrosion themselves.

There is a poster that many mock, but it is the ultimate test of honest love: "If you love something, set it free. If it comes back to you, it is yours. If it doesn't, it never was." The glue that binds any relationship, from the spousal to the international, is trust, and trust is impossible without honesty. Where honesty is too painful, love is impossible.

Levels of Love

There is a spectrum in the legitimate uses of the word *love,* ranging from the unthinking need-love of an infant for its mother to Sydney Carton's sacrifice of his life to save the husband of the woman he loved: need-love, affection, friendship, romance, sexual involvement (a spectrum in itself), *Eros* (a true soul commitment sexually expressed), and selfless charity (giving up one's life—often without dying—for others).

Need-Love

C.S. Lewis discovered he had been wrong to disparage need-love as "mere selfishness." A child is not selfish if she runs to her mother with a skinned knee, nor is a husband who turns to his wife for compassion when he feels a failure. Need-love is, in fact, a gift to the loved one: an act of trust, a gift of one's weakness more difficult to give than a gift of one's strength. Only the narcissist has no need-love at all.

Even mother-love—the archetype of genuine loving—has within it an element of need-love: needing to be needed. At times I wonder if my need-to-be-needed isn't selfish or at least self-doubting, as if I lose my value when someone doesn't depend on me (at the very least for a boot in the butt). But each of us, legitimately, needs a sense that we serve a purpose. The love of a parent or a teacher, of course, is to render one's service and oneself unnecessary.

Often charitable acts are unwittingly motivated by a need to feel good about myself or to assuage guilt. But it's better than nothing; someone's hurt is also assuaged, no matter what the motive. Perhaps a less slippery and less self-serving word than *charity* is *kindness.* Charity can be faked; kindness can't.

Love, as Plato saw, is a child of poverty. The instant an infant is born, it knows loneliness and alienation for the first time.

Therefore, as soon as possible it must be put back against that heartbeat it has known for nine months. For the rest of life, we need others if we are to know anything, even ourselves.

For the next two years, most of us felt (without doubt) unconditionally loved. Anything we did was acceptable. Then gradually—but still disconcertingly—parents began to set limits, to ask for cooperation, and (at least from the child's unreasoned point of view) to put *conditions* on being loved. That growing sense of the need to be "acceptable" in order to be loved then fanned out beyond the parents into the whole web of social relationships: siblings, peers, neighbors, then teachers, bosses, lovers, spouses, children.

That time of weaning, potty-training, and "No, no!" is a critical moment in a child's life whose effects can perdure until death, the individual soul submitting unthinkingly to the belief that "That's the way things are": unless I succeed, I won't be loved. There are many responses to that unfounded belief: anti-social ("T' hell with all of you, then!"), obsessive ("I'll be acceptable no matter how much pain it costs"), narcissistic ("I'm OK no matter what they want of me"), all of which can foreclose the possibility of honest love for a lifetime.

Much of psychotherapy is trying to sort out which need-loves are legitimate and which are self-accepted delusions.

Affection

Even animals feel and need affection. Monkeys, separated from their mothers, very quickly pine away and die, but if they are put to cling on a fuzzy doll fitted with a heater and a ticking clock, they can survive. Any pet owner knows the symbiotic need the two share, one content to scratch, the other content to be scratched.

Affection is probably the least reasoned of the loves, but it is nonetheless genuine and life-enhancing for both, whether it is human and animal or human and human. Like any unbalanced virtue, of course, it can become silly. For many childless couples or people living alone, affection for their pets can become more important (or at least more secure) than dealing with people and therefore self-impoverishing.

No one "plans" affection; it just happens. Some people just fasten onto us and we don't feel the need to brush them off. Symbiotic, like the elephant and the tickbird: the tickbird gets her sustenance, and the elephant gets rid of his ticks.

Often affection happens when the object has no apparent fitness to arouse it or receive it: Don Quixote and Sancho Panza; Rosencrantz and Guildenstern; Pickwick and Sam Weller; Mole, Rat, Badger, and Toad in *Wind in the Willows;* Vladimir and Estragon; Henry Higgins and Eliza. No matter how dissimilar, each gives the other the familiar, taken-for-granted, homely, comfortable feeling of an old pair of slippers. First one falls in with another, then endures him or her, then begins to enjoy just having them around, and finally begins to cherish them.

Friendship

Friendship is the least physical of the loves, the least prone to jealousy, and surely the least complex. Men enjoy having someone with whom to talk shop or sports; women enjoy klatching about family and the limitations of males. That forms a matrix of companionship out of which closer friendships can emerge. For that reason, people who simply "want friends" can never make any, because to have friends is to want together something *other* than just to have friends, whether it is golf or physics or rap music or a shared passionate detestation of the bosses. It is close to impossible to share a romantic love with others, but it is enriching to share a good friendship.

When I try to ponder the faces of friendship with students, I draw an enormous circle on the board. Inside the circle is "You"; the whole room outside the circle is all the people you will probably never know—old grandmas in China, sheep men in Australia, wanderers in the African bush. Those are the "Anonymous." Then I draw a very tiny circle adhering to the inside of the big one; those are "Best Friends," the people you'd tell anything, no matter how shaming, and feel secure.

At one time, your best friends were anonymous. What was the first thing that had to happen to bring them from way out there into way in here? The students look puzzled, as if I'd asked for a one-sentence explanation of the quantum theory, even though they've all been through this. (They aren't much given to reflection.)

> "You meet them."
> Even before that.
> "You say hello."
> Even before that.

Finally, someone comes up with it: "You've got to notice them." Until that happens, there's no chance. Yet we brush by thousands of potential friends each day with blinders on, not *wanting* to notice them, impoverishing ourselves for the sake of security. Once someone steps into the circle, he or she becomes an "Acquaintance," probably with a name to separate that face from the faceless. That's where most of the people you "know" reside: The Outer You. "Yeah. I've met her."

Then I draw two smaller circles around the tiny "Best Friends" circle: The larger one is "Friends," the smaller one is "Pals"—friends being those you don't mind sitting with at lunch, pals being people you simply expect to sit with. How does someone get from "Acquaintance" to "Friends"? Again, puzzlement, but someone comes up with the fact you have common interests. Most friends came by accident; you didn't go looking for them: same job, same part of the alphabet, same club, but you've shared time and talk.

What moves someone from "Friends" to "Pals" is that you've shared experiences, often harrowing, and each has found the other trustworthy in a pinch. You not only do the same things, but *care* about them with the same intensity.

How does someone move from "Pals" to "Best Friends"? Yet again, intrigued confusion (the only place from which to learn). One young woman came up with the perfect answer: "You cry together." Your best friends are the ones you've invited behind the tapestried exterior, allowed them to look at all the snarls and knots, and he or she says, "So? We're still friends." Your best friends didn't happen because you went to the circus together but because you went through hell together.

Each juncture from "Acquaintances" to "Best Friends" was a calculated risk, an act of faith. (Loving is all about faith, you see.) If I notice her, she might snag me in conversation and slow me down; if I sit with him, he might be a boor or a bore; if I trust her with this secret, she could betray me; if I tell him I'm gay, he'll drop me flat, if not deck me.

Not many of us are very trusting. Not many of us feel comfortable with risk. Which is why so many of us love—and live—so little. Cats live nine-lives-in-one because they are curious, willing to take the risk of dying, again, and yet again, each time with no less pain. But no one is reborn without dying.

Romance

Here we come to the most complex of the loves, the most slippery and susceptible to misuse of the word, because quite often you're discussing it with someone pixilated on love potion and completely incapable of seeing the objective truth.

Here, too, it is helpful to think in the ambiguous gradations of a spectrum (more/less), rather than with the comforting certitude of bins (either/or)—calling a relationship love when it is considerably less than the real thing. Romance often moves from the platonic being-in-love of George and Emily in *Our Town* (a phase often short-lived in the *Playboy* ethos), through a sexual relationship with no commitment, through such a relationship where there is some commitment, but hesitations or impediments hinder full commitment: *Eros*.

The word *romance* comes from the French *roman,* a novel. Therefore, romance is storybook love like the courtly love of Arthurian tales: The brave knight worships (chastely) the flawless lady: his inspiration, the ideal who moves him to nobility, spirituality, refinement. Romance is a fine antidote to the patriarchal need to dominate arising in the boy from his newfound maleness. For both, it is a temporary way to feel "at home" again, a sense of wholeness neither has felt since their forced separation from their mothers. At least for a magical time, one feels unconditionally loved once again. A blissful blindness.

Being in love is what Eric Fromm calls an "immature form of love," not really full-blown love but rather a complex of involuntary feelings which make the soul soar, because it is unhampered by the deadweight of reality. It usually brings with it a selective myopia; as Lucretius wrote, "She becomes 'svelte' and 'willowy,' when she is really too skinny to live."

Being in love also infects its victims with a raging proclivity for hyperbole, exclamation points, and italics: "You're my *every-thing!* . . . I'd *die* without you! . . . I would give my very *soul* and not regret it!" Or the poet Carlos Almaran: "Always you were the reason for my existence; To adore you for me was religion." It is the illusion "we were meant for each other," as if the gods had engineered the linkage, unaware of the caprice of the gods or that what is fated, as with Tristan and Iseult, is often fatal.

Thus, their passion is usually *passive,* a kind of "possession" of which they are the victims, needful of the other rather than giving. One "falls for" the other; "You can't drop me; I *need* you!" Young people themselves immediately nod when you suggest there might be similarities between being-in-love and chemical addiction. You feel "above it all," cut loose from the pedestrian, feeling the jolt of what at least seems fulfillment. But it is, they admit, a dependency. And the high doesn't last long. Reality creeps in. The prince begins to resent being account-able for every moment away; the princess pouts. Either the two begin the difficult process of loving, or they part.

Very often, being in love can become a narcissism-built-for-two, and it is difficult for an outsider (and surely an insider) to distinguish between *relating* to another person and *using* the other person as a lightning rod for our own projections. What Margaret Mead wrote of romance in 1949 remains true (at first):

> The boy who longs for a date is not longing for a girl. He is longing to be in a situation, mainly public, where he will be seen by others to have a girl, and the right kind of girl, who dresses well and pays attention.[4]

Falling in love can often be what psychologists call *transference* in which we project onto other people aspects of ourselves of which we are unaware and we think the other person embodies them—superlatively and flawlessly. She, a princess; he, a prince. Each becomes what Morton Kelsey calls "a hook on which we hang our projections." Too often a male "dumps off" his anima on the female, the female her animus on the male.

Today, because of TV, two-sex dating starts far earlier than it did even in the '60s. Reading Margaret Mead fifty years later, describing adolescent sexual experimentation in 1949, is like watching reruns of *The Waltons,* when men wore fedoras and women wore girdles. A boy got his first pair of long pants in fifth grade, and a girl didn't have her ears pierced (if at all) until she was in high school. If Booth Tarkington were writing *Seventeen* today, he'd have to call it *Ten*.

What Mead says about petting back then is still true, if only in the eyes of parents: "The boy is expected to ask for as much as possible, the girl to yield as little as possible." Therefore the girl was both a participant and the referee. But in our permissive ethos, where a girl is either "with it" or frigid, she suffers some conflict which has less to do with sexuality than with acceptability. Thus, we have the phenomenon of date rape, where the girl has obviously said no, but the boy "knows" she doesn't mean it, that she "wants it" just as much as he does. After all, he's seen TV. It is a matter of "the new sexual freedom." The folks on *Melrose Place* appear to be adult while acting like horny adolescents, unaware that their "freedom" makes them slaves to their hormones, moods, and need to be wanted.

Whenever a young woman asks, "What if he says, 'Honey, if you really loved me, you'd let me do it'?," I tell her, say, "Honey, if you really loved me, you wouldn't ask me to prove it."

They are unaware also that in order to give away yourself you must first possess yourself, which few have the time or inclination to do. In mature love, each preserves his or her own integrity, becoming a "we" while remaining an "I." In one's childhood, the good mother—the touchstone of real love—not only tolerates the child's independence of her but encourages it. So, too, with people who claim genuinely to love one another.

Sexual Friendships

It is somewhat too facile to assert that every single sexual relationship short of permanent commitment is reprehensible, but like all tried-and-true dogmas it is not a bad guideline in nearly every case, as long as one admits of exceptions (though not too hastily). Sexual relations can occur casually, disinterestedly, even brutishly, what *Time*'s Richard Corliss called "frantically perfunctory bouts of sex-making."

It is pleasure that goes no further than the senses, an event within one's *own* body and only in the most peripheral way a concern about the other: the more pleasure the other has, the more pleasure *I* have.

She can be "taken" (but not seriously); she on her part never "gives" herself away. The immorality (less than humanness) of nonmarital intercourse arises not because something untoward was given, but that not enough was given.

In such cases, a man doesn't "want a woman," and a woman doesn't "need a man." Each wants merely an animated sexual apparatus warmer than an inflatable doll. Judge the truth of that by how each feels about the other *after* "It" is over. The honest person can differentiate need-pleasure from appreciative pleasure. Subhuman encounters hardly qualify as acquaintance, much less friendship, and only the incurably narcissistic would call them "making love."

But *Playboy* and the media have had a greater influence on our sexual attitudes than any parent or pastor. Casual erotic romps are merely one step removed from prostitution, a mere means, nonbinding. Very often that gives rise to "anticipatory anxiety." Like the stammerer focusing on his disability, thus unable to speak, and the insomniac worried about sleeping and therefore staying awake, many who focus on sex as a means focus not on the partner but on the act and, therefore, on their ability to "perform" well—and therefore they often can't perform at all.

As a longtime teacher of young men whose crossing the bar of puberty is not that far behind them, I have had more opportunities than many to clarify the distinction between sex-as-selfish and sex-as-selfless. Few realize I've heard, "C'*mon!*

If she wants it as much as you do, who's gettin' hurt?" more times than God has heard the Lord's Prayer. To that interjection, I have the reflexes of a veteran gunslinger: If she *wanted* to be your slave—"Hitch me to your plow and *beat* me," would that justify your using her? If she desperately wanted you to help her commit suicide, would that make your assistance a moral, human act?

But one time, the skies opened. After that habitual back-and-forth, a smart young man said, *"Look"* (he was being patient), "if you like each other, it's only *natural*. When you're thirsty, you get a glass of water. When you're horny, you call your girlfriend."

Suddenly, it came to me. "Okay," says I, "there are two words for having sex. What are they?"

Of course, at least five worthies obliged me with the F-word.

"And the other one?"

And the boy who had challenged me said, "Making love."

I leaned down and said, "They *don't* call it making *like.*"

His face closed up like a fist. After about six or eight go-rounds on the question, he suddenly *understood*. That afternoon I left and said to myself, "Yep. I can do it another year."

Puberty comes from ambush. No matter how much talk the child has heard from open-minded parents or narrow-focused pals, the reality far outreaches the explanations. The teenager's task is to integrate this new upheaval into his or her psyche. At first sexuality is an aimless urge; anyone will do: Don Juan, Madonna, masturbation. It is the yearning of empty "selves."

Then at the deeper stage of romance and infatuation, sexuality becomes focused on one person: companionship, affection, understanding, tenderness. Few in their teens could conceivably go *beyond* sex, beyond the body to the soul. Contentment with and desire for a monogamous sexuality is the criterion for mature sexuality. A problem exterior to an adolescent sexual relationship is the effect on the rest of the individual's life: narrowing of interests, limitation of mental horizons; the easy pleasure drowns out all other concerns.

The problems which elude the "bin mentality" about active sexuality without permanent commitment (on both the permissive and the restrictive sides) arise when there is, in fact, a real but impermanent commitment. Permanent commitment is desirable but "impractical": they have to get through college; they have no jobs; they're dependent on their parents, both financially and psychologically; they're not ready to make an "at home" yet. The "fault," if there is one, is not theirs; if they had financial stability, they'd get married next Saturday. This is real love.

But one could ask if they have a legitimate right to the benefits of active "married" sex without having paid the price. More importantly, just from the way human beings are made, the honeymoon after marriage helps two people get through the unexpected confusions of surrendering autonomy for commitment. For those unused to it, sex can wipe out many of the conflicts that arise in those first couple of years. But if they have had the honeymoon for two or three years *before* the commitment, they can't expect another. That's just the way things are, not because of what religions say but what human nature says. That's the reason more than half the couples who live together and then get married break up. The cards are stacked against them.

One good question to ask in the case where there is some-but-incomplete commitment: Suppose someone more beautiful, charming, funny, and wise came along? It's possible. Or if he or she died, and you were offered a perfect physical and temperamental clone, would you know the difference? If it is merely a self-deceptively sexual and emotional union, you would hardly care. In genuine sex, *Eros,* it is not a connection between bodies or even between personalities, but between two souls.

Perhaps the best test of a sexual friendship: Does this connection make both more joyful, openhearted, lively, and generous *outside* the relationship? Or does it make them both more secretive, touchy, inaccessible, and devious? Nifty test.

Eros

Lovemaking without love lacks the main ingredient no animal can offer: soul. Love is the surrender not just of the body but of the inner self. "I bow to the divine in you." As C. S. Lewis writes: "The fact that she is a woman is far less important than the fact that she is herself." Eros says, equivalently, "I'd rather be unhappy with you than happy with someone else."

In true loving, as in *Beauty and the Beast,* looks hardly count. A man who truly loves a woman wouldn't want her to have liposuction, and a woman who loves a man would tell him his hairpiece makes him look silly. Love isn't blind; being-in-love is blind. Real loves lets us truly see—without wincing.

The essential condition for genuine loving is overcoming one's own narcissism. Narcissists care only about what is rewarding or threatening to them. The opposite of narcissism is *objectivity:* to see things and people as *they* really are, and seeing not only with the analytical left brain but with the empathic right brain. *Eros* is not only humble before the facts, the unchangeables, but rejoices in them.

If true loving is, as Erich Fromm maintains, an art, then it requires the faithful, pedestrian practice any art like playing the piano or carpentry requires: discipline, concentration, patience, commitment, and the willingness to "start small" and practice the art often. Yet the prevailing attitude is hostile to all those habits. We chafe against discipline and long to shuck it off like a corset on Friday afternoon. Concentration is rare outside work; rather we are diffused into distractions. Patience can no longer be a virtue when everything has to be quick: fast food, zero to sixty in sixty seconds, have it for me by yesterday. Commitment is confining; keep your options open. That's why so many sexual friendships fail. If love means commitment, love can't last long without it.

Real sexual love accepts that the bedroom is important, but that there are other rooms in the house in which they must live more. Genuine love is very undramatic: cutting down on the drinking love, "No, I'll get up and change her" love, letting go of the grudge love, forgiving love. Not the rhapsodic union of Cinderella and Charming, nor the drama of George and Martha in *Who's Afraid of Virginia Woolf,* but the easygoing comfort with one another of Tevye and Golde in *Fiddler on the Roof.*

No matter what one thinks of Saint Paul's theology, his psychology of love is pretty much squarely on target:

> Love is long-suffering and kind; love is not jealous
> or conceited or vain; love is not ill-mannered or
> selfish or irritable; love does not have a long
> memory for wrongs; love is not happy with evil,
> but is happy only with the truth. Love never gives
> up: its faith, hope, and patience never fail.[5]

If a relationship you call "love" is touchy, ungracious, suspicious, patronizing, discourteous, narcissistic, quarrelsome, grudge-bearing, self-deceptive, unable to stand up to the unexpected—then you are misusing the word and deluding the other and yourself, but most likely no one else.

Chapter Thirteen

BECOMING MARRIED

Cinderella and the prince
lived, they say, happily ever after,
like two dolls in a museum case
never bothered by diapers or dust,
never arguing over the timing of an egg,
never telling the same story twice,
never getting middle-age spread,
their darling smiles pasted on for eternity.
Regular Bobbsey Twins.
That story.

Anne Sexton—*"Cinderella"*[1]

Getting David and Rick Nelson conceived must have taken
some contriving, since in the days of *America Graffiti* and *Father
Knows Best,* Ozzie and Harriet always slept in twin beds, despite

the fact that anything they did behind closed doors was, one supposes, ratified by the state of California if by no one else.

In no area is the dramatic, though gradual, transformation of American attitudes since the '50s more manifest than in the media's treatment of sexuality, marriage, raising children, and divorce—and therefore our society's attitudes toward sexuality, marriage, raising children, and divorce. A recent study[2] showed all the women interviewed who married in the '50s were either virgins or pregnant at the altar, whereas none of those married during the '80s and '90s was a virgin. In the '50s, the economy was stable, no real worries about layoffs, little anxiety about divorce. It is obvious how we have been not only disenchanted but disillusioned from an ethic our parents and most of us on the far side of fifty took as unchallengeable.

Even today we are not so cynical that marriage does not still begin in fantasy: everything will be happily ever after. This person will continue to make me whole, protect me, make me feel good, true, and beautiful forever. Since the demise of Victoria, romance is an absolute requisite for marriage. Without the breathless blindness that makes each an only slightly flawed god and goddess, no one in their right mind would take on such an unlimited liability for someone else. Who would walk up to a relative stranger, known maybe a year or so and say, "You seem a terrific person. Here's all my money"? Most wouldn't do that to a sibling we've known all our lives.

Yet people who won't speak to strangers in elevators, won't lift their hands at meetings, didn't commit themselves to choose a college till the last minute—bet their lives on marriage. You've got to be a bit crazy to do that, right? Yet most of us do it—some more than once.

In some states, there might be a required blood test, but no insistence that either person has a job and sufficient means to support the two of them, no need to prove either did not spend several years in a prison or asylum, no tribal elder to give wise and binding advice from a longer perspective. One needs to prove more to get a driver's license or a gun permit than a wedding license, and one needs no license at all to beget a child. For neither of those does one need to give evidence he or she is a personally validated self, a person of character—which is the only true assurance of healthy marriage and parenthood. On the other hand, it would be difficult to imagine what such a test would be.

In a '70s survey, couples lined up for marriage licenses were asked if they thought this marriage would last "till death do us part." Sixty-three percent said no. Somewhere in the inaccessible part of themselves, they knew they were entering a minefield without proper intelligence or even a map, knowing they *didn't* really know one another yet, yet unaware that growth—at great sacrifice—is still both possible and necessary.

The absolute requisite for fostering not only physical but psychological intimacy is vulnerability. Ironically, one must be confident before one dares be trusting. To offer an inner self to another, one must have explored and *owned* that self, warts and all. When we share our deepest fears and secret impulses with a marital partner, there is a profound risk. But it is worth the risk. As Herbert Anderson writes:

> Nothing promotes greater intimacy than the relief
> of a burden no longer carried alone and the
> deepening of trust that comes when our hidden
> self is recognized and accepted by the one we love.[3]

When the partners can share truths about themselves that they hardly want to acknowledge themselves, before the marriage, as really best friends can do, they have a strong assurance that they can weather just about any future failings. But such absolute trust in one another—and in oneself—is rare, especially in a romantic love where one wants to offer the other "the best self" one can, even though every secret has an ominous ticking inside.

Unreserved commitment also becomes more conditional in an ethos fogged with awareness of divorce courts now so common in the papers and on television or even experienced firsthand with their own parents. Even though it is unconscious, many couples feel bound only by legal commitments rather than by more human, person-to-person commitments rooted in their souls; they may still have a felt responsibility for the children but no longer for one another. To my mind, anyone who has made a premarital financial agreement has already invalidated the marriage.

Even more ironically, freedom to divorce *restricts* the freedom of a couple trying to preserve and deepen a marriage. When divorce was pretty much unthinkable, a spouse could indulge quarreling, sulking, neglectfulness within a long-range, fundamental commitment that kept that phase in perspective. When divorce becomes relatively common, each new quarrel can quicken the question: Does that mean we're through?

Most marital problems arise because neither has, in fact, achieved a positive, confident self—chosen a personal map, forged a keel that will take the self (and therefore the couple) through inevitable storms and conflicts. After the euphoria of the honeymoon (if in fact it is their *first* honeymoon), such a couple go back to playing the same old games they played in childhood—scapegoating, projection, pouts—because, although they may still have a physical union, they have yet to build an adequate psychological union. When "The Child" in either or both takes over for too long, the marriage begins to toddle.

Most lovers would probably find it demeaning to their love to take the very practical step of sitting down with a pad long before their wedding, drawing a line down the center, and writing out the things they love about the other on the left side and the things they honestly dislike on the right. If there are no—or very few—items on the right, the scribbler is purblind and heading toward an abyss. Without such an objective assessment, the partners risk entering the Fun House and quickly detouring into the House of Horrors. They may call it "blind faith." To my mind, blind faith is a synonym for "sheer idiocy."

Marriage, like any act of faith, is a calculated risk. The more calculation, the less risk. But tell that to a young woman and man with moonbeams in their eyes.

The best definition of a marriage I have seen is in Thornton Wilder's *The Skin of Our Teeth*. Maggie's husband, George, has just come from a "conversation" with Sabina Fairweather, with whom he intends to decamp. Maggie says:

> I didn't marry you because you were perfect. I didn't even marry you because I loved you. I married you because you gave me a promise. That promise made up for your faults. The promise I gave you made up for mine. Two imperfect people got married, and it was the promise that made the marriage. And when our children were growing up, it wasn't a house that protected them; and it wasn't our love that protected them—it was that promise.[4]

Maggie cuts through the flab and even the gristle to the bone: Marriage is a *promise*. Not a feeling, but a pledge of commitment, without reservations, crossed fingers, or "yes, but what ifs." No jury makes a commitment when there is "reasonable doubt." Nor should any couple. Unfortunately, the daze of romance, the urge to get-it-done, and (frankly) the fear of appearing cowardly often nudge them onto a bridge they are really not ready to cross. "Take this ring as a sign of my love and fidelity." We read that as sexual fidelity, but faithfulness goes much further. It means "I'll stick with you even when I haven't liked you for a long time." Hard words; hard truth.

The wedding is only *one* focal event in a process that begins before the engagement and ends only with death. They are *becoming* married every day of their lives so that on their twentieth anniversary, a couple are a lot *more* married than on their wedding day. A marriage is not an event but a process. It doesn't just "happen," it's *built*. It's not a given; it's a triumph.

The Good Marriage

Although there are shelves of books on divorce, Judith Wallerstein's *The Good Marriage* is probably the only anecdotal study of fifty couples who have been happily married from ten to forty years, judged by their friends, neighbors, and themselves. The study is somewhat skewed insofar as it was restricted to northern California, college-educated, predominantly white, middle-class couples, and unless her collaborator edited their responses, they are remarkably articulate. However, if this chapter has no other value, it can serve as an unsolicited promo for a book every engaged couple, every seminarian, every clergy person, and anyone involved in counseling about marriage ought to read carefully.

Her study is thorough, compassionate, and clear-eyed:

> Marriage counselors like to tell their clients that there are at least six people in every marital bed— the couple and both sets of parents. I'm here to say that a crazy quilt of conflicting personal values and shifting social attitudes is also in that bed. The confusion over roles and the indifference of the

community to long-term conjugal relationships are there, as are the legacies of a self-absorbed, me-first, feminist-do-or-die, male-backlash society. The ease of divorce and changing attitudes about the permanence of marriage have themselves become centrifugal forces.[5]

Four Types of Marriages

Wallerstein isolates four types of marriage: (1) the traditional marriage, a clear division of roles in which the mother creates the family and the father supports it; (2) the romantic marriage, a lasting, passionate relationship; (3) the rescue marriage, in which one or both partners had a quality the other lacked but the wounded partner wanted to develop; (4) the companionate marriage (now most common), in which both spouses balance the demands of the marriage, full-time careers, and children.

Since the beginning, the *traditional* marriage has been the stereotype. In such a union, the husband and wife willingly accept the conventional roles society has ordinarily assumed males and females would undertake: the male breadwinner and the female homemaker (as distinguished from "housekeeper"). Most of us admit the unfairness of stereotypes, but there *are* in fact men and women who are unregenerately "typical"! There are women who genuinely enjoy creating a physical—and psychological—space in which spouses and children can feel "at home," flourish, share crises, know they are safe and loved.

As with any job, there are elements a homemaker could well live without. Teachers love to challenge minds so much they are willing to endure swamp-gas essays, mindless proc- toring assignments, and lobotomizing teachers' meetings. Physicians are so fascinated with healing they are willing to deal with bodily indignities most of us avert our eyes from even on a medical TV show. So, some women love caring for a family so much they can take wiping the same dust from the same surfaces week after week.

It is important to note, however, that in Wallerstein's study every woman in a happy traditional marriage had a significant involvement *outside* the home which kept her psychologically more alive—and interesting—than the Stepford Wives one sees on oven-cleaner commercials. To thrive in a traditional marriage, a woman has to maintain a *self,* rather than defining herself as "the wife of this husband, the mother of these children." But in general in the traditional marriage, the primary focus is on the children rather than on career, companionship, or even sex—though all of those remain essentials.

One can only stand in awe at the *romantic* marriage, especially in a culture so fixated on individualism and incessant change. Contrary to the conventional wisdom, the study shows 15 percent of the couples had maintained a continuing romantic relationship—sometimes for forty years—as vibrant or more than when they were dating. Part of the reason is probably as elusive as "chemistry." But another element is the ability of both spouses to yield, to sense the needs and moods of their partner, to be unreservedly generous, to "mother" one another.

The successful *"rescue"* marriage is not the relationship in which each partner "supplies" what the other lacks as a healthy psychological self, not the complementarity Plato envisioned in a primeval fusion of couples who were then severed and forced to roam the world in search of "the right fit." In a rescue marriage, one partner triggers in the other an awareness of a human potential he or she has repressed or denied through fear of disapproval. He is all work and no play: she jollies him into taking himself less seriously. She has been sexually repressed; he painstakingly eases her into a more human understanding not only of his needs but more especially of her own. One partner does not supply a quality the other lacks but summons the other to discover and cultivate what the other already has.

As a result of the women's movement and the change in the economy, nearly all new marriages are *companionate,* both spouses working, even with very young children. Also, very many of what had been traditional marriages have given a greater emphasis to equal partnership in all aspects of the marriage. If parents want their teenagers to go to more advantageous private schools, the mother is going to have to get a job, even if she had stayed at home during the important early formative years.

It is the most difficult form of marriage to maintain. Founded on the shared belief that both are equal and *all* roles are completely interchangeable, it requires high levels of confidence in oneself and in the other. Each can stand alone but rejoices that neither has to. Each counts on a wedding promise that makes breaking up inconceivable, which in turn allows each the enriching challenge of discovering unsuspected areas of their own selves, both inside and outside the home. For young people, it is a marriage quite different from the marriages their parents modeled for them. For older couples, it can be a renaissance.

As with any style of marriage, there are problems. Some couples solve the problem of sharing home jobs by doing what each likes or doesn't mind doing: he would rather cook, she hates it. What they must negotiate are jobs neither likes: those they take turns at. Juggling the demands of a career, the needs of the kids (real and imagined), sharing housework means a couple simply has to make a conscious decision to set apart time every week to be alone: to work on the marriage which is at the heart of the family. And they have to have time when they aren't too fatigued and stressed out to keep up a loving sexual relationship.

Time is a chronic problem in many families today. It is no secret that work intrudes on family life. Longer hours at the office mean fewer hours with the kids. To compensate, many parents subscribe to the concept of "quality time"—short periods of especially loving or devoted interaction with their children that supposedly distills the essence of good parenting. But children do not buy into the concept of quality time; they are foolish enough to clamor for "time time"—bedtime, playtime, story time, soccer time, just-being-together time, and not watching the clock time. They don't go for nouvelle-cuisine parenting no matter how prettily presented, for they have figured out that the helpings are too small and only leave them hungry for more.[6]

One's love is not quantifiable, but one's energy is. At times couples feel "the pie is too small to meet everyone's needs." That's when the couple must make time to *reassess* the priorities, before the everyday demands of job, house, taxes, braces, hockey equipment, grandparents, and on and on smother the couple's relationship until they become functionaries rather than lovers and parents. When that happens, divorce becomes less untenable than before. Many marriages break up simply because the couple has been so busy doing the jobs that embody their love for their families they have no time to remain best friends.

Nine Tasks for Any Marriage

From her many years of working with divorced couples—during which she found which challenges couples had failed to face (which led to a breakup of the marriage and the family) and which challenges had been successfully negotiated by the happily married couples she studied more recently—Judith Wallerstein has delineated nine tasks that are part of any marriage, needs that are inevitable—and yet, ironically, avoidable. They will surely arise, but a couple is free to ignore them, deny them, walk away from them. If so, the marriage is in jeopardy, if not self-doomed.

The tasks are, briefly:

1. Separation from original families;

2. Building intimacy without losing a self;

3. Opening to children without losing privacy;

4. Forging an ability to face crises together;

5. Creating a haven in which to voice differences;

6. Protecting a sexual relationship from work and family;

7. Using laughter to keep perspective;

8. Providing nurturance for one another;

9. Keeping alive the early romantic image of one another.

Further, "If pregnancy occurs before the work of these tasks has progressed significantly, parenthood begins at a grave disadvantage for the child and for the married couple."

1. Letting Go: Few married people often recall the unnerving disequilibrium of uprooting oneself from one's birth family with all its comforting reassurances, its unquestioned customs, a room of one's own with all its "specially chosen junk," the security of parents who usually had a handle on things, its decades of a shared story, its . . . "at-homeness." Getting married is not rejecting the birth family but developing a completely different kind of connectedness to them. This couple is no longer a son and daughter in the same way. Now they have to begin dealing with their parents as adults-to-adults.

This is not just a physical separation but a moral independence. Their primary loyalty is now to the spouse, not to their parents. If the reasonable desires of the birth families and the new marriage conflict, the marriage wins. This can be difficult, since the relationship with the parents has been deepening for twenty years or more, while the relationship with the spouse is comparatively recent. But it's a challenge they must surmount.

2. Partnership / Autonomy: Just as an adolescent ought to develop an identity as a self, the couple now must build a new identity as a "we"—without losing their own identities. Until quite recently, a woman "had to" learn to sacrifice her autonomy; today, *both* spouses have to, and both have to tend the marriage as if it were their first child—as indeed it is. They have to look at the marriage as an *entity in itself,* the bond between them, which cannot be lost sight of, no matter what the demands of the job, extended family, or even their own children.

They have to discover what each wants and needs and, as important, what each doesn't want and need. They have to learn that in some marriages what one partner perceives as nagging is often objectively only the request that he or she grow up. Most important, they have to remind themselves, again and again, that they will never go to bed angry, no matter what the cost, that preserving the marriage is far more important than any disagreement, no matter how strongly felt.

Another difficult but essential element of a good marriage is confident and unfearful *self-disclosure.* The couple must learn openly to share life stories, because they are now fusing long-separate stories into one new story. You can't complete writing a novel already begun if you haven't read the first chapters. This is an intimacy *beyond* the sexual and far more profound. It is, in fact, what differentiates "making love," *Eros,* from merely "having sex." Self-revelation is often more difficult for a male because of the ego boundaries he's used to define himself, first as different from his mother and then as different from his father. Also, because of the debilitating male stereotype, he has had to box in his feelings. Many men aren't even aware they have feelings. But in this new relationship he has to be capable of telling his wife not only "I'm angry" but also "I'm scared."

In the male or female, it is mother-love which heals, an empathy that knows the other is hurt even when—as with a child—he or she can't put it into words.

3. Parenthood: Having a child forever changes the marriage relationship, often to the point parents begin to refer to one another as "Dad" and "Mom," even when the children are gone, rather than by their first names. Even before the child is born and surely after, its schedule dictates the whole rhythm of the household, and it can be exhausting, even when every task is shared, taking its toll not only on the parents' energy but on their souls—precisely what they have to offer one another and the child: their selves. Once they have both finished the day, they both need "mothering."

Also, Wallerstein insists:

> It's so important that new fathers be forewarned of
> the powerful, difficult emotions they will naturally
> have about this "intruder." But our society does
> not offer such advice to men.[7]

A new father has to understand and calmly accept the fact that this woman who has been "all his" is no longer all his, that someone else is making constant physical and emotional demands on her which he would tolerate from no one else, male or female. That is why it is so much more helpful in companionate marriages that the father do as much as he can to share what were formerly tasks "only a mother can take care of."

Just as, at the start of their marriage, they had to open their lives to accommodate one another, without losing their selfhood, they have to open to the child, while still tending their marriage. It is a film and TV cliché that, just as the couple begin to cuddle, the child comes in and says there's a monster under her bed. So she crawls in with them. For the moment, the child takes precedence over the sex.

Still they have to resolve, for instance, that one night a week they are going out alone to dinner and that the children will not even be on the agenda. They need time once a week to say "there are things bothering me," not just about the spouse but about everything. It is wise, even if it's a *severe* strain on their budget, that a few times a year the couple leave the kids with someone else and go off for a couple of days alone. Renewing the marriage is caring for the *heart* of the family, more important than a new carburetor or music lessons or braces. It is important not only for the two as a couple but for the children's sense of security: that they see and feel a love between their parents so obvious they can take it for granted.

4. Coping with Crises: Crises are a given. Some are foreseeable: challenges involved with children, especially in adolescence when they become confused and confusing; then they will surely leave the parents to cope again with being just "us"; the death of grandparents, growing old, retirement. Others are unforeseeable: job loss, sudden death or injuries, natural disasters.

One opportunity a crisis offers is to let us see what is truly important: the fire destroyed our home, but it's more important we all survived; the breast lost to a mastectomy is not as important as my wife; sooner or later we have to get back to living the one life we have left. In the best marriages, the couple do not allow tragedy to dominate their lives too long.

More and more common today is the loss of a job (especially in midlife) which has been central to one's self-image.

There is the fear of unspoken accusations, resentment, or pity. Often it becomes easier to feel angry than helpless, letting fly at the partner as a handy lightning rod. Also, the partner may be unable to look beyond the anger to the hurt that causes it.

The spouse who is at the moment stronger can't just "let things take their natural course," at least not for long. He or she has to take a deep breath, step in, and say, "All right, now what do we do? For a while, we'll have to compromise with less, but we can do more than just endure it; we can survive it." This particular task will be far less traumatic if the couple has done a reasonable job on the other tasks.

5. A Space for Conflict: From the first day of the marriage there are bound to be conflicts neither partner ever expected: Do we sleep with the window open? Do we put the toilet roll over-shot or undershot? ("My mother always . . . ") Do we smoke, watch the Super Bowl, eat liver? Whose parents do we visit at Christmas? Who always drives? And the big whopper: Who controls the TV remote? Unlike college or business or athletics, where every policy is spelled out, the two selves in marriage are left to improvise and compromise. The object of this enterprise is not to get one's own way. If either "wins," both lose.

If his dream has been to be a high school English teacher and her past has led her to take membership in a country club for granted, they ought to have taken a great deal more thought before they even got engaged. If she sets her sights on becoming a surgeon and he is climbing in a company that frequently uproots and moves executives, they have a lot of heavy thinking ahead. There are bound to be conflicts on the allotment of money, especially if there are two incomes.

Even continuous, honest communication can't weed out all conflicts. It's neither possible *nor* desirable. Honest confrontation gives each a chance to see the other in a new light—provided both agree beforehand (in writing if necessary) that when the battle is over, they'll put their arms around one another. Both have to be secure in the realization that their marriage is far more important than *any* specific issue.

One woman when asked what made a good marriage replied, "A bad memory." But she might have said "forgiveness." If I had only one wedding gift to give a couple—and the power to give it—it would be that finest of graces: forgiveness.

In Wallerstein's study, it is surprising—and refreshing—how many (both men and women) described their partners admiringly as tolerating "no bullshit." Clarity is of the utmost importance to a marriage relationship, so that neither partner has to go around wondering and worrying about what the hell the other *might* be thinking.

6. Keeping intimacy: Many find the security of marriage makes sex less arousing. No matter what form the marriage takes, there is no arguing with fatigue. Even priapists and nymphomaniacs get tired once in a while. After a few years of marriage, working, keeping ahead of bills, dealing with children, sex no longer seems the overwhelming need it once was—except for that admirable and enviable 15 percent in romantic marriages. To an adolescent, having to make an act of will to have sex seems as inconceivable (to crack the wind of the phrase) as refusing it.

But preserving that active sexual engagement adds powerful strands to the web they are weaving, strengthens self-confidence, and validates one another by lowering the emotional barriers with which they defend themselves during the day from intrusions of work and family. Any couple who can't recall the last time they made love is either headed for the divorce court or has settled for a life of willing servitude. It is a celibate who speaks.

7. Sharing Laughter: When any relationship, even marriage, becomes too serious, some virtue like dutifulness or some vice like a sense of total inadequacy has run amok. Again, one or other has to remember—or be reminded—"Hey! Wait a minute! What's *really* important here?" And the only sane answer is "Us!" This demands not just trading the latest jokes from the office but bantering. Teasing. Tickling. Defusing the bruised ego. Surprising one another. All the virtues of the Trickster.

What was the first stupid gift he gave her that he couldn't afford? I wonder if they still make them. Where are the slides showing him at his absolute worst? What if I put them together with background music from Spike Jones? She'll hate it at first, but let's go bowling, the way we did when we couldn't afford anything "better." The most wonderful thing about a good marriage is the ways we can surprise one another.

8. Providing Soul Nurturance: The absolute essential to a good marriage is paying attention, observing, hearing what is *not* said. Again the model of genuine loving is the good mother. The loving couple must be attuned to one another with the same calm alertness a mother has for an infant. Each must be aware of the other's body language—a skill we learned at the breast, mutely aware when the mother was happy or anxious, a skill we often lose when our focus narrows to ourselves. Each must know when to probe and when to let be, when to josh and when to stroke. Often in studies of divorce one or other partner will say, "I never had the slightest idea she was upset at all."

Each needs support when they feel failure, disappointment, anxiety, discouragement, inadequacy, and they also need someone with whom to share the euphoria of a job well done. When I've directed a show that brought an audience to their feet, I help clean up, lock up, then go back to my room in the dorm, crack a beer alone, and flick on the late news. But I've committed myself to that. It could never keep a marriage together.

Again, we consider "at home" as mother-love, a place to shuck off the armor of forced geniality and gentility. It is most important, no matter what the form of the marriage, that each recognize *both* people need comfort at the end of the day.

> The need for sympathy and for restoration of battered self-esteem, which receives much less press than the search for sexual adventure, is a major component in infidelity.[8]

9. Remembering Romance: Once again, every human being needs time once a week—if not every day—to pause and ponder, regain a sense of self and perspective in the midst of the maelstrom, to give a tune-up to the soul. After all, the soul is at the center of it all. Even more true for a wife and husband balancing commitments like juggling Indian clubs. Not only together but each separately has to take time to let the dishes crash for about fifteen minutes and become calm.

One subject for renewing rumination ought to be "The Way We Were." When did you first meet? Where? How would your life have changed if you'd never taken that very first step of noticing? When was the first time you suspected he or she was worth knowing better? When did you first suspect "this is the one"?

You need time to see how precious he or she is, how precious your marriage is, and if you're honest, how precious you are.

A "We" Made of Two "I's"

Every morning in spring when I walk from my room in the dorm to my office, I pass a dogwood tree. At first it looks like an ordinary dogwood, curly and frothy and white. But then you realize half is white but half is pink. The same tree. Then I found out a crafty gardener had grafted a pink dogwood onto a white dogwood tree. Or vice versa. No one could tell.

And that's what a marriage is all about.

The King James Version of Genesis says, "Therefore shall a man leave his father and his mother, and shall cleave to his wife: and they shall be one flesh." The word *cleave* has two contradictory meanings. One is to sever, to part or disunite, just as the gardener had cut a white (or pink) branch from another dogwood. But the other, opposite meaning of the word *cleave* is to join, to fuse, as the gardener grafted the one branch into the other living tree. And the two became one tree. But neither changed color. White stayed white; pink stayed pink.

A good marriage is a union, but it is neither a 50–50, you-do-your-share-I'll-do-mine legal commitment, nor is it a 100–100, everything-I-have-and-am-is-*yours!* selfless oblation. It's trickier than that. It is a total gift of the self, yet—ironically—without losing a sense of still being a unique human being. We have a fusion of life stories here, and yet there are still two quite different voices telling it.

Even in a fusion as intimate as a marriage, you have to have "a room of your own," a place you can retreat and *be* a self. Otherwise, you become *absorbed* in the other, and by that very fact, you have nothing left to give. And part of the paradox of a good marriage is giving the other person the freedom to be an integral part of who-I-am and yet "not-me." The best guarantor in a relationship without built-in guarantees is the ability to stand alone—together.

You may have noticed I used the word *ironically* several times in this chapter. There's a reason for that.

You can be pink. I can be white. We're still one tree.

There is only one rule: We can work it out.

Chapter Fourteen

—❦—

FORMING THE SOUL OF A FAMILY[1]

It is easier to govern a kingdom than a family.
—Chinese proverb

The humbling delights of Robert Bly's *Iron John* consistently provoke the unguarded response: "I should have thought of that!" One insight is that mythology is full of bad fathers: jealous giants, son-swallowers, absent adventurers. There are no good fathers at all in the major Greek myths (Daedalus, perhaps) and few in Hebrew Scripture or other cultural myths: Cronos, Zeus, Ulysses, Abraham, Isaac, and Jacob come immediately to mind as heartless to sons.

Nor were fathers too commendable in their disposition of daughters: Antigone, Iphegenia, Jephthah's daughter, the female progeny of so many princes, not to mention uncountable female Chinese infants and Inca virgins. Fathers seemed to focus elsewhere, on more important matters than their children. But a major thesis of Bly's book is that, according to those with whom he's spoken in workshops, there are many parent-inflicted wounds on modern young men and women as well.

Like the act which occasions it, the birth of a child automatically sets up an objectively more profound human (therefore, moral) relationship between the two parents and between the parents and the child. But in an age of open minds and options, when commitments are far more precarious than ever before, the rise in statistics on divorce and overt child abuse show, in our day, that objective moral responsibility is less often subjectively acknowledged and fulfilled than it was by the Waltons.

For the first couple of years, other than the goo-goo eyes, there isn't much return from the child for all the time, energy, money, toil, and availability a parent is called upon to surrender. In fact, the parent-infant relationship is strictly one-way: unconditional, no matter what the infant does. But for young parents trained by the media never to submit even to inconvenience and whose interest in school or work lasts only as long as the rewards are consistently forthcoming, the commitment to the child can wear very thin, very fast.

The fulcrum on which the family balances is the fusion of the parents. If there are unheeded and unhealed cracks in that balancing point, it is only a matter of time before the child begins to sway dizzyingly and pay psychologically—often for a lifetime—for shortcomings he is neither aware nor guilty of.

What's more, although there are whole libraries of books for new parents, at least to my knowledge there are not many about dealing with children—and with one another—once the child has graduated from the pediatrician. If such books exist and are read, they haven't worked in far too many pitiful cases.

All but the best parents seem to have unquestioningly accepted the Spartan way as a guide to handling children. Too many (especially fathers) narrow their role in the child's psychological growth to caring administrators: providers, arbitrators, life-managers. Their task is to "give them the best" and keep them from hurting others, themselves, and the family. Many children describe a parent more like a waspish Gradgrind than the imperturbable Atticus Finch. (In accepting the assessment, be careful to check the vested interests of the source.)

Even the kindliest parents seem to believe that for an unacceptable act there must be some kind of "eye for an eye," that saying you're sorry—or even just asking forgiveness—is not enough. For the good of the child. Left-brain justice in the name of—and too often instead of—right-brain love.

This surely has been mirrored (if not even caused by) the habitual treatment of the undisciplined by civic and religious authority: a defendant or penitent must disgorge the particulars of at least each serious offense and be given a salutary punishment or penance to "make amends." This surely can't help but affect the attitudes of diligent parents toward their children's breaches of "the rules."

Discerning / Deciding

Parents could do worse than read or reread Harper Lee's *To Kill a Mockingbird*—or rent the film—to find at least provocative clues to good parenting. In one scene, because a spiteful, sickly old woman has accused Atticus Finch of being "no better than trash" for defending a Negro in court, his son, Jem, has—with equal spite—uprooted the old woman's garden. Atticus doesn't impose an arbitrary sanction on the boy "in reparation." Instead, he says,

> Son, I have no doubt you've been annoyed by your contemporaries about me lawing for niggers, as

> you say, but to do something like this to a sick old
> lady is inexcusable. I strongly advise you to go over
> and have a talk with Mrs. Dubose.[2]

Not "order"; "I strongly advise." The boy is free to take responsibility for his actions. Or not. Atticus is trusting enough to let the decision twist around *within* the boy's own conscience, rather than "setting things right" with a father's fiat. The persuasive factor is not that Atticus has the *political* authority of the "office" of father; rather, he has the consistently proven *moral* authority of being a wise man. Wisdom is not "bestowed" by physical parenthood; it is achieved, beginning long before Atticus was a father. And the result is that the act of conscience goes on inside the boy, not just outside. Jem's soul is more important to Atticus than Mrs. Dubose's garden.

As a result, Jem himself suggested he work on Mrs. Dubose's garden until it grew back. Wouldn't it be better if a parent said, "Could you help me understand why you did that?"—*first,* before imposing punishment? Atticus shows he understands—empathizes with—the "reasons" that impelled his son to such an impetuous act. But his *way* of making the boy understand has more to do with helping the boy understand his relationships with other people than his relationship to the law—which was formed for people who didn't have parents like Atticus. Rehabilitation is more important than retribution.

Would parents be better off, then, holding back the heat of their own anger, to ask, "What do you think would be a good way to make it up—not just for her sake, but for your sake, so you could go back to feeling good about yourself?" Better that than the easier-to-hand—and therefore more usual—"God says . . . It was a sin . . . You broke the law . . . You're grounded! . . . Because I said so!"

If some action is immoral—less than human—a parent has to find a motivation based sheerly on *reason* alone. To the young, appeal to the Bible is appeal to an unread book. For most, God is a distant and shadowy figure. What's more, God becomes involved only as the heavy, like "You wait till your *father* comes home, young lady!" (Odd, too: when they're skateboarding or frolicking in the pool, they're just kids; when they've done something wrong, it's "young man, young lady." Worth pondering.)

"Because I said so" quite often "does the job," that is, it closes the question and ends the dispute. But nothing's changed *inside* the child. If the task of all teachers, including parents, is to render themselves unnecessary, to help a child evolve a self who will act morally—not because it is the law or because "everybody knows" or because "I say" but because the child *wants* to do what is humanly right, then the parents have to find ways to *convince* the child that this action is right and that action is wrong. Doing that takes longer than a quick, decisive decree. But it also lasts longer.

You can get lots more mileage when you can prove *whatever* you claim sheerly on the basis of reason, especially about morality, and most especially about sexual morality. Our young—and some not-so-young—have the ludicrous idea such-and-such is a sin *because* the law-church-Bible say so. That, of course, is ridiculous. It was wicked for Cain to slay Abel, even though civil law, commandments, and churches didn't yet exist. Rather, reason shows that this act is beneath the dignity of humans—perpetrator and victim—and therefore the law is formed. Unless we find convincing evidence for what we teach from *reason alone,* we are preaching to the deaf.

Unlike any other teachers, parents must show not only *that* an action is unseemly or unacceptable but *why* that is true. Unlike any other teachers, they are trying not only to fill them with data but to change beliefs and behavior.

Morality "v." Compassion

Morality is incumbent on us merely on the basis of our common human nature. Every fair-minded atheist holds the same tenets about moral behavior to outcasts, the disenfranchised, prisoners of war, or atomic bombs as any religious believer. But believers—and sensitive atheists—take upon themselves the further burden of compassion even for those who don't "deserve" it: the victims of societally unacceptable or personally induced suffering—the homosexual; the chemical addict; the pregnant teenager; the divorced; the suicidal; the third-generation welfare recipient. Difficult to elicit compassion for such victims in the young, even though supposedly brainwashed by parents for 20 years. And much of that resistance, sadly, comes from their parents.

They've also told the same kids: "Never talk to strangers; push down all the door buttons; don't be a sucker."

I'm not sure I know how to *teach* compassion. I always thought kids learn empathy intuitively from parents, or not. Yet a family's task is not merely to produce law-abiding citizens but people of compassion. No matter how obdurate the audience.

My mentor, Atticus Finch, puts it as well as I've ever heard it when he tells his daughter, Scout: "You never really understand a person until . . . you climb into his skin and walk around in it." But every year I give a reaction paper asking students to pick out the greatest "outcast" in their year and "get inside that person's skin and walk around in it awhile; tell me what it's like to face a typical day *as* that person." Almost without exception, the descriptions are totally from the *out*side: how others react to that person, not how the person feels inside. They "feel sorry" for the person, but they can't bring themselves to *become* that person, to have compassion for him or her—not *pity,* but fellow-feeling, which is what, in fact, compassion means: "I suffer *with* you." But perhaps it's unfair to ask kids to understand what it's like inside someone else's skin when they can't understand the person walking around in their own skin.

Vulnerability

Too many parents put the children's need for security above the children's need to grow, despite the evident fact that insecurity —disequilibrium—is the requisite for growth as a human individual. Judith Guest's novel *Ordinary People* (or the Robert Redford film) is another casebook for parents, this time about the disintegration of a family.

After the unexpected tragedy of one son's drowning and the other's attempted suicide out of guilt for surviving, the mother copes by attempting to keep everything "in control": the napkin rings, her son's frayed collars, the neighbors' opinions. When Conrad, the survivor, sees a psychiatrist, what he wants is "control," and when in the end he and his father finally speak to one another as friends, sharing their separate weaknesses, he says, "I always used to think you had a handle on everything."

Too many parents try—from the best of motives—at least to give the appearance they have "a handle on everything," in order to shield children from suffering. But as Jung points out, neurosis is always a defense against *legitimate* suffering. Life is difficult and uncertain; to shield at least adolescents from that truth is not kindness. Parents' credibility is not threatened but rather enhanced by an honest and vulnerable sharing of their own acknowledged shortcomings. It is the only way the child can get inside the *parents'* skin and walk around in it awhile. To shield children from the truth is to shield them not only from life but from developing compassion.

It would cost parents a great deal more to share their past mistakes with their children than to openly admit them to one another. No difficulty (for the parent) in recalling one's Horatio Alger childhood, trudging through the snow to school ("Right! Uphill both ways."). But parents claim they feel they must project a kind of "dependable ideal" to give children a sense of security. Some truth in that, but one wonders if the real reason is it would be so embarrassing to the parents.

There are at least three reasons to entertain the possibility of speaking openly with adolescents about past weaknesses.

First, warnings that "You're going to regret that, young lady" give the youngster the idea the parents have some kind of crystal ball or else some morbid appetite for authority, when in fact the parents have been around the track far more than the youngster and have seen—or experienced—again and again, exactly the same situation *and* its inevitable outcome.

Second, how would the relationship between parent and child change if, instead of "Don't do that . . . Stop doing that," the father said, "Look, son, I had troubles with masturbation too," and the mother said, "Honey, I know what it's like to be boy crazy and have catty girlfriends. You know what I did once?" Sharing weakness is not a weakness.

Third, it is always easier for anyone to confess mistakes to a wounded healer. If children know the "impeccable" parents made mistakes, too, their own mistakes become no less real but less needful of being kept hidden.

Too many children ultimately end up going to psychiatrists because they have never been able honestly to vent their feelings and confusions to their own parents. "My God! He'd be the *last* one I'd tell!" The suppressed feelings—justified or not—don't go away; they retire inward and build up steam that will sooner or later demand release, sometimes volcanically.

It behooves parents at least to consider mechanisms for venting that frustration, analyzing it calmly together, and coming to at least a tentative conclusion. One such way might be to take a tip from the old practice in monasteries of "Chapter," in which each member of the family is allowed (tactfully and charitably) to air his or her beefs about the "community": preferential treatment, rules that seem unreasonable, etc. Bring the wounds out into the air to be acknowledged and perhaps healed. Then, when the session is over, everybody (again, even under blood-oath beforehand!) has to give everybody else a heartfelt hug and leave the grudges in the middle of the table.

There are also at least three basic elements to a happy family: communication, compassion, and forgiveness—all of which can be summed up in one word: vulnerability.

Communication is an easy word for counselors of all types to bandy about. But we often forget—I surely do—that genuine communication is not just telling the other person all you know, even your most shameful secrets. That's only one side of a two-way street. You also must *listen,* really listen, looking the other person right in the eyes. You can't do that and tinker with a faucet or finish the ironing at the same time. Quite often—maybe *most* often—you won't have any personal, inherent interest in what the child is saying. But that's where the love comes in: the child is more important than what he or she is saying.

What's more, you can't teach a child until you know where the child is, until you hear their words with their minds, setting aside your own cherished convictions and surefire solutions. In short, getting inside his or her skin yourself. That legitimates my writing about teenagers: I'm incessantly giving surveys, questionnaires, and reaction papers—to see what they really think. Before I try to change their minds, I have to find where their minds are.

The overall effect on a person who is genuinely listened to is an increase in self-esteem: somebody affirms that what I say—or at least *I*—am worth listening to. And without self-esteem, no one can have the courage to get inside somebody *else's* skin and walk around in it awhile.

Not a bad idea for spouses (the fulcrum) too. Maybe he's not interested in her story about the dingbat at the drugstore, and she's not overwhelmed by his day with the Dweeb account. That's not the question; the question is whether they're genuinely interested in one another. Romance—being-in-love—is effortless; love is in an act of will. Love is hard work.

It is very difficult to get *outside* one's own preconceptions and inside someone else's skin. How does a parent, for instance, put aside for a moment all the principles he or she has wrestled a lifetime for—to say nothing of the blind biases we can't even admit—in order to understand and *forgive* a son who declares he's homosexual or a daughter who's pregnant?

How do parents get around the wound inflicted on *them* by their child's wounds? How does a youngster lay aside the confusion and hurt in order to understand and forgive the alcoholic mother or the father who went off with someone else? How does a sister understand and forgive a brother who has betrayed her trust? That's what parents must teach. Otherwise, the pain moves inward and festers forever.

At times, of course, the understanding and compassion are there, but the words are not. At times, the shared truth is too enormous for words, as at a wake, and the only answer is arms around one another and mute tears. The family which has a barrier against touch and tears will find their mutual life far more difficult than families more comfortable with vulnerability.

And in that one word, I think we come at last to the bedrock answer: vulnerability—the one quality which ultimately separates human beings from animals. Animals always have their guard up, are always defensive, always frightened by change. And we are partly animals, even though our human nature is an invitation to go further: to know more, to love more, to grow more. But that invitation to be more than merely high-level animals can be refused, as witness serial murderers. Again, there is a whole spectrum of "human," stretching from Hitler to Helen Keller.

What's more, even though we do accept the invitation to grow beyond our animal origins, we never leave our animal natures behind. If we did, we could pension off all soul-healers.

No parent can compete with a biology teacher. Whenever I give a survey that says "Self-preservation is the most basic law of specifically *human* life," almost all invariably check "True." Try vulnerability with that bunch. But it is the bunch we have.

And without vulnerability humanity is impossible. If we differ from our animal forebears in that we can learn and love, vulnerability is the sine qua non.

How can we learn unless we're vulnerable to the truth, no matter where the truth leads, no matter how much acknowledging the truth threatens what we've so long cherished? You can prove inescapably that casual sex is less than human, merely two animals coupling, and therefore immoral (less than human). But will youngsters set up a howl! Why? Because accepting the truth would mean they have to give up something they like very much.

How can one love unless he or she is vulnerable to the beloved, no matter how inconvenient the beloved's requests, no matter how unlikable the beloved is at the moment? If you want a reason so many recent marriages break up, there it is: a union of two Teflon invulnerabilities. Once the love potion neuters down, it's time to dig out the prenuptial agreement.

And compassion is impossible without the self-esteem which allows one to be vulnerable. How can you get inside someone else's skin when your own skin is a fortress, beyond which everything becomes less and less "real" the further it gets from the focus of all reality? How can you genuinely understand another, yield your defenses to his or her pain? How can even a parent say, "I'm ashamed you did that. But right now your shame is more important than my shame"?

That, of course, is what a liberal education is for—or ought to be: to give people the ability to read books, climb inside other people's skins and walk around in them awhile. But my experience in more than a few schools says the analytical left brain reigns supreme. Poems, plays, and novels are intended not to move the soul but to serve as analysis fodder. Beyond the empty rhetoric of the catalogues, the hard-nosed transcript and the SAT scores are what really count. Vulnerability seems harder and harder to come by.

But I don't think it's impossible. One real way to educe vulnerability in the young is extracurricular activities, and parents who allow a child to leave school at the last bell ought to get a third of their taxes or tuition back. Being on a team forces you to put your trust in someone else, which is the beginning of vulnerability. Most especially plays are a way to get inside another person's skin and walk around in it awhile, to explore the motivations of someone you may not even particularly like.

And when that curtain goes up, you're out there swingin' slowly, slowly in the wind. What'll happen if you forget your lines? What'll happen if whoever's supposed to come on *doesn't* come on? But at the curtain calls you find in a way beyond words or question: being vulnerable pays off. As one teary football player said after his first play (in which he *danced)*, "I never realized. In a play, everybody wins."

I've been thinking of that reaction paper about getting inside an outcast's skin, the one that failed. I now think I have at least *an* answer. Next time, I'm going to ask them to close their eyes and pretend there's a full moon and, like Wolfman, they're slowly metamorphosing into that outcast: "Your hair is slowly changing into her hair, her skin, her clothes, her smells; look at the family picture on her desk and her parents and siblings become your parents and siblings; now, walking inside her body, describe an average lunch in the cafeteria."

You see? The problem isn't in the kids; the problem's in me. I'm the adult. If a communication doesn't get through, it's always the sender's fault, not the receiver's. As the psychologist Jerome Bruner said, you can teach anything to any child, at any stage of his or her development, *provided* you can adapt it to their receptivities. That's every parent's job.

Kids *want* to be vulnerable; they *want* to be an organic part of something bigger than themselves; they *want* to know and love. After all, that's their *human nature,* inviting them. But they're afraid. Afraid to be hurt again. What we have to do is be relentless in our efforts to build their trust, their self-esteem, their willingness to risk losing something good—like their security—in order to get something better—like love.

My patron saint as a teacher is Annie Sullivan. How many weeks did she draw incomprehensible signs in Helen Keller's stubbornly resistant hands? But she trusted; she trusted Helen, and more importantly she trusted herself, that she *would* find a way inside Helen's defenses.

There's a way into every kid's skin. And I have a hunch a loving, patient parent can find it.

Chapter Fifteen

⁓᠙ ⋅⋆⋅ ᠙⁓

THE SOUL OF THE EARTH

I think it pisses God off if you walk by the color purple in a field somewhere and don't notice it. . . . People think pleasing God is all God care about. But any fool living in the world can see it always trying to please us back. . . . It always making little surprises and springing them on us when we least expect. . . . Everything want to be loved. Us sing and dance, make faces and give flower bouquets, trying to be loved. You ever notice that trees do everything to git attention we do, except walk? . . .

Man corrupt everything. He on your box of grits, in your head, and all over the radio. He try to make you think he everywhere. Soon as you think he everywhere, you think he God. But he ain't. Whenever you try to pray, and man plop himself on the other end of it, tell him to git lost. Conjure up flowers, wind, water, a big rock.

Shug to Miss Celie in Alice Walker's *The Color Purple*[1]

We've considered the soul in itself and within the web of human relationships which is society. Now might be time to move further out, beyond the visible web, not yet to a transcendent divine, if such exists, but at least to a sense of the transcendent which each of us—probably without exception—has personally experienced. It is, perhaps, the vapor trail of the divine.

The premise of the profane world is that no one who watches TV or uses an electric razor or a computer can believe in the immaterial and intangible. Which implies that we moderns do have an unadulterated, clear-eyed view of what *can* be real. Yet by far most of the realities in the rooms where I type and you read are there, but unseen: electrons whizzing about, fanning out into rays then sucking in their tummies to become pellets; radio signals leaking around every room, and all you have to do is plug in a set to prove it; we see hardly any of the light spectrum—not ultraviolet, infrared—and yet they're there. "There are more things in heaven and earth, Horatio, than are dreamt of in your philosophy." Is it possible angels and demons go on existing despite our inability to accept them? Neutrinos do.

Yet we are most often too busy even to consider such things, much less sense them. There is too much noise and neon, too many serious problems in the papers, too many promises to keep.

As Hopkins wrote more than a century ago:

> And all is seared with trade; bleared, smeared with
>   toil;
> And wears man's smudge and shares man's smell:
>   the soil
> Is bare now, nor can foot feel, being shod.[2]

In the utilitarian society we develop a numbness, the incapacity to feel. Monkeys raised away from their mothers become sullen and irritable. The same is true of us when we are no longer "at home"; we exude a protective sheath of indifference because there is just too much there to cope with. Walking down a corridor at the office or school, pushing through the crowd on a street, we armor ourselves from seeing or hearing— except perhaps the pounding defense of the Walkman. Sometime, make up your mind really to *focus* on the faces you walk past day after day and count how many you have never seen before. Never "allowed" to become real.

Our inner cities are jungles, populated by humans unaware they have a higher calling. Old tires, abandoned appliances and furniture, paper, garbage, rusty cars, forsaken houses, weeds, noise. We never notice them anymore unless they are blatant. The soullessness. No one feels the smothering, inhuman rage that sprayed the graffiti. Rationalism, opportunism, enlightened self-interest have freed us from the gods of the wood, from superstition, but we've lost our souls. We don't turn to devils but to anesthesia. The Earth Mother is demythologized into nothing more than dirt, which we cannot even feel, "being shod." We are so weakened by spiritual anemia we have lost even our sense of evil.

Yet there are moments, rare but real, when we are ambushed by a sense of human life, of the universal animatedness of every-thing, the atoms carousing, the neutrinos roadrunning through it all, hardly slowed down, even by the whole earth. There's a suspicion of more, much more than we see or suspect.

At times we are suddenly caught by the breathtaking fire-folk hanging overhead in the dark of a summer night, an endless display of stars whose light began to travel toward Earth before there were humans. Or less dramatically, we suddenly become aware of the rhythm of the rain, the keening of wind through the arms of trees, the harrumph of waves on a beach. The athlete "loses" himself in the game, yet never felt more a self. We feel the precarious magic of being alive when we walk away from an accident, hear the call to stand down from battle, know "she's going to pull through." As surprising and unexpected as a rainbow.

Such flashes of unreasoned insight and delight snatch us by surprise because for some reason we were caught "off guard" a moment. No one can force them to happen, only be *open* to them, which we rarely allow ourselves to be: open to the awesome. Awe is not simply an emotion; it is an intuitional insight into the largeness and richness of our *context*. We sense a *presence* around us, more than meets the eye. And unlike the momentary highs from LSD or mescaline, we don't feel let down afterward.

The poet James Russell Lowell captures such a moment:

> I remember the night, and almost the very spot on
> the hilltop, where my soul opened out, as it were,
> into the Infinite, and there was a rushing together
> of the two worlds, the inner and the outer. . . . I
> could not any more have doubted that *He* was
> there than that I was. Indeed, I felt myself to be, if
> possible, the less real of the two.[3]

Such experiences, momentous or modest, are moments of ecstasy (*ekstasis,* standing outside). Not the transports of mysticism, yet not unlike them: a chance to stand outside the everyday, the pedestrian, the commonplace.

These are experiences of the *numinous,* an elevating "presence" which is real but inexplicable. William James writes:

> It is as if there were in the human consciousness
> a sense of a reality, a feeling of objective presence,
> a perception of what we may call "something
> there," more deep and more general than any of
> the special and particular senses.[4]

They are natural experiences of nonphysical reality, when we enter a real world within but beyond the "real" world—at one time both immanent and transcendent, a place with its own rules and a unique sacredness: falling in love, art, music, story-telling, play (especially running, when after a couple of miles you break "out of time"), sports (when they're really sportive), genuinely loving sex. It is a rare time of honest, humble *appreciation*. Each experience is ecstatic in the sense we do "stand outside" ourselves for a few moments. Humor, for instance, lets us see our tense human strivings as they really are—not only see but feel, and we have to chuckle. At least for the moment we are freed from the empirical, this-worldly, secular, pragmatic, utilitarian, contractual and hedonistic.

A dynamic contact with the numinous cannot be caused by an arbitrary act of the will, any more than we can preprogram our dreams. On the contrary, it seizes and controls the human subject, who is always rather its victim than its creator. It is the influence of an invisible *presence* to which or to whom I am fully present, a moment of attentive consciousness without content. What Gerald May calls a "unitive experience," Maslow called "peak experiences," and Heidegger called *dasein:* "being there"—when you gain authentic elevation as a human being.

Peak experiences can't last. We couldn't endure them longer any more than our hearts could stand an hour-long orgasm. But the difference between a unitive experience and a drug high is that it gives way to serenity and can last, like fireflies in a bottle. It revivifies our hope in what life can deliver.

In a 1945 letter to P. W. Martin, Carl Jung wrote:

> The main content of my work is not concerned with the treatment of neuroses but rather with the approach to the numinous. But the fact is that the

approach to the numinous is the real therapy and inasmuch as you attain the numinous experiences you are released from the curse of pathology.[5]

Our incapacity for delight arises not only because of intrusions from a noisy, demanding, heartless ethos but also from within: from all we've surrendered to become adults—or at least to seem like adults. Holden Caulfield saw it, far too clearly: most adults are "phony bastards" who have forsworn the innocence of children like Phoebe and Allie, who have abdicated imagination, wonder, awe, the willingness to be overwhelmed— because that would mean we must put down our guards, which in a society of constant low-grade paranoia seems suicidal, a death wish, when it is in fact precisely the opposite.

> [Wonder] is a quality, like playfulness, that is found in nearly all children unless they have had it stamped out of them. The insatiable thirst for learning emerges out of wonder. . . . The world for children has a magical quality, and it is still possible to have faith in Love. We also find the same quality in the greatest scientists, such as Einstein, Heisenberg, Jung, Madame Curie, and Gödel. This quality is also the essence of scientific discovery.[6]

Nor is imagination at odds with knowledge. It is indeed a way of *illuminating* facts. But insights through imagination will be more ambiguous, more open-ended than strict formulas and definitions. When asked what a dance meant, the great choreographer Martha Graham said: "Mean? Darlings, if I could *tell* you, I wouldn't have *danced* it!" If you want to "understand" Handel's *Messiah,* I don't hand you the score. If you want to know why fans love baseball, it will be of little help to study the physics and geometry of the game. In all those cases—and in the case of the numinous—you have to experience them. And you have to develop a sensitivity to it, to evolve the *potential* within you, in order to apprehend the sacred in our midst.

The root of the word *ecology* is the Greek *oikos,* "home." Just as our humanity invites us to evolve a soul so we can feel "at home" within ourselves, within our marriages, within our families, so it invites us to contact the *anima mundi,* the soul of the earth. The soul is the source of aliveness: the spirit. When it is gone, I am gone. We *share* life with everything on this planet and are meant to feel "at home" here. Native Americans felt it profoundly. When the government wrote Chief Seattle in 1852 with an offer to buy Indian land, he wrote back:

> The earth does not belong to man, man belongs to the earth. All things are connected like the blood that unites us all. We did not weave the web of life, we are merely a strand in it. Whatever we do to the web, we do to ourselves. . . . Your destiny is a mystery to us. What will happen when the buffalo are all slaughtered? The wild horses tamed? What will happen when the secret corners of the forest are heavy with the scent of many people and the view of the ripe hills is blotted by talking wires? . . . The end of living and the beginning of survival.[7]

In experiences of that numinous presence of which Seattle was so well aware, we can be suspended in an "eternal present," having a sense there is more to life than we've settled for. It is an intuition of the eternal in the temporal, perhaps contact with the Beyond in our midst.

Chapter Sixteen

———— ❦ ·•· ❦ ————

THE ULTIMATE MYSTERY

The world is charged with the grandeur of God.
It will flame out, like shining from shook foil.

Gerard Manley Hopkins—*"God's Grandeur"*[1]

The philosopher Thales of Miletus said "Everything is full of gods." All round us, if we are not totally unaware, we sense rumors of something more, challenging the world of triviality with which most of us fear we must content ourselves: another rock star overdoses; another housewife induces her teen lover to kill her husband; another legend divorces and remarries. Is that all there is? Resignation to a world where abuse, litigation, hostile takeovers, betrayals are merely "the order of things"?

Whether a terminus of the soul's fulfillment exists or not, something healthy in our souls yearns for something "steady" in our lives, something unsullied, not "seared with trade;

bleared, smeared with toil." Just as our souls want to be "at home" in the chaos of the world, we also want to be "at home" even in the face of death, even in the face of endless space. We long for something *not* transitory, *not* untrustworthy, *not* corruptible. We want something permanent, dependable, sacred.

We get hints—vapor trails.

Oddly, we seem the only species with a sense of the sacred—odd, since like so many other human potentials (the hunger for answers, the desire to survive death) such a hankering makes no sense if in fact the universe, the environment, and we ourselves are no more than machines reacting to electrochemical stimuli.

This sense of the sacred, as we saw, seems not just wishful thinking but an involuntary reaction to "something" actually *there.* On one hand we hesitate to yield to it because it smacks so naively of primitive religion, the animism which "gave" not only life but divinity to thunder, waterfalls, mountains. Yet on the other hand, except in the most shallowly sophisticated, the hankering persists. Perhaps no more than an atavistic throwback, like uneasiness passing a graveyard at night or unwillingness to walk under a ladder, no matter how silly it seems. Yet this yearning for the sacred is not a negative reaction of fear, but a desire for something quite positive: affirmation, enlivening, a *connection* with the source of this energy we catch hints of.

The key, I think, is to separate a sacredness we *impose* on an object from a sacredness we *respond* to. Humans have charged objects with holiness from the beginning: totems, amulets, stones—objects set aside from the secular and mundane. But we forget such an investiture of power was *not* the beginning, that before the tribe hallowed an object or place, the people had *felt* a presence there and only afterward solemnized it.

This historical "smearing" is paralleled in a smearing of words. We take holy to mean "completely good," in the moral sense of being uncorrupted, without sin (negative). But the Greek, Semitic, and Latin meanings go *beyond* morality to a real quality: the presence of the numinous (positive), the *transcendent,* the supernatural *in* our immanent world, what Bonhoeffer called "the Beyond in our midst."

Further, pictures we see in churches, cartoons of heaven, lead us unconsciously to believe that *supernatural* means physically above us, as in "superstructure": above the clouds, over the rainbow. But if there is in fact a dimension to reality independent of the immanent limitations of time and space, "above" has no meaning in that way of being real. Nor do "before and after."

Rather, supernatural means highly intensified, as in *supercharged,* an infusion of greater aliveness from another dimension of being real, which permeates and enlivens the nature which was already there. In fact that supernatural infusion—what many have called "grace"—does make us truly "superhuman." The objective foundation for such a belief, of course, is impervious to testing by scientific method or mechanical means. The only norm to validate its presence is in the *effects* in the everyday lives of those who claim to have made a connection to that transcendent energy: Do they in fact lead "supercharged" lives? Are their habitual ways of living more graceful, more gracious?

We are not speaking of formal religion here (nor will we), but of a lowercase religion, since the word *religare* does mean "to connect." What we ordinarily think of when we use the word *religion* or *religious* is people who regularly attend a church, mosque, synagogue. Such activities can indeed energize, uplift, supernaturalize human lives, but they are not automatically efficacious, like dropping in to the mechanic's for a tune-up. What's more, high-church worship can easily devolve into artistic performance and response to it, and low-church worship can easily devolve into moral challenge and uplift.

Both response to art and moral challenge are very laudable and even effective in energizing the heart and soul and bringing about positive social change—but they are still stranded on the strictly human, natural level. Henry James went into raptures about the beauties of Chartres, but he had no connection with the experience which motivated its creation. Humanly valuable, but still not supernatural. Unless there is a genuine receptivity within the participants, a true vulnerability to a transcendent "connection," there is no real religion, just worthy humanism.

Perhaps one can capture the difference in a homely way by considering tourists. Some "pass through," snapping pictures at every turn, the Parthenon, the Venus de Milo, Stonehenge, so they can "possess" them and when they get home prove to their friends (and themselves) that they were "there."

Other tourists don't travel nearly so widely or quickly. They become enthralled with the curves and heft and sheen of Michelangelo's David and just stand in awe. There is a "connection," this-worldly to be sure, but enlivening of the human soul. A true religious experience is that same connection, but beyond the human.

Like the link between the viewer and the numinous presence in the sublime "emanations" in art and nature, the link between the "victim" of a supernatural experience and its source is not an experience one can possess or even comprehend in any way to be able to communicate the experience satisfactorily to someone else. But we can *encounter* it, relate ourselves to it. We can't manipulate it, but we can allow ourselves to manipulated by it.

Empiricism / Mystery

Experience of the sacred is no more irrational than experience of sex is irrational. As explaining orgasm to a 10-year-old is impossible, so explaining communication with the transcendent is futile. With both, one has to experience it to have even the remotest beginnings of understanding it.

What's more, we've known since 1932, when Heisenberg won the Nobel Prize for the Principle of Uncertainty, that even models of *physics* are no more than approximate metaphors for realities we can't see. As Jung wrote, "It is almost ridiculous prejudice to assume existence can be only physical." And in the end, the exclusively secular world's denial of the supernatural becomes the triumph of the trivial, since all medals, profits, condominiums, and skyscrapers shrivel into Lilliputian perspective in the face of the ultimate Gulliver—Death.

Even at the heart of physical science, then, there is a core of mystery, which led Einstein to say, "The most beautiful thing we can experience is the mysterious." We work on the unspoken belief that all questions are solvable. Yet the Hebrew story of the gentile Job poses at least one mystery for which we have no satisfying solution, much less a dogmatic scientific certitude: the existence of unmerited suffering, especially of children. It rankled in Ivan Karamazov as well, the injustice of it if there is a provident God, the absurdity of it if there is not.

The "solution" at the end of Job is not a solution at all, at least not a solution of Job's rational craving for an answer but rather a solution of his soul's agony. Job does not "solve his problem," rather, he "sees the light." The Presence which comes to him in the depths of the hurricane does not *give* an answer but *is* the answer, which Job does not possess but *experiences.* "In the past I knew only what others have told me, but now I have seen you with my own eyes."[2] What Job understands at the end of his torment is the humbling, disturbing truth that if God exists God is not answerable to us.

Socrates offered a similar insight when he said the first requirement for someone in search of wisdom is *humility.* Only those are wise who sincerely confess they are not.

Any human person is another example of a mystery. You can accumulate the vital statistics, the family tree, the full survey of opinions, the SATs, the Meyers-Briggs, thematic apperception results, credit rating, and so forth, but you still have no more than a left-brain stereotype, perhaps a rough map to start out with. But the person remains uniquely elusive. What you have is no more the person than a play script is a performance.

The only alternatives to making peace with mystery are the futile attempt to "solve" it or the impoverishing choice to ignore it. Chesterton said poets don't go mad, chess players do; chess players try to cross the infinite sea, thus making it finite, while poets simply float on the infinite sea and enjoy its infinite mysteries. Spiritual "understanding" is not like other understandings, dealing with realities that can be objectified, captured, mastered, used—the way one might break and use a mustang. On the contrary, if we are humble enough, it captures us, masters us, uses us.

Hard-eyed rationalism works on the belief that what is can be known, which is as naive as saying, if there was a murderer, he *will* be found—as he is in murder "mysteries" (which are not mysteries at all but only problems, whose solution the author already has, otherwise the book would never be published). And each of us has unquestionable and repeated experience of questions for which we can find no satisfying answers, not even in a lifetime: the mystery of love, the ease of evil and the cost of honor, the prosperity of the devious and the failure of the good-souled, the meaning of suffering, the persistence of death—and of the question of what may or may not lie behind it.

A mystery is always "beyond words," not because it can't be discerned but because one can begin to understand its inner truths only by going through a process—not just a routine rite but a vulnerable submission to a soul-experience. Siddhartha left the Buddha because wisdom can't come through words but only through *contemplation*.

A Mind Behind It All

Nevertheless, the rationalist hesitation persists even in the most open-minded. In fact, the fear of being hoaxed by a rootless spiritualism is the prime obstacle even to giving a chance to a soul-experience. After all, many atheists have been geniuses (as have many believers). Many are agnostic, incapable of commitment one way or other because there is no evidence sufficient to compel assent to the existence of a deity, a Mind Behind It All. The only fourth alternative is complete indifference to the question, which appears to be the most common response, dealing with the problems on your plate and leaving such conundrums to philosophers. "Who *cares* about these questions?" People who think.

A well-researched atheism is an honorable position, as is a well-researched theism. Agnosticism is honorable, but only for so long. Like committing to a marriage, if you wait to commit yourself on the God question until you have Cartesian certitude—"so clear and distinct I have no occasion to doubt it," you will stand at the crossroads forever. Such evidence doesn't exist.

Of the four postures on the existence of a Supreme Being, only indifference is dishonorable. If someone insists the question is unimportant, put him or her in a foxhole with tracers whizzing overhead, or at the wake of a 17-year-old murdered for five dollars, or in a dayroom filled with impaired children. If they still insist the question of a Mind Behind It All is inconsequential, they have "said" more about their own intelligence and sensitivity than about the question.

"The Mind Behind It All" is nonspecific. It does not limit itself to Yahweh, the Trinity, the Oversoul, Allah, or any other attempt by a particular creed to capture it. (Nor will we.) The only issue is whether there is an Entity outside our minds to *validate* the idea of a Supreme Being, which even atheists have.

Finally, whatever answer one arrives at will never enjoy the certitude a genuine agnostic craves. The best one can hope for is a high degree of *probability* that either atheism is the truth or theism is. There is no other alternative; *either* a Higher Power exists or not, just as one is either pregnant or not. If that Power exists, all our denials will not make it go away; if it doesn't exist, the most profound belief will not make it real. One can only search the clues and see which is the *more* probable answer. "Scientific proof" could offer no better.

Atheism

Atheism has its appeal and its drawbacks. In the first place, no one has literally seen God; you can argue scientifically only from visible effects to invisible causes. We can be sure of the existence of invisible subatomic particles because the only plausible explanation for certain effects is the existence of such causes. An atomic explosion is pretty solid evidence. But, atheists argue, you can't set up such an experiment to validate the existence of an invisible God.

An even more suasive argument is the existence of evil, both physical and moral. If there were a benevolent and all-knowing creator, would that Mind have consented (as Ivan Karamazov demanded) to create a universe in which even one innocent child suffered? Would such a supposed Deity give freedom to apes?

However, if atheism is the truth, we face a bleak life and a bleaker death. "If there is no God," Ivan says, *"anything* is permissible." And he is right. If there is no power higher than human who differentiates between objective good and evil, then there is no such thing as right and wrong, and as Nietzsche insisted, the liberated soul who grasps that truth realizes "I, then, am God." The Superman *legislates* right and wrong, arbitrarily according to his lights and whims. Worse, if there is no Higher Power, death wipes out *all* as far as each of us is concerned. All achievements, triumphs, integrity, loves are annihilated as cleanly as a power outage on a computer, since that is all death actually is.

We are freed from guilt, but we know the handsome prince will never come, and hell began the day we were born.

Theism

What solid evidence and reasoning do I have to validate my belief that there is a greater probability of a Mind Behind It All? I believe I have both notional and real evidence.

Notional knowledge is secondhand, academic, and probable—depending on the thoroughness of my research and argument. I have only notional knowledge of the value of honesty over dishonesty, why I am particularly apprehensive today, whether my friend's profession of affection is genuine or sham. But I start from the real effects and reason, by induction and deduction, to their most probable causes. I have only notional evidence that China, atoms, or the *e coli* virus exist, since I've never experienced them, but I take it on the word of more knowledgeable people who have no apparent motive to lie.

Real knowledge is firsthand, experiential, and certain. I don't *believe* I'm sitting at this machine; I'm sure of it. Seeing is not believing; seeing is knowing. I don't argue to a belief that I should be a teacher; I know it; a lifetime of experience has validated it. I have no firsthand experience at the moment of our kitchen, but common sense tells me there's little likelihood someone cleared it out while I've been tap-tap-tapping away.

Let me lay the evidence out schematically first to serve as a reference as we go:

NOTIONAL EVIDENCE
    —A. Reason: my intelligence
        —1. no effect > causes
            —a. Intelligence
            —b. Universe
            —c. Evolution
        —2. human hungers
            —a. for answers
            —b. for survival
            —c. for justice
    —B. Expert testimony: example

REAL EVIDENCE
    —A. Firsthand experience
    —B. A lifetime of testing
    —C. Common sense: Pascal's Wager

Notional Evidence

A. My Intelligence

Reason begins from evidence which is certain and works carefully toward conclusions which are probable. So I start with something I'm sure of: my intelligence. I know I have it (sometimes I wish I didn't, but I do).

1. No Effect > Causes: My undeniable intelligence tells me no effect can be greater than its causes. If I put a watermelon on a table and it began to belt out "Hey, Big Spender," you'd have to surmise there was a speaker inside, because a watermelon, all by itself, can't produce that effect without some internal help.

a. So I apply that principle to my intelligence itself. In *Cosmos,* Carl Sagan simply assumes that, given water, intelligent life was a foregone conclusion, but I fail to grasp the basis for his assertion, especially since only one insignificant species (at the time) "achieved" intelligence. Chemicals have power, but they don't seem able to change their minds. Plants have adaptability, but I have no evidence they *choose* to change. Animals show a shrewdness and trainability, but I don't expect even the smartest dog to write *"Hamlet."* I have no right to deny there *could* be some hitherto unknown entity to account for my speculative intelligence. Perhaps some space aliens came and zapped us into cognition. But whatever the source of intelligence, I know for sure it wasn't passed on by King Kong.

The effect eludes a mindless cause. To deny a Mind Behind It All, I have to deny my own intelligence.

b. The universe comes to me ("The tree comes to me") as a stunningly ordered piece of work. I don't impose the periodic table on the material cosmos. Further, everywhere (according to better experts than myself) the physical laws of nature are the same. Difficult to get "law" out of "luck," but that is what I'm stuck with if there is no ordering Mind.

If I look at the universe, every single object is doing the same thing: rotating on an axis, and further it revolves around another object, and that system revolves around another system, and so on. Predictably. If I go to the other extreme and peer at a droplet of ditch water through a microscope, what do I find? The *same* dance! How do you get predictability out of sheer chance? Having directed 30-some musicals, I find that pretty damned impressive, without a Choreographer.

I have no trouble with a Big Bang, but I do have difficulties with its unvaryingly predictable results. If I accept that the ordered universe came about by sheer accident and has continued to work without intention, then I must accept the equal possibility that, if I dropped an atom bomb on Pike's Peak, the result just might be a working Disneyland.

The effect eludes a mindless cause. To deny a Mind Behind It All, I have to deny the demands of my own intelligence.

c. The theory of evolution, at least in its larger outlines, seems beyond dispute. In fact, unlike fundamentalists, I find the evidence of science in general and evolution in particular not only no threat to belief but a massive support.

Evolution at least appears to be a *plan*. But if you use the word *plan,* you have ipso facto ruled out accident; there can't be a plan without a mind. To speak of "natural selection" not only begs the question but is at the very least a misuse of words, since only a mind can see alternatives and *select* among them. Yet in *Cosmos,* Sagan says, "One day, quite by accident, a molecule arose that was able to make crude copies of itself."[3] I wrote in the margin, "That was one *helluva* clever molecule!"

Later, in speaking of the herds of trilobites which carpeted large sections of the earth: "They stored crystals in their eyes to detect polarized light."[4] The use of the word *to*—as in "in order to"—implies a purposefulness no animal I know of can muster. And how did they even "know" there was light if they had no eyes? At times I find I could use an extra eye in the back of my head, but I'll be hornswoggled if I can find out how to evolve one, though a brainless trilobite could. So much for my degrees.

"It is only by the most extraordinary coincidence that the cosmic slot machine has this time come up with a universe consistent with us."[5] Indeed. If the earth were not tilted at 23 degrees, we would have no seasons; if its crust were ten feet thicker, we would have no atmosphere; if the moon were closer, we would be inundated by tides twice a day; if the subcontinent of India had not shouldered up into Asia and created the Himalayas, the whole climatic pattern of the earth would be different. "Extraordinary coincidence" is far too feeble.

If I accept that all those uncountable pieces fell comfortably into place at just the right time, even given billions of years, I would have to accept at least the possibility that if you put the pieces of a clock (a relatively simple mechanism) onto a sheet, and at each corner tireless Titans hurled them into the air, sooner or later part A would affix itself (correctly) to Part B, and A–B would attach itself to C, and so on, until you had a working clock. Difficult to digest.

The effect eludes the purported cause. To deny a Mind Behind It All, I must deny the evidence of my own intelligence.

2. Human Hungers: Besides the electrochemical businesses being conducted in me all unknown, I have discovered I share with every other human being internal soul-hungers which I have no evidence trouble animals: (a) a hunger for answers, (b) a hunger to survive death; (c) a hunger for ultimate justice. Hungers so invariant I have to conclude that they are integral to humanity.

a. More than any other question that troubles my soul is asking the reason my cousin, Judy, has suffered cerebral palsy for over 50 years, why it took my mother so many years to die, why young people I've known died unexpectedly at 17 while other shriveled souls last even longer than three-score-years-and-ten.

If there is no Mind, then the very intelligence that drives me to ask the question is a curse, since there are no answers; it is a hunger for which there is no food. As my gifted student John Hoeffel wrote: "If there is no God, life is an Easter egg hunt. And there are no Easter eggs."

b. I don't want to die, but if I must something unregenerate in me longs to survive. Some very learned folks tell me that irrational hope is precisely what creates the illusion of God. Perhaps that is the truth of it. But if it is, my hunger for permanence is a curse written in my very nature. To my knowledge no pig either knows it will die or yearns to survive it. Better to have been born a pig.

If there is no "food" for that hunger to survive, then evolution took one blind, cruel, accidental step too far and created a species who know—by their very *nature*—that everything they do is ultimately futile. Such unfulfillable hungers violate the constitution of every other nature I know. Surely the law of "the survival of the fittest" would have bred them out of us by now. And yet, ironically, those very hungers are what keep us going and allow us to survive.

c. I don't have to teach a little girl that if another little girl cops her doll, that's not right. Maybe I have to spend time teaching her the other girl has rights, too, but I don't have to teach her that primal sense of justice. I have a reasoned conviction that every human being has self-evident rights. There must be ultimate justice for the millions who died in the Nazi camps. But if there is no transcendent justice, then their deaths—and lives—were all the more obscene.

To summarize: the evidence of my intelligence, its reasoning about the provenance of intelligence itself, the universe, and evolution, and its hungers are either purposeful or purposeless—or worse, curses.

All of this notional evidence is enough to convince me there must be a Mind Behind It All. Notice I didn't say "prove"; I said "convince." It is a *calculated* risk, with evidence enough at least for me sufficient to bet my life on it.

B. Expert Testimony

I have read atheists, and some seem a surprisingly noble lot; Albert Camus is one shining example. But most seem, for all their jigs and japes, a very honest but very dour lot; Samuel Beckett and Jean Genet come to mind. Conversely, a good many of my fellow believers are stupefyingly rigid, puritan, small-minded, vindictive, parsimonious, juiceless, and joyless. But I find they separate themselves from those who strike me as authentic believers in the *way they live their lives*. They tend to be dogmatic, restrictive, ungiving and unforgiving, gnostic and filled with certitudes. "By their fruits you will know them." I sense in the lives of the inquisitors and the ayatollahs none of the energy, the superhumanizing effect that must come from an authentic "connection" to a transcendent, liberating Power. There is power in them, to be sure, but *their* power.

On the other hand, I do sense such a connection in the lives of Dag Hammarskjöld, Pearl Bailey, Thomas More, Helen Keller, Einstein, Dorothy Day. Gandhi, Schweitzer, Golda Meir.

When Claire Booth Luce was considering a conversion to belief, she looked at believers and said in her mind, "You say you have the truth. Well, the truth should set you free, give you joy. Can I *see* your freedom? Can I *feel* your joy?" A good enough test for me of *authentic* religion.

All I know is that, if all those radiant human beings were stupid to believe, I want to be stupid with them.

Real Evidence

A. Firsthand Experience

Atheists say that, unlike experiments to validate the presence of unseen atoms, there are no experiments to validate the presence of an unseen Deity. Theists disagree. They insist we can engage in an experiment: praying—not "saying prayers" or engaging in liturgical worship, but opening our selves with as complete vulnerability as we are able and allowing our souls to be manipulated by the Beyond in our midst.

Like everyone else, I have had "twinges" which suggested I was not alone. But one time, when I was at rock bottom, in the "wilderness," I received a jolt of certitude about the existence of a transcendent in our midst which belies denial or question as clearly as the evidence that I exist. (Realize, of course, for me this was real, existential evidence; for the reader it is notional: testimony.)

Since I was old enough to be aware of what a breech birth must have done to my mother, I was convinced that unless I succeeded, I wouldn't be loved—to the point that, every year on *my* birthday, I gave a present to my mother since she had done all the work. Because neither of my parents had been schooled and my sister had been a failure at it, every month or so I brought home a report card with nothing less than 90s—like a cat delivering a mouse to the door in exchange for Nine Lives.

Then when I entered the seminary and began competing for inclusion in the upper quintiles with some of the brightest men in my generation, my grades slipped from superlative to mediocre to something less than that: My "mother" was telling me something. And my entire sense of self-worth had been grounded on grades for 30 years. Finally, after 6 years of—equivalently—"He is unable to achieve mediocrity," I was literally ready to kill myself. I stood in a fourth-floor window and could find no other reason not to jump than that I'd probably botch that too.

It was the year of my ordination, and they sent me (mercifully) to a psychiatrist, an extraordinarily good man. But he said that, in therapy, I should never think of such a definitive commitment. So on a January Sunday when everyone else went to lunch and then out to skate, I dragged myself to my room, unable to be with normal people. I paced, fussed, fretted. "Yes, I should; no I shouldn't." Finally, I couldn't take it anymore. I had to get away from it. I'd lie down and sleep. So I lay down, but I didn't sleep. The only way I know it lasted two hours is that I lay down at noon and "came out of it" at two.

For two hours, the only way I can describe it is like "drowning in light." I had no slightest awareness of time and space, the room, myself. And I *knew*—diametrically against everything I thought of myself—that I was *accepted,* more unconditionally than even my own mother had accepted me. When it faded, I sat up, and I said—for the first time in 30 years—"I'm a *good* man, and I'll be a good priest, because I'm a good man." I grabbed my skates and went down to the skating lake (everyone was back inside by then), and I skated around in big circles, and I *shouted* it out: "I'm a *good* man! And from now on I *never* have to have anybody prove that to me!"

The next day I sat down with my doctor and said, "Before we start, I want to say something. I'm going to be ordained, no matter what you think of me." That fine man smiled, pinched his mouth against the tears, and said, "Good!"

I was free! As free as Helen Keller when she pulled away from that pump. And that searing enlightenment has never left me. When I sin, and I do sin, I know it's a good man that made a dumb mistake, not a poor klutz forever doomed to sully himself.

Unlike the self-surrender one can offer during prayer, I had not opened myself purposefully to invite God into my soul. How could someone so wretchedly unworthy offer such accommodations? But in a very true sense my self-savaging had hollowed me out, a vacuum empty even of myself. I didn't prepare myself. But I believe deeply that I was *being* prepared.

Since that moment, all the notional knowledge has been like the essential but ultimately disposable first stage of a rocket. I am not certain, not in the Cartesian sense. But I am as certain of a Mind Behind It All as I am certain that my friends who claim to love me do love me.

B. A Lifetime of Testing

That happened in 1963; I write this in 1995. It's worked. That's 32 years, 12,000 days of work, love, anger, trust, frustration, joy, betrayal, triumph, failure—even a brush with spurious fame on the old silver screen. And I've never doubted once, not for a watch-tick, that God was with me, even—especially—when I least "deserved" it.

I look at my life before that moment—hag-ridden with self-doubt, convinced of ugliness inside and out, joyless, an unprofitable servant. Now, I need no Nobel Prize (though I wouldn't spurn one). But I am, by *God,* the world's luckiest man.

If you can find a better offer, take it.

C. Common Sense

As we saw before, speaking of an afterlife, Blaise Pascal (d. 1662) saw that if there are only two alternatives, one hideous (annihilation), the other promising (*some* kind of going-on), and we have no idea which it is, we might as well opt for the happy option. And we'll never find out we were wrong!

What If . . . ?

Science says there can be no reality faster than light. Yet science also delights in playing "what if." Well, what if there were a light, an energy, faster than light? It would be moving so fast it would be everywhere at once. Like God. So dynamic it would also be utterly at rest. Like God. And science now believes when it cracks open the last building block of matter it will find nonextended energy. Like God. $E = mc^2$ means matter *is* energy. There is an insight there.

Couple that modern insight with the insight of Exodus. When Moses asked Yahweh his name, he was asking for much more than a label. For a Hebrew, one's name designated his or her role in the community. And God's reply was "I am who am." What is God's role in the community? Existence. God is the pool of existence out of which anything that is gets its "is." At least in that sense, insofar as the power of God is immanent,

God *is* the *anima mundi*. When we react in awe and revere
to the numinous in nature, we are reacting to the Source of its
aliveness and energy: "The world is charged with the grandeur
of God."

There's got to be something more than Gradgrind! There's
got to be something more than Didi and Gogo boring one
another toward death, and Gregor Samsa worrying about
missing a train, despite the fact he is now a gigantic cockroach.

The very depth of their seriousness demands that we
dance! And if they are right and I am wrong, if we all are
indeed on the Titanic, then we might as well go down singing,
hoping, trusting.

Chapter Seventeen

CONNECTING WITH THE HOLY

Batter my heart, three-personed God; for you
As yet but knock, breathe, shine, and seek to mend;
That I may rise and stand, o'erthrow me and bend
Your force to break, blow, burn and make me new. . . .
Take me to you, imprison me, for I
Except you enthrall me, never shall be free,
Nor ever chaste, except you ravish me.

John Donne—*"Batter My Heart"*[1]

In *The Idea of the Holy*, Rudolf Otto calls encounter with the Holy a contact with the *mysterium tremendum,* "the overwhelming mystery"—awe before something objective, truly-there, outside myself, which causes an involuntary feeling of smallness. Augustine felt that confluence of exaltation and humility when he wrote:

> What is that which gleams through me and smites my heart without wounding it? I am both ashudder and aglow. Ashudder insofar as I am unlike it, aglow insofar as I *am* like it.

This response is not the same as being "humiliated" by a bully, but rather being "humbled" by unexpected love. One has the sense (not a concept) of being so small in the face of something so powerful and enormous. We feel, at one and the same time, submissive yet elated. "Ashudder insofar as I am unlike it, aglow insofar as I *am* like it."

Tremendum. The root of the word is *tremens,* "quivering," not from fear but from astonishment. Nor is it the same as "eerie, weird, dreadful," as listening to stories of ghosts or demons. It is, rather, awe. Today, we overwork *awesome;* now it means nothing more than "rather good." But it really means "breath-taking, wondrous, inspiriting." This is fear only in the sense of fear before stored-up Energy, daunting yet fascinating, intoxicating, urgent, compelling, alive. At such moments we have come in contact with the living God rather than merely with the idea of God. This is the root of *all* authentic religion.

Islam means "surrender," and as John Donne's poem indicates, what the soul needs from the Divinity is not mending but rending. For us to be genuinely free, God must enslave us; to be chaste, we must submit to God's ravishment. Not many of us have heard that message from pulpits; far too many unsavory hints of sex and violence there—*and* in unseemly reference to God. Yet had we heard it, religion might not have devolved in our minds into pious preachments and pallid practices. As the Christian epistle says, "It is a fearsome thing to fall into the hands of the living God."[2] It is what Job discovered: glorious servitude.

From the start, I have examined our culture's resistance to the unquantifiable and intangible, its obsession with the empirical, this-worldly, secular, pragmatic, utilitarian, contractual, and hedonistic, an addiction that makes evolving a human soul unlikely, if not impossible. Vulnerability—surrender—does not fare well in our society. We don't like to be the subjects of passive verbs: "I told 'em all to go t' hell; I can do it by myself; don't tread on me!" But the objective fact is I *was* conceived, *was* carried nine months, *was* born. If I believe there is a Mind Behind It All, I must by that very fact accept the corollary that I *was* created without my cooperation or deserving.

When we come, then, to the process of supernaturally energizing that human soul, even the worthiest of us feels resistance. In the preceding chapter, I referred to "the 'victim' of a supernatural experience," and the word was carefully chosen. To be fully *human,* we must yield to the truth, wherever it leads; we must succumb to the needs of those we love, no matter how inconvenient.

To be *supernaturally* energized, our souls need to yield to Job's truth: God is not answerable to us; we are answerable to God. This does not require the passivity of "an old man's staff" or a robotic slave or an open tape recorder. That passivity in fact would deflect the intrusion of God. What is required is that, before God, each of us—male and female—must be actively *receptive,* fertile, "feminine."

Just as evolution of our humanity calls for turning away from self-absorption, the evolution of the supernatural soul needs turning away from the need to dominate, to be in charge, to go it alone, to fancy ourselves the lead, center stage. If there is a Mind Behind It All, we are not the lead. As Eliot's Prufrock confesses, hearkening back to Polonius: "I am not Prince Hamlet, nor was meant to be."

That turnabout—that conversion from laudable and hard-won self-sufficiency to dependence again—is wrenching. The physical conversion of a child to an adolescent is out of our hands, like the emergence of a butterfly. But from that point on, no evolution of the soul can take place without our coopera-tion—often, in fact, not without our suffering: our surrender of a height achieved at great effort in order to go higher. Then we plunge into a forest of paradoxes: conversions and reconversions.

The growth of a child-soul to an adult-soul may never take place because it means a painful conversion: the effort to establish a personally validated, independent self, leaving behind secure victimhood to the Id and Superego. Even in that very process, we have to suffer yet another conversion: opening that self to accommodate others in ever widening circles of aware-ness and concern. What's more, each male must struggle against stereotypical expectations to access the power of his feminine anima and each female her masculine animus, and then—yet another turnabout!—return to repossess the assets of their own maleness and femaleness. If one aspires further—beyond the self, the marriage, the family, friends, community, nation, the human family, out into fellowship with God, there is yet another spiritual conversion: to reaccess the resources of a child.

We shed many valuable human assets on our climb to adult self-possession and responsibility. In exchange for duti-fulness, punctuality, dependability, decisiveness, commitment, we often gave up spontaneity, wonder, awe, time to pause and ponder, the susceptibility that can be drawn into time-free contemplation of bugs under a rock, the freedom and humility to say, "Wow!"

Although the odyssey to self-possession and responsibility is written by the Creator into our very nature, God can't readily deal with world-beaters. To attain human fulfillment, we have—at least some times in the midst of our chaotic week—to pull aside from progress and simply "let go," to yield center stage, to put everything back into its real perspective.

We need to remind ourselves that we really live in a larger dimension than the world's selfish interests, beyond even the legitimate demands of family, career, and community. We need to *feel* a friendly continuity with a Higher Power and surrender to it, to shift the emotional center of our lives to peaceful acceptance of what is. We need time really to *transcend* our limited selves, the opinions of the small-souled, to reassess our attitude toward unmerited suffering. We have to *know* that somewhere in the crapstorm, there is light. We need to accept that the wrath of God often *is* the love of God, assessed by a fool.

Saint Teresa, no mean hand at evolving souls, said that from the perspective of eternity, the most wretched life on earth will seem like one unpleasant night in a grubby hotel. That perspective is at hand whenever we choose to avail ourselves of it.

Another great soul, Simone Weil, wrote:

> In order that a new sense should be formed in us to enable us to hear the universe as the vibration of the word of God, the transforming power of suffering *and* of joy are equally indispensable. When either of them comes to us we have to open the very center of our soul to it, just as a woman opens her door to messengers from her loved one. What does it matter to a love if the messenger be polite or rough, so long as he delivers the message?[3]

The trick, of course, is to be "at home" when the messenger arrives. He doesn't call ahead. Therefore, you have to be ready to receive him at any time.

Praying

There is a difference between praying and "saying prayers,"
although there's nothing wrong with saying prayers. Some say
they no longer use made-up prayers because they can't focus on
the content of the words. They miss the whole point. Going
over and over the prayers of a Buddhist or Catholic rosary
or reading the Hebrew Psalms one after another may not
stimulate any deep insights one can later write down as "lights
from prayer." (The intrusion even into prayer of the need to
make progress, to have a product.) Prayer is a conversation
(sometimes without words, like an old couple in the front seat
of their car).

Any conversation is really two conversations: one is
the words which pass back and forth and which are rarely
worth etching in bronze; the other beneath the audible one
says, "I feel at home with you." That's all saying prayers need
be, like a Zen mantra, repeated over and over, *so that* the
words cease to have meaning but remain only a focus of the
real connection.

In recent years, I sort of gave up on petitionary prayers:
"Oh, God, please do this," or "Make me want to do what I
don't want to do." The reason was it didn't "work." I prayed
incessantly for three years that God would release my mother
from agony, but God apparently had other plans my mind was
too small to encompass. On a theoretical level, I began to
wonder if it wasn't slightly arrogant of me, trying to change
God's mind, to manipulate, dominate, control. Others tell me
they gave up praying altogether because God never answered
their prayers, not realizing "No" is, in fact, an answer.

But I think I was wrong, first of all because petitionary
prayers are unavoidable. For many of us our turning to God is
almost always out of need-love. In that foxhole with the tracers

overhead, you helplessly cry out, "God, help me!" Also I began
to realize that, in rough times, you automatically turn to a friend
and unburden, not because you expect him or her to give "the
answer," much less reverse the situation. All you want is just to
be heard. Now when I feel that need, I try to pray without
offering suggestions, like Mary at the wedding, not "Would you
please take care of this wine situation?" much less "After all I've
done for *you*, young man." Just "They have no wine."

Finally, in made-up or petitionary prayers, the important
thing is not the words or the intention but the felt *connection*.
You can set aside time to take a walk just "hangin' out with
God," mulling things over, watching the first crocuses pop up
to slurp the pale sun, and that's praying—as long as it's *together*.

Contemplation

Unitive experiences of God can happen when we are caught
off guard by the numinous. Or they can be prompted by need.
But they can also happen by choice rather than by chance. That
doesn't mean any time you choose to contact God you will
suddenly be wafted off into the seventh heaven, ablaze with
light, perhaps even wheeling around the ceiling. That's more
like the raptures of being-in-love. Like real love, real union with
the energizing power of God is ordinarily as undramatic as a
couple sitting in an airport lounge, he stroking her shoulder
while he reads a book, she staring at nothing with her hand
resting on his knee.

Prayer by choice is setting aside time consciously to *let down*
your guard, the dukes-up posture with which most of us have
to face most of the week, to lose the surface self in order to
access the real self and open that soul to the Ultimate Spirit.

Contemplation offers the most fundamental
meeting ground for psychology and religion; it is

at once a psychological condition and a religious attitude. In traditional religious usage, the term "contemplation" implies a totally uncluttered appreciation of existence, a state of mind or a condition of the soul that is simultaneously wide-awake and free from all preoccupation, preconception, and interpretation. It is a wonder-filled yet utterly simple experience.[4]

Just as with the art of loving, the art of praying takes time, discipline, concentration, patience, commitment, willingness to start simple and practice often—like learning to walk. But we have little experience of self-sufficient solitude. When we're alone in the house, the ordinary thing is to turn on the radio. And stereo. And television. The first step in praying is to understand the difference between loneliness and solitude.

Contemplation is not a matter of the willful mastery we were encouraged to desire in school and which plays so much a part in "getting ahead." Rather, it is willing self-surrender to a mystery one can never understand but can experience, not a matter of comprehension but *appreciation*. Like the two different kinds of tourists we saw before, this is not a time for progress. It is a time merely to be-with.

Perhaps the following exercise might help, but there are many books to help anyone serious about contacting God.[5]

First, find a place you can be relatively undisturbed: no phone, no sirens, no TV, a room where you can shut the door on the world for a few moments or a secluded part of a park. Sit quietly, eyes closed. Roll your head around your neck and get rid of all the tensions, all the obligations, and let them drain down from your head into your shoulders, into your back, then down your back into your seat and away. Peace.

Then focus on your breathing, but really *deep* breaths: in for five full counts, out five full counts. Over and over until you feel a soothing rhythm. Then consider your breath. That air keeps you alive. We have no idea where it's been, but we use it and pass it on. Ponder that for as long as it "feeds" you.

Then expand your awareness—and your self—beyond the little circle of peace where you sit, out into the surroundings, beyond the walls or the trees. In your imagination, move gradually beyond this city, this county, this state, this country. The air that enlivens us moves eastward across the country, across the Atlantic, Europe, Asia, the Pacific, and back to us. There you are, focused, at the center of that enormous enlivening reality.

Finally, realize the word for breath is *ruah, pneuma, anima:* spirit. "Oh, morning, at the brown brink eastward, springs— Because the Holy Ghost over the bent World broods with warm breast and with ah! bright wings."[6] Open yourself to that Spirit.

That is your true "home."

ENDNOTES

Introduction

1. The Beatles, "Eleanor Rigby."
2. Maslow, Abraham H., *The Farther Reaches of Human Nature,* p. 175, Viking Penguin.
3. Johnson, Robert, *We,* p. 3.
4. Gardner, John W., *Self–Renewal: The Individual and the Innovative Society,,* p. 13, Norton.
5. Doestoevsky, Fyodor, *The Brothers Karamazov,* Vol I, p. 298, Random.
6. Heschel, Abraham J., *Who is Man?* p. 23, Stanford University Press.
7. Rock, Leo, S.J., *Making Friends With Yourself: Christian Growth and Acceptance,* p. 103, Paulist Press.

Chapter One

1. Kafka, Franz, *The Metamorphosis,* p. 1, Copyright, Schoken Books, Inc.
2. Lee, Peggy, "Is That All There Is?" copyright 1966 by Yellow Dog Music, Inc., /Hudson Bay Music, Inc, NY.
3. Shakespeare, William, *Macbeth,* Act V, Scene v, lines 21–30.
4. Lewis, C. S., *The Abolition of Man,* p. 88, Macmillan.
5. Dickens, Charles, *Hard Times,* p. 1, Afterword copyright 1961 by the New American Library of World Literature, Inc.
6. Kelsey, Morton, *Companions on the Inner Way: The Art of Spiritual Guidance,* p. 133, Crossroad.
7. Fitch, Robert, *What is the Nature of Man?,* passim.
8. Eliot, T.S., "The Hollow Men," *Collected Poems 1909–1935,* Harcourt, Brace & Co., Inc.
9. Campbell, Joseph, with Bill Moyers, *The Power of Myth,* p. 144, Doubleday.

Chapter Two

1. Yeats, William Butler, "The Second Coming," from *Collected Poems of William Butler Yeats,* Macmillan.
2. Marcuse, Herbert, *One–Dimensional Man,* pp. 127, 157, 232 Beacon Press.
3. *The World Almanac and Book of Facts,* 1955 and 1995.
4. Neuhausler, *What Was It Like In Concentration Camp Dachau?* Trustees for the Monument of the Atonement, ND, p. 63.
5. Quoted in Marcuse, *One–Dimensional Man,* p. 80.
6. Milgram, *Human Relations,* Vol 18 (1965), No. l, pp. 57–76.
7. Miller, Arthur, *Death of a Salesman,* pp. 17–18, Amereon Ltd..

8. Ibid., pp. 19–20.
9. Williams, Tennessee, *Cat on a Hot Tin Roof,*, p. 75, Signet.
10. Ibid., p. 81.
11. Fitch, *What is the Nature of Man?*, p. 60.
12. Fitch, *The Decline and Fall of Sex*, p. 109, Greenwood Press.
13. *1995 Information Please Almanac*, p. 744.
14. Taylor, "Don't Blame Me!," *New York*, 3 Jun 91, p. 30.
15. Vonnegut, Kurt, *Cat's Cradle*, p. 164, Dell.
16. Huxley, Aldous, *Jesting Pilate*, p. 300, George Dorn.
17. Horney, Karen, *New Ways in Psychoanalysis*, p. 174, Norton.
18. Mannes, Marya, *More in Anger*, p. 184, Lippincott.
19. Johnson, *We*, p. 21.

Chapter Three
1. Arlen, "Over the Rainbow."
2. Marcuse, *One–Dimensional Man*, p. 125.
3. Amy Lowell, "Wind and Silver," from *What's O'Clock*, Houghton Mifflin, Co., ND.
4. Traherne, *Centuries of Meditations*, i. 12.
5. Aristotle, *Nichomachean Ethics*, 1004 B.
6. Lewis, C.S., *The Abolition of Man*, p. 56, Macmillan.
7. Lemonick, Michael, "Glimpses of the Mind," *Time* July 17, 1995.
8. May, Gerald, *Care of Mind / Care of Soul*, p. 23, Harper & Row.
9. Ibid., p. 129.
10. Frankl, *Man's Search for Meaning*, p. 194.
11. Miller, Walter M. Jr., *A Canticle for Liebowitz*, p. 305, Bantam.

Chapter Four
1. Mead, Margaret, *Male and Female*, p. 184–5, Morrow.
2. Hammarskjöld, Dag, *Markings,* p. 205, Ballentine.
3. See Bettelheim, Bruno, *The Roots of Enchantment*.
4. Campbell–Moyers, *The Power of Myth*, p. 144, Doubleday.
5. Keen, Sam, *Hymns to an Unknown God,* p. 112, Bantam.

Chapter Five
1. Keen, *Hymns to an Unknown God*, p. 61.
2. Fitch, *The Decline and Fall of Sex,* p. 113.
3. Heschel, *Who Is Man?* p. 35.
4. *1995 Information Please Almanac,* pp. 841, 844.
5. Matthew 5: 48.

6. Bettelheim, "Freud and the Soul," *The New Yorker,* 1 May 1982, p. 52.

7. Quoted by Bettelheim, ibid, p. 64.

8. Ibid., p. 79.

9. Ibid, p. 84.

10. Ibid., p. 85.

11. Ibid., p. 54.

12. Quoted, ibid., p. 84.

13. Quoted, ibid., p. 86.

14. Horney, Karen, *New Ways in Psychoanalysis,* p. 99, Norton.

15. Goethe, Johann Wolfgang von, "The Sorrows of Werther," *Permanent Goethe,* p. 393, Dial.

16. Emerson, Ralph Waldo, "Self–Reliance," *Selected Writings,* p. 250, Modern Library.

Chapter Six

1. Conrad, Joseph, *Under Western Eyes,* Anchor (1963), 1.2.

2. Erikson, Erik, *Identity and the Life Cycle,* p. 72, Norton.

3. Frankl, *Man's Search for Meaning,* p. 158.

4. Kohlberg, *The Psychology of Moral Development,* passim.

5. Gilligan, Carol, *In a Different Voice,* passim.

Chapter Seven

1. Maslow, *The Farther Reaches of Human Nature,* p. 154.

2. Belenky, et al., *Women's Ways of Knowing,* p. 128.

3. Johnson, *She.*

4. Nathanson, Paul, *Over the Rainbow: The Wizard of Oz as a Secular Myth of America,* SUNY Press.

Chapter Eight

1. Frankl, *Man's Search for Meaning,* xiii.

2. Kreeft, Peter, *Making Sense of Suffering,* p. 58.

3. Frankl, op. cit., p. xiii.

4. Ibid, pp. 106–7.

5. Ibid., pp. 96–7.

6. Quoted in Fitch, *Of Love and Suffering,* pp. 151–2.

7. Hopkins, Gerard Manley, "Spring and Fall: To a Young Child," *Poems of Gerald Manley Hopkins,* Oxford U. Press, 1948.

8. Sagan, Carl, *The Dragons of Eden,* Ballantine, 1978, pp. 14–15.

9. MacLeish, Archibald, "The End of the World," from *Poems 1924–1933,* copyright Archibald MacLeish, 1933.

Chapter Nine

1. Shakespeare, Sonnet XCIV.
2. Kevorkian, *Free Inquiry,* Fall 1991, p. 14.
3. Bellah, et al., *Habits of the Heart,* pp. 75–6.

Chapter Ten

1. The substance of this chapter was first published in *Human Development,* Fall, 1993.
2. Irving, Washington, "The Wife," *The Sketch Book of Geoffrey Crayon, Gent.*
3. Quoted in Horney, *New Ways in Psychoanalysis,* p. 103.
4. Belenky, et al., *Women's Ways of Knowing,* p. 69.
5. Quoted in Lahr, "Dealing with Roseanne," *The New Yorker,* July 17, 1995, p. 48.
6. Loc. cit., p. 52.
7. Belenky, et al., op. cit., p. 119.
8. Harris, Maria, *The Dance of the Spirit,* Bantam Doubleday Dell.
9. Ibid., p. 182. (Italics hers.)

Chapter Eleven

1. Alfred, Lord Tennyson "Ulysses."
2. Mead, *Male and Female,* p. 189.
3. Wilbur, Richard, "Parable," *Ceremony and Other Poems,* Harcourt Brace.
4. Students of the Enneagram will see some correlation. The Pilgrim is analogous to the Enneagram Four (Artist) with the resolve of the Three; Patriarch is like Eight (the Leader); Warrior is like Three (Climber) with Six (Team Player); Magician is like Five (Thinker); Wildman is like Seven (Sampler); Healer is like Two (Helper); Prophet is like One (Reformer); Mediator is like Nine (Peacemaker); and Trickster is also like Seven (Sampler). As with the Enneagram, the purpose of this reflection is not to pigeonhole a man into a "type," but to develop the assets of each archetype and avoid the liabilities of its shadow.

Chapter Twelve

1. Huxley, Aldous, *Tomorrow and Tomorrow and Tomorrow,* Harper, 1956, p. 151.
2. Quoted by Fitch, *Of Love and Suffering,* p. 45.
3. Peck, *The Road Less Traveled,* p. 102.
4. Mead, *Male and Female,* p. 286.
5. 1 Corinthians 13:4–7. (My translation.)

Chapter Thirteen

1. Sexton, Anne, "Cinderella," *Collected Poems,* p. 258.
2. Wallerstein, *The Good Marriage,* p. 13.
3. Anderson and Fite, *Becoming Married,* p. 126.
4. Wilder, *The Skin of Our Teeth,* from *Three Plays by Thornton Wilder,* Copyright 1957 by Thornton Wilder. Reprinted by permission of HarperCollins Publishers.
5. Wallerstein, *The Good Marriage,* p. 7.
6. Ibid., pp. 194–5.
7. Ibid., p. 76.
8. Ibid., p. 240.

Chapter Fourteen

1. The substance of this chapter was originally published as "Atticus Finch and the Family," *America,* May 11, 1991.
2. Lee, Harper, *To Kill a Mockingbird,* Harper & Row, 1960, pp. 112–3.

Chapter Fifteen

1. Shug to Miss Celie, Walker, *The Color Purple,* pp. 178–9.
2. Hopkins, Gerard Manley, "God's Grandeur," *Poems of Gerard Manley Hopkins,* 3rd edition, Oxford U. Press.
3. Quoted by James, *The Varieties of Religious Experience,* p. 61.
4. Ibid., p. 55.
5. Jung, C. G., *Letters, 1906–1950,* p. 377.
6. Kelsey, *Companions on the Inner Way,* p. 102.
7. Quoted in Campbell, *The Power of Myth,* p. 34.

Chapter Sixteen

1. Hopkins, "God's Grandeur," *Poems of Gerard Manley Hopkins,* 3rd edition, Oxford U. Press.
2. Job, 42:5.
3. Sagan, *Cosmos,* Random House, 1980, pp. 30, 338.
4. Ibid., p. 32.
5. Ibid., p. 260.

Chapter Seventeen

1. Donne, John, "Batter My Heart," *The Complete Poems and Selected Prose of John Donne,* edited by M. H. Abrams, Norton, 1979.
2. Hebrews 10:31.
3. Weil, *Waiting for God,* p. 132.
4. May, Gerald, *Will and Spirit,* p. 25.

5. O'Malley, *Dangerous Prayer: Being Vulnerable to God,* Liguori.
6. Hopkins, "God's Grandeur," *Poems of Gerard Manley Hopkins,* 3rd edition, Oxford U. Press.

BIBLIOGRAPHY

Anderson, Herbert and Robert Fite. *Becoming Married*. John Knox, 1993.

Arendt, Hannah. *The Human Condition*. U. of Chicago Press, 1958.

Belenky, Clinchy, Goldberger, Tarule. *Women's Ways of Knowing*. Basic Books, 1986.

Bellah, Robert, et al. *Habits of the Heart*. Harper and Row, 1985.

Berger, Peter. *A Rumor of Angels*. Anchor, 1970.

Bergson, Henri. *The Two Sources of Morality and Religion*. Henry Holt, 1935.

Bettelheim, Bruno. "Freud and the Soul." *New Yorker,* 1 March 82.

———. The Uses of Enchantment. Vintage, 1977.

Bly, Robert. *Iron John*. Addison-Wesley, 1990.

Browne, Fishwick, Browne. *Dominant Symbols in Popular Culture*. Bowling Green, 1990.

Campbell, Joseph, with Bill Moyers. *The Power of Myth*. Doubleday, 1988.

Cook, Frank. *The Corrupted Land*. Macmillan, 1966.

Dolan, Frederick. *Allegories of America*. Cornell, 1994.

Dostoevsky, Fyodor. *The Brothers Karamazov*. Penguin, 1958.

Douglas, Mary. *Natural Symbols*. Barrie and Rochliff, 1970.

Eliade, Mircea. *The Sacred and the Profane*. Harcourt Brace, 1959.

Emerson, Ralph Waldo. "Self-Reliance." *Selected Writings of Ralph Waldo Emerson*. Modern Library, 1950.

Erikson, Erik. *Identity and the Life Cycle*. Norton, 1980.

Fitch, Robert. *The Decline and Fall of Sex*. Harcourt, Brace, 1951.

———. *The Limits of Liberty*. College of the Pacific, 1952.

———. *Of Love and Suffering*. Westminster, 1970.

———. *Odyssey of the Self-Centered Self*. Harcourt, Brace & World, 1960.

Frankl, Viktor. *The Doctor and the Soul*. Vintage, 1986.

———. *Man's Search for Meaning*. Washington Square, 1963.

Fromm, Erich. *The Art of Loving*. Harper & Row, 1956.

Gardner, John W. *Self-Renewal*. Harper & Row, 1963.

Gilligan, Carol. *In a Different Voice*. Harvard, 1982.

Harris, Maria. *Dance of the Spirit*. Bantam Doubleday Dell, 1989.

Harris, Thomas. *I'm OK—You're OK*. Avon, 1973.

Heschel, Abraham. *Who is Man?* Stanford, 1965.

Hitchcock, James. *The Recovery of the Sacred*. Crossroad, 1974.

Horney, Karen. *New Ways in Psychoanalysis*. Norton, 1939.

James, William. *The Varieties of Religious Experience*. Longmans Green, 1902.

Johnson, Robert. *He*. Harper & Row, 1977.

———. *She*. Harper & Row, 1977.

————. *We.* Harper & Row, 1983.

Jones, Alan. *Soul Making.* HarperCollins, 1989.

Jung, C. G. *Man and His Symbols.* Doubleday, 1964.

————. *Modern Man in Search of a Soul.* Harvest, 1933.

————. *Psychology and Religion.* Yale, 1933.

Keen, Sam. *Fire in the Belly.* Bantam, 1991.

————. *Hymns to An Unknown God.* Bantam, 1994.

Kelsey, Morton. *Companions on the Inner Way.* Crossroad, 1983.

Kreeft, Peter. *Making Sense Out of Suffering.* Servant, 1986.

Lacayo, Richard. "Are Music and Movies Killing America's Soul." *Time,* 12 June 1995.

Langer, Suzanne. *Philosophy in a New Key.* Harvard, 1951.

Lasch, Christopher. *The Culture of Narcissism.* Warner, 1979.

Lewis, C. S. *The Abolition of Man.* Macmillan, 1947.

————. *The Four Loves.* Harcourt, Brace, Jovanovich, 1960.

Maslow, Abraham. *The Farther Reaches of Human Nature.* Penguin, 1976.

May, Gerald. *Care of Mind / Care of Spirit.* Harper & Row, 1982.

————. *Will and Spirit.* Harper & Row, 1982.

May, Rollo, ed. *Symbolism in Religion and Literature.* Braziller, 1960.

Mead, Margaret. *Male and Female.* Morrow, 1949.

Miller, Arthur. *Death of a Salesman.* Viking, 1949.

Miller, Walter. *A Canticle for Liebowitz.* Bantam, 1976.

Moore, Thomas. *Care of the Soul.* Harper, 1992.

Nathanson, Paul. *Over the Rainbow: The Wizard of Oz as a Secular Myth of America.* SUNY Press, 1991.

Niebuhr, Reinhold. *The Godly and Ungodly.* Faber and Faber, 1959.

————. *Human Nature.* Scribners, 1941.

O'Malley, William. *Building Your Own Conscience.* Tabor, 1992.

Otto, Rudolf. *The Idea of the Holy.* Oxford, 1923.

Peck, M. Scott. *The Road Less Traveled.* Simon & Schuster, 1978.

Rock, Leo. *Making Friends With Yourself.* Paulist, 1990.

Rohr, Richard. *Quest for the Grail.* Crossroad, 1994.

Roszak, Theodore. *Unfinished Animal.* Harper and Row, 1975.

Sagan, Carl. *Cosmos.* Random House, 1980.

————. *The Dragons of Eden.* Ballantine, 1978.

Tannen, Deborah. *You Just Don't Understand.* Morrow, 1990.

Taylor, John. "Don't Blame Me!" New York, 3 June 1991.

Verhalen, Philip. *Faith in a Secularized World.* Paulist, 1976.

Walker, Alice. *The Color Purple.* Washington Square Press, 1982.

Wallerstein, Judith, and Sandra Blakeslee. *The Good Marriage.* Houghton-Mifflin, 1995.

Weil, Simone. *Waiting for God.* Harper & Row, 1951.